Donald Grant Mitchell

Wet Days at Edgewood

With old farmers, old gardeners, and old pastorals

Donald Grant Mitchell

Wet Days at Edgewood
With old farmers, old gardeners, and old pastorals

ISBN/EAN: 9783337083199

Printed in Europe, USA, Canada, Australia, Japan

Cover: Foto ©ninafisch / pixelio.de

More available books at **www.hansebooks.com**

WET DAYS

AT EDGEWOOD

WITH

Old Farmers, Old Gardeners, and Old Pastorals

BY THE AUTHOR OF

"MY FARM OF EDGEWOOD."

New York

CHARLES SCRIBNER'S SONS

1899

Original Dedication

PREFATORY NOTE.

A CONSIDERABLE portion of this book was published more than a score of years ago in the
pages of the *Atlantic Monthly*. The articles thus contributed—under the name of *Wet-Weather-Work*—were
afterward revised, large additions made to them, and
published at the instance of my friend, the late Mr.
Charles Scribner — to whom I dedicated the volume,
under its present title.

That dedication I repeat upon this edition of twenty
years later — that it may stand there so long as this
book is issued, in token of my high regard for his
memory, and of my warm recollections of his kindly
nature, and of his many and unabating offices of
friendship.

DONALD G. MITCHELL.

EDGEWOOD, 1883.

CONTENTS.

FIRST DAY.

SECOND DAY.

SIXTH DAY.

SEVENTH DAY.

EIGHTH DAY.

NINTH DAY.

FIRST DAY.

Without and Within.

IT is raining; and being in-doors, I look out from my library-window, across a quiet country-road, so near that I could toss my pen into the middle of it.

A thatched stile is opposite, flanked by a straggling hedge of Osage-orange; and from the stile the ground falls away in green and gradual slope to a great plateau of measured and fenced fields, checkered, a month since, with bluish lines of Swedes, with the ragged purple of mangels, and the feathery emerald-green of carrots. There are umber-colored patches of fresh-turned furrows; here and there the mossy, luxurious verdure of new-springing rye; gray stubble; the ragged brown of discolored, frostbitten rag-weed; next, a line of tree-tops, thickening as they drop to the near bed of a river, and beyond the river-basin showing again, with tufts of hemlock among naked oaks and maples; then roofs, cupolas, ambitious lookouts of suburban houses, spires,

belfries, turrets: all these commingling in a long line
of white, brown, and gray, which in sunny weather is
backed by purple hills, and flanked one way by a
shining streak of water, and the other by a stretch of
low, wooded mountains that turn from purple to blue,
and so blend with the northern sky.

Is the picture clear? A road ; a farm-flat of party-
colored checkers ; a near wood, that conceals the sunk-
en meadow of a river; a farther wood, that skirts a
town, — that seems to overgrow the town, so that only
a confused line of roofs, belfries, spires, towers, rise
above the wood; and these tallest spires and turrets
lying in relief against a purple hill-side, that is as far
beyond the town as the town is beyond my window;
and the purple hill-side trending southward to a lake-
like gleam of water, where a light-house shines upon a
point; and northward, as I said, these same purple hills
bearing away to paler purple, and then to blue, and
then to haze.

Thus much is seen, when I look directly eastward;
but by an oblique glance southward (always from my
library-window) the checkered farm-land is repeated in
long perspective: here and there is a farmhouse with
its clustered out-buildings; here and there a blotch of
wood, or of orcharding; here and there a bright sheen
of winter-grain ; and the level ends only where a slight
fringe of tree-tops, and the iron cordon of a railway

that leaps over a marshy creek upon trestle-work, separate it from Long Island Sound.

To the north, under such oblique glance as can be caught, the farm-lands in smaller enclosures stretch half a mile to the skirts of a quiet village. A few tall chimneys smoke there lazily, and below them you see as many quick and repeated puffs of white steam. Two white spires and a tower are in bold relief against the precipitous basaltic cliff, at whose foot the village seems to nestle. Yet the mountain is not wholly precipitous; for the columnar masses have been fretted away by a thousand frosts, making a sloping débris below, and leaving above the iron-yellow scars of fresh cleavage, the older blotches of gray, and the still older stain of lichens. Nor is the summit bald, but tufted with dwarf cedars and oaks, which, as they file away on either flank, mingle with a heavier growth of hickories and chestnuts. A few stunted kalmias and hemlock-spruces have found foothold in the clefts upon the face of the rock, showing a tawny green, that blends prettily with the scars, lichens, and weather-stains of the cliff; all which show under a sunset light richly and changefully as the breast of a dove.

But just now there is no glow of sunset; raining still. Indeed, I do not know why I should have described at such length a mere landscape, (than which I know few fairer,) unless because of a rainy day it is

always in my eye, and that now, having invited a few
outsiders to such entertainment as may belong to my
wet farm-days, I should present to them at once my
oldest acquaintance, — the view from my library-window.

But as yet it is only coarsely outlined; I warn the
reader that I may return to the outside picture over
and over again; I weary no more of it than I weary
of the reading of a fair poem; no written rhythm can
be more beguiling than the interchange of colors —
wood and grain and river — all touched and toned by
the wind, as a pleasant voice intones the shadows and the
lights of a printed Idyl. And if, as to-day, the cloud-
bank comes down so as to hide from time to time the
remoter objects, it is but a cæsural pause, and anon the
curtain lifts — the woods, the spires, the hills flow in,
and the poem is complete.

In that corner of my library which immediately
flanks the east window is bestowed a motley array of
farm-books: there are fat ones in yellow vellum; there
are ponderous folios with stately dedications to some
great man we never heard of; there are thin tractates
in ambitious type, which promised, fifty years and more
ago, to overset all the established methods of farming;
there is Jethro Tull, in his irate way thrashing all down
his columns the effete Virgilian husbandry; there is the
sententious talk of Cato, the latinity of Columella, and

some little musty duodecimo, hunted down upon the quays of Paris, with such title as " Comes Rusticus" there is the first thin quarto of Judge Buel's " Culti vator " — since expanded into the well-ordered state-liness of the " Country Gentleman " ; there are black-letter volumes of Barnaby Googe, and books compiled by the distinguished " Captaine Garvase Markhame " and there is a Xenophon flanked by a Hesiod, and the heavy Greek squadron of the " Geoponics."

I delight immensely in taking an occasional wet-day talk with these old worthies. They were none of them chemists. I doubt if one of them could have made soil analyses which would have been worth any more, practically, than those of many of our agricultu-ral professors. Such powers of investigation as they had, they were not in the habit of wasting, and the results of their investigation were for the most part compactly managed. They put together their several budgets of common-sense notions about the practical art of husbandry, with good old-fashioned sturdiness and pointedness. And, after all — theorize as we will and dream as we will about new systems and scientific aids — there lies a mass of sagacious observation in the pages of the old teachers which can never be outlived, and which will contribute nearly as much to practical success in farming as the nice appliances of modern collegiate agriculture. Fortunately, however, it is not necessary to go to the pages of old books for the traces and aims of that sagacity which has always underlaid the best practice. Its precepts have become traditional.

And yet I delight in finding black-letter evidence of the age of the traditions and of the purity with which they have been kept. An important member of the County Society pays me a morning visit, and in the course of a field-stroll lays down authoritatively the opinion that "there's no kind o' use in ploughing for turnips in the spring, unless you keep the weeds down all through the season." I yield implicit and modest assent; and on my next wet day find Ischomachus remarking to Socrates,* — "This also, I think, it must be easy for you to understand, that, if ground is to lie fallow to good purpose, it ought to be free from weeds, and warmed as much as possible by the sun." And yet my distinguished friend of the County Society is not a student of Xenophon. If I read out of the big book the same observation to my foreman (who is more piquant than garrulous), he says, — "Xenophon, eh! well, well — there's sense in it."

Again, the distinguished county member on some Sunday, between services, puts his finger in my buttonhole, as we loiter under the lee side of the porch, and says, — "I tell *you*, Squire, there a'n't no sort o' use in flinging about your hay, as most folks does. If it's first

---

* *Œconomicus; Chap. XVI. § 13*

year after seedin', and there's a good deal o' clover in
it, I lay it up in little cocks as soon as it's wilted; next
morning I make 'em bigger, and after it's sweat a day
or so, I open it to dry off the steam a bit, and get it
into the mow;"— all which is most excellent advice,
and worthy of a newspaper. But, on my next rainy day,
I take up Heresbach,* and find Cono laying down the
law for Rigo in this wise:—

"The grasse being cut, you are to consider of what
nature the grasse is, whether very coarse and full of
strong weedes, thicke leaves and great store of peony-
grasse, or else exceeding fine and voyd of anything
which asketh much withering; If it be of the first kind,
then after the mowing you shall first ted it, then raise
it into little grasse Cockes as bigge as small molehills,
after turne them, and make them up again, then spread
them; and after full drying put them into wind rowes,
so into greater Cockes, then break those open, and after
they have received the strength of the Sunne, then put
three or four Cockes into one, and lastly leade them into
the Barns."

If I read this to my foreman, he says, "There's sense
in that."

And when I render to him out of the epigram-
matic talk of Cato, the maxim that "a man should farm

---

* "*The whole Arte of Husbandry*, first written by Conrade Heresbatch, and translated by Barnaby Googe, Esquire;" Book I.

no more land than he can farm well," and that other,
" that a farmer should be a seller rather than a buyer,"
Mr. McManus (the foreman) brings his brown fist
down with an authoritative rap upon the table that ies
between us, and says, — " That 's sense ! "

In short, the shrewd sagacity, the keen worldly prudence, which I observe to lie at the root of all the
farming thrift around me, I detect in a hundred
bristling paragraphs of the Latin masters whose pages
are before me.

" Sell your old cattle and your good-for-nothing
sheep," * says Cato ; and, true to the preachment, some
thrifty man of an adjoining town tries to pass upon me a
toothless cow or a spavined horse. " Establish your farm
near to market, or adjoining good roads," † says the Roman, and thereupon the New-Englander pounces down
in his two-story white house upon the very edge of the
highway. And not alone in these lesser matters, but
in all that relates to husbandry, I take a curious interest
in following up the traces of cousinship between the
old and the new votaries of the craft; and believing
that I may find for a few wet days of talk, a little parish
of country livers who have a kindred interest, I propose
in this book to review the suggestions and drift of the

---

* " Vendat boves vetulos . . . . oves rejiculas [and the old heathen
scoundrel continues] servum senem, servum morbosum."
† " Oppidum validum propè siet . . . . aut via bona."

various agricultural writers, beginning with the **Greeks,** and coming down to a period within the memory of those who are living. I shall also take the liberty of relieving the talk with mention of those pastoral writers who have thrown some light upon the rural life of their days, or who by a truthfulness and simplicity of touch have made their volumes welcome ones upon the shelves of every country library.

The books practical and poetical which relate to flower and field, stand wedded on my shelves and wedded in my thought. In the text of Xenophon I see the ridges piling along the Elian fields, and in the music of Theocritus I hear a lark that hangs hovering over the straight-laid furrows. An elegy of Tibullus peoples with lovers a farmstead that Columella describes. The sparrows of Guarini twitter up and down along the steps of Crescenzi's terraced gardens. Hugh Platt dibbles a wheat-lot, and Spenser spangles it with dew. Tull drives his horse-hoe a-field where Thomson wakes a chorus of voices, and flings the dappling shadows of clouds.

Why divorce these twin-workers towards the profits and the entertainment of a rural life? Nature has solemnized the marriage of the beautiful with the practical by touching some day, sooner or later, every lifting harvest with a bridal sheen of blossoms ; no clover-crop is perfect without its bloom, and no pasture hill-

side altogether what Providence intended it should be,
until the May sun has come and stamped it over with
its fiery brand of dandelions.

Hesiod and Homer.

HESIOD is currently reckoned one of the oldest
farm - writers; but there is not enough in his
homely poem ("Works and Days") out of which to
conjure a farm-system.   He gives good advice, indeed,
about the weather, about ploughing when the ground is
not too wet, about the proper timber to put to a plough-
beam, about building a house, and taking a bride.   He
also commends the felling of wood in autumn, — a
suggestion in which most lumbermen will concur with
him, although it is questionable if sounder timber is
not secured by cutting before the falling of the leaves.

> "When the tall forest sheds her foliage round,
> And with autumnal verdure strews the ground,
> The bole is incorrupt, the timber good, —
> Then whet the sounding ax to fell the wood." *

The old Greek expresses a little doubt of young folk

> "Let a good ploughman years ared to forty, drive :
> And see the careful husbandman be fed
> With plenteous morsels, and of wholesome bread:

* Cooke's *Hesiod;* Book II.

The slave who numbers fewer days, you'll find
Careless of work and of a rambling mind."

He is not true to modern notions of the creature comforts in advising (Book II. line 244) that the oxen be stinted of their fodder in winter, and still less in his suggestion (line 285) that three parts of water should be added to the Biblian wine.

Mr. Gladstone notes the fact that Homer talks only in a grandiose way of rural life and employments, as if there were no small landholders in his day; but Hesiod, who must have lived within a century of Homer, with his modest homeliness, does not confirm this view. He tells us a farmer should keep two ploughs, and be cautious how he lends either of them. His household stipulations, too, are most moderate, whether on the score of the bride, the maid, or the "forty-year-old" ploughman; and for guardianship of the premises the proprietor is recommended to keep " a sharp-toothed cur."

This reminds us how Ulysses, on his return from voyaging, found seated round his good bailiff Eumæus four savage watch-dogs, who straightway (and here Homer must have nodded) attack their old master, and are driven off only by a good pelting of stones.

This Eumæus may be regarded as the Homeric representative farmer, as well as bailiff and swineherd, — the great original of Gurth, who might have prepared a supper for Cedric the Saxon very much as

Eumæus extemporized one upon his Greek farm for Ulysses. Pope shall tell of this bit of cookery in rhyme that has a ring of the Rappahannock:—

> " His vest succinct then girding round his waist,
> Forth rushed the swain with hospitable haste,
> Straight to the lodgments of his herd he run,
> Where the fat porkers slept beneath the sun;
> Of two his cutlass launched the spouting blood;
> These quartered, singed, and fixed on forks of wood,
> All hasty on the hissing coals he threw;
> And, smoking, back the tasteful viands drew,
> Broachers, and all."

This is roast pig: nothing more elegant or digestible. For the credit of Greek farmers, I am sorry that Eumæus had nothing better to offer his landlord, — the most abominable dish, Charles Lamb and his pleasant fable to the contrary notwithstanding, that was ever set before a Christian.

But there is pleasanter and more odorous scent of the Homeric country in the poet's flowing description of the garden of Alcinous; and thither, on this wet day, I conduct my reader, under leave of the King of the Phæacians:—

> " Four acres was the allotted space of ground,
> Fenced with a green enclosure all around,
> Tall thriving trees confined the fruitful mould;
> The reddening apple ripens here to gold.
> Here the blue fig with luscious juice o'erflows,
> With deeper red the full pomegranate glows;

The branch here bends beneath the weighty pear,
And verdant olives flourish round the year.
The balmy spirit of the western gale
Eternal breathes on fruits untaught to fail:
Each dropping pear a following pear supplies;
On apples apples, figs on figs arise:
The same mild season gives the blooms to blow,
The buds to harden and the fruits to grow.

"Here ordered vines in equal ranks appear,
With all th' united labors of the year;
Some to unload the fertile branches run,
Some dry the blackening clusters in the sun;
Others to tread the liquid harvest join,
The groaning presses foam with floods of wine.
Here are the vines in early flowers descried,
Here grapes discolored on the sunny side,
And there in autumn's richest purple dyed."

Is this not a pretty garden-scene for a blind poet to
lay down? Horace Walpole, indeed, in an ill-natured
way, tells us,* that, "divested of harmonious Greek and
bewitching poetry," it was but a small orchard and vineyard, with some beds of herbs and two fountains that
watered them, enclosed by a thick-set hedge. I do not
thank him for the observation; I prefer to regard the
four acres of Alcinous with all the Homeric bigness
and glow upon them. And under the same old Greek
haze I see the majestic Ulysses, in his tattered clothes
flinging back the taunts of the trifling Eurymachus,

* Lord Orford's Works, 1793; Vol. II. p. 520.

and in the spirit of a yeoman who knew how to handle
a plough as well as a spear, boasting after this style: —

> " Should we, O Prince, engage
> In rival tasks beneath the burning rage
> Of summer suns; were both constrained to wield,
> Foodless, the scythe along the burdened field;
> Or should we labor, while the ploughshare wounds,
> With steers of equal strength, the allotted grounds;
> Beneath my labors, how thy wondering eyes
> Might see the sable field at once arise!"

To return to Hesiod, we suspect that he was only a
small farmer — if he had ever farmed at all — in the
foggy latitude of Bœotia, and knew nothing of the sunny
wealth in the south of the peninsula, or of such princely
estates as Eumæus managed in the Ionian Seas. Flaxman has certainly not given him the look of a large
proprietor in his outlines : his toilet is severely scant,
and the old gentleman appears to have lost two of his
fingers in a chaff-cutter. As for Perses, who is rep-
resented as listening to the sage,* his dress is in the
extreme of classic scantiness, — being, in fact, a mere
night-shirt, and a tight fit at that.

But we dismiss Hesiod, the first of the heathen farm-
writers, with a loving thought of his pretty Pandora,
whom the goddesses so bedecked, whom Jove looks on
(in Flaxman's picture) with such sharp approval, and

* Flaxman's Illustrations of *Works and Days;* Plate I.

whose attributes the poet has compacted into one **resonant** line, daintily rendered by Cooke, —

" Thus the sex began
A lovely mischief to the soul of man."

Xenophon.

I NEXT beg to pull from his place upon the shelf, and to present to the reader, General Xenophon, a most graceful writer, a capital huntsman, an able strategist, an experienced farmer, and, if we may believe Laertius, "handsome beyond expression."

It is refreshing to find such qualities united in one man at any time, and doubly refreshing to find them in a person so far removed from the charities of to-day that the malcontents cannot pull his character in pieces. To be sure, he was guilty of a few acts of pillage in the course of his Persian campaign, but he tells the story of it in his "Anabasis" with a brave front; his purse was low, and needed replenishment; there is no cover put up, of disorderly sutlers or camp-followers.

The farming reputation of the general rests upon his "Œconomics" and his horse-treatise ('Ἱππική).

Economy has come to have a contorted meaning in our day, as if it were only — saving. Its true gist is better expressed by the word *management*; and in that old-fashioned sense it forms a significant title for Xen-

ophon's book: management of the household, management of flocks, of servants, of land, and of property in
g*n*eral.

At the very outset we find this bit of practical wisdom, which is put into the mouth of Socrates, who is
replying to Critobulus: — "Those things should be
called goods that are beneficial to the master. Neither
can those lands be called goods which by a man's un-
skilful management put him to more expense than he
receives profit by them ; nor may those lands be called
goods which do not bring a good farmer such a profit
as may give him a good living."

Thereafter (sec. vii.) he introduces the good Ischomachus, who, it appears, has a thrifty wife at home, and
from that source flow in a great many capital hints upon
domestic management. The apartments, the exposure,
the cleanliness, the order, are all considered in such an
admirably practical, common-sense way as would make
the old Greek a good lecturer to the sewing-circles of
our time. And when the wife of the wise Ischomachus,
in an unfortunate moment, puts on *rouge* and cosmetics,
the grave husband meets her with this complimentary
rebuke: — "Can there be anything in Nature more
complete than yourself?"

"The science of husbandry," he says, and it might
be said of the science in most times, "is extremely profitable to those who understand it; but it brings the

greatest trouble and misery upon those farmers who undertake it without knowledge." (sec. xv.)

Where Xenophon comes to speak of the details of farm-labor, of ploughings and fallowings, there is all that precision and particularity of mention, added to a shrewd sagacity, which one might look for in the columns of the " Country Gentleman." He even describes how a field should be thrown into narrow lands, in order to promote a more effectual surface-drainage. In the midst of it, however, we come upon a stercorary maxim, which is, to say the least, of doubtful worth : —
" Nor is there any sort of earth which will not make very rich manure, by being laid a due time in standing water, till it is fully impregnated with the virtue of the water." One of his British translators, Professor Bradley, does, indeed, give a little note of corroborative testimony. But I would not advise any active farmer, on the authority either of General Xenophon or of Professor Bradley, to transport his surface-soil very largely to the nearest frog-pond, in the hope of finding it transmuted into manure. The absorptive and retentive capacity of soils is, to be sure, the bone just now of very particular contention; but whatever that capacity may be, it certainly needs something more palpable than the virtue of standing water for its profitable development.

Here, again, is very neat evidence of how much

2

simple good sense has to do with husbandry : Socrates,
who is supposed to have no particular knowledge of the
craft, says to his interlocutor, — " You have satisfied me
that I am not ignorant in husbandry ; and yet I never
had any master to instruct me in it."

" It is not," says Xenophon, " difference in knowledge
or opportunities of knowledge that makes some farmers
rich and others poor ; but that which makes some poor
and some rich is that the former are negligent and lazy,
the latter industrious and thrifty."

Next, we have this masculine *ergo :* — " Therefore we
may know that those who will not learn such sciences
as they might get their living by, or do not fall into
husbandry, are either downright fools, or else propose
to get their living by robbery or by begging." (sec. xx.)

This is a good clean cut at politicians, office-holders,
and other such beggar-craft, through more than a score
of centuries, — clean as classicism can make it : the
Attic euphony in it, and all the aroma of age.

Once more, and it is the last of the " Œconomicus,"
we give this charming bit of New-Englandism : — " I
remember my father had an excellent rule," (*Ischomachus loquitur,*) " which he advised me to follow : that,
if ever I bought any land, I should by no means purchase that which had been already well-improved, but
should choose such as had never been tilled, either
through neglect of the owner, or for want of capacity

to do it; for he observed, that, if I were to purchase improved grounds, I must pay a high price for them, and then I could not propose to advance their value, and must also lose the pleasure of improving them myself, or of seeing them thrive better by my endeavors." *

When Xenophon wrote his rural treatises, (including the Κυνηγετικός,) he was living in that delightful region of country which lies westward of the mountains of Arcadia, looking toward the Ionian Sea. Here, too, he wrote the story of his retreat, and his wanderings among the mountains of Armenia; here he talked with his friends, and made other such *symposia* as he has given us a taste of at the house of Callias the Athenian; here he ranged over the whole country-side with his horses and dogs: a stalwart and lithe old gentleman, without a doubt; able to mount a horse or to manage one, with the supplest of the grooms; and with a keen eye, as his book shows, for the good points in horse-flesh. A man might make a worse mistake than to buy a horse after Xenophon's instructions, to-day. A spavin or a wind-gall did not escape the old gentleman's eye, and he never bought a nag without proving his wind, and handling him well about the mouth and ears.

* It is worthy of note that Cato advises a contrary practice, and urges that purchase of land be made of a good farmer. "Caveto ne alienam disciplinam temere contemnas. De domino bono colono, bonoque ædificatore melius emetur." — *De Re Rustica,* I.

His grooms were taught their duties with nice speciality: the mane and tail to be thoroughly washed; the food and bed to be properly and regularly prepared: and treatment to be always gentle and kind.

Exception may perhaps be taken to his doctrine in regard to stall-floors. Moist ones, he says, injure the hoof: "Better to have stones inserted in the ground close to one another, equal in size to their hoofs; for such stalls consolidate the hoofs of those standing on them, beside strengthening the hollow of the foot."

After certain directions for rough riding and leaping, he advises hunting through thickets, if wild animals are to be found. Otherwise, the following pleasant diversion is named, which I beg to suggest to sub-lieutenants in training for dragoon-service : — " It is a useful exercise for two horsemen to agree between themselves, that one shall retire through all sorts of rough places, and as he flees, is to turn about from time to time and present his spear; and the other shall pursue, having javelins blunted with balls, and a spear of the same description, and whenever he comes within javelin-throw, he is to hurl the blunted weapon at the party retreating, and whenever he comes within spear-reach, he is to strike him with it."

Putting aside his horsemanship, in which he must have been nearly perfect, there was very much that was grand about the old Greek, — very much that makes us

strangely love the man, who, when his soldiers lay be-
numbed under the snows on the heights of Armenia,
threw off his general's coat, or blanket, or what not,
and set himself resolutely to wood-chopping and to
cheering them. The farmer knew how. Such men win
battles. He has his joke, too, with Cheirisophus, the
Lacedæmonian, about the thieving propensity of his
townspeople, and invites him, in virtue of it, to *steal* a
difficult march upon the enemy. And Cheirisophus
grimly retorts upon Xenophon, that Athenians are said
to be great experts in stealing the public money, especially the high officers. This sounds home-like! When
I come upon such things, — by Jupiter! — I forget the
parasangs and the Taochians and the dead Cyrus, and
seem to be reading out of American newspapers.

Theocritus and Lesser Poets.

IT is quite out of the question to claim Theocritus as
a farm-writer; and yet in all old literature there is
not to be found such a lively bevy of heifers, and wanton kids, and "butting rams," and stalwart herdsmen,
who milk the cows "upon the sly," as in the "Idyls" of
the musical Sicilian.

There is no doubt but Theocritus knew the country
to a charm : he knew all its roughnesses, and the thorns
that scratched the bare legs of the goatherds; he

knew the lank heifers, that fed, "like grasshoppers,"
only on dew; he knew what clatter the brooks made,
tumbling headlong adown the rocks; * he knew, moreover, all the charms and coyness of the country-
nymphs, giving even a rural twist to his praises of the
courtly Helen:—

> "In shape, in height, in stately presence fair,
> Straight as a furrow gliding from the share." †

A man must have had an eye for good ploughing and
a lithe figure, as well as a keen scent for the odor of
fresh-turned earth, to make such a comparison as that!

Again, he gives us an Idyl of the Reapers. Milo and
Battus are afield together. The last lags at his work,
and Milo twits him with his laziness; whereupon Battus
retorts,—

> "Milo, thou moiling drudge, as hard as stone,
> An absent mistress did'st thou ne'er bemoan?"

And Milo,—

> "Not I,—I never learnt fair maids to woo;
> Pray, what with love have reaping men to do?"

Yet he listens to the plaint of his brother-reaper, and
draws him out in praise of his mistress—"charming

* The resounding clatter of his falling water is too beautiful to be
omitted:—

— ἀπὸ τᾶς πέτρας καταλείβεται ὑψόθεν ὕδωρ·

† Elton's translation, I think. I do not vouch for its correctness

Bombyce," — upon which lóve-lorn strain Milo breaks
in, rough and homely and breezy: —

> " My Battus, witless with a beard so long,
> Attend to tuneful Lytierses' song.
> O fruitful Ceres, bless with corn the field;
> May the full ears a plenteous harvest yield!
> Bind, reapers, bind your sheaves, lest strangers say,
> ' Ah, lazy drones, their hire is thrown away! '
> To the fresh north wind or the zephyrs rear
> Your shocks of corn; those breezes fill the ear.
> Ye threshers, never sleep at noon of day,
> For then the light chaff quickly blows away.
> Reapers should rise with larks to earn their hire,
> Rest in the heat, and with the larks retire.
> How happy is the fortune of a frog:
> He wants no moisture in his watery bog.
> Steward, boil all the pease: such pinching 's mean,
> You 'll cut your hand by splitting of a bean."

Theocritus was no French sentimentalist; he would
have protested against the tame elegancies of the Roman Bucolics; and the *sospiri ardenti* and *miserelli
amanti* of Guarini would have driven him mad. He is as
brisk as the wind upon a breezy down. His cow-tenders
are swart and barelegged, and love with a vengeance.
It is no Boucher we have here, nor Watteau: cosmetics
and rosettes are far away; tunics are short, and cheeks
are nut-brown. It is Teniers rather: — boors, indeed;
but they are live boors, and not manikin shepherds
There is no miserable tooting upon flutes, but an up

roarious song that shakes the woods; and if it comes to a matter of kissing, there are no "reluctant lips," but a smack that makes the vales resound.

I shall call out another Sicilian here, named Moschus, were it only for his picture of a fine, sturdy bullock: it occurs in his "Rape of Europa": —

> "With yellow hue his sleekened body beams;
> His forehead with a snowy circle gleams;
> Horns, equal-bending, from his brow emerge,
> And to a moonlight crescent orbing verge."

Nothing can be finer than the way in which this "milky steer," with Europa on his back, goes sailing over the brine, his "feet all oars." Meantime, she, the pretty truant,

> " Grasps with one hand his curved projecting horn,
> And with the other closely drawn compressed
> The fluttering foldings of her purple vest,
> Whene'er its fringèd hem was dashed with dew
> Of the salt sea-foam that in circles flew:
> Wide o'er Europa's shoulders to the gale
> The ruffled robe heaved swelling, like a sail."

Moschus is as rich as the Veronese at Venice ; and his picture is truer to the premium standard. The painting shows a pampered animal, with over-red blotches on his white hide, and is by half too fat to breast such " salt sea-foam" as flashes on the Idyl of Moschus.

Another poet, Aratus of Cilicia, whose very name has a smack of tillage, has left us a book about the weather (Διοσημεῖα) which is quite as good to mark down a hay-day by as the later meteorologies of Professoɪ Espɣ or Judge Butler.

Besides which, our friend Aratus holds the abiding honor of having been quoted by St. Paul, in his speech to the Athenians on Mars Hill:—

" For in Him we live, and move, and have our being; as certain also of your own poets have said : ' For we are also His offspring.' "

And Aratus, (after Elton,) —

> " On thee our being hangs; in thee we move;
> All are thy offspring, and the seed of Jove."

Scattered through the lesser Greek poets, and up and down the Anthology, are charming bits of rurality, redolent of the fields and of field-life, with which it would be easy to fill up the measure of this rainy day, and beat off the Grecian couplets to the tinkle of the eave-drops. Up and down, the cicada chirps; the locust, " encourager of sleep," sings his drowsy song; boozy Anacreon flings grapes ; the purple violets and the daffodils crown the perfumed head of Heliodora ; and the reverent Simonides likens our life to the grass.

Nor will I part company with these, or close up the Greek ranks of farmers, (in which I must not forget the great schoolmaster, Theophrastus,) until I cull a sample of the Anthology, and plant it for a guidon at the head of the column, — a little bannerol of music, touching upon our topic, as daintily as the bees touch the flowering tips of the wild thyme.

It is by Zonas the Sardian : —

Ἀ! δ' ἄγετε ξουθαὶ σιμβληΐδες ἄκρα μέλισσαι,

κ. τ. λ., —

and the rendering by Mr. Hay : —

> "Ye nimble honey-making bees, the flowers are in their prime;
> Come now and taste the little buds of sweetly breathing thyme,
> Of tender poppies all so fair, or bits of raisin sweet,
> Or down that decks the apple tribe, or fragrant violet;
> Come, nibble on, — your vessels store with honey while you can,
> In order that the hive-protecting, bee-preserving Pan
> May have a tasting for himself, and that the hand so rude,
> That cuts away the comb, may leave yourselves some little food."

Cato.

LEAVING now this murmur of the bees upon the banks of the Pactolus, we will slip over-seas to Tusculum, where Cato was born, who was the oldest of the Roman writers upon agriculture ; and thence into the Sabine territory, where, upon an estate of his father's, in the midst of the beautiful country lying northward of the Monte Gennaro, (the Lucretilis of Horace,) he learned the art of good farming.

In what this art consisted in his day, he tells us in short, crackling speech : — "*Primum*, bene arare se-

cundum, arare; *tertium,* stercorare." Foi the rest, ho says, choose good seed, sow thickly, and pull all tho weeds. Nothing more would be needed to grow as good a crop upon the checkered plateau under my win dow as ever fattened among the Sabine Hills.

Has the art come to a stand-still, then ; and shall we take to reading Cato on fair days, as well as rainy ?

There has been advance, without doubt ; but all the advance in the world would not take away the edge from truths, stated as Cato knew how to state them. There is very much of what is called Agricultural Science, nowadays, which is — rubbish. Science is sound, and agriculture always an honest art ; but the mixture, not uncommonly, is bad, — no fair marriage, but a monstrous concubinage, with a monstrous progeny of muddy treatises and disquisitions which confuse more than they instruct. In contrast with these, it is no won- der that the observations of such a man as Cato, whose energies had been kept alive by service in the field, and whose tongue had been educated in the Roman Senate, should carry weight with them. The grand truths on which successful agriculture rests, and which simple experience long ago demonstrated, cannot be kept out of view, nor can they be dwarfed by any im- position of learning. Science may explain them, or illustrate or extend ; but it cannot shake their pre- ponderating influence upon the crop of the year. As

respects many other arts, the initial truths may be lost
sight of, and overlaid by the mass of succeeding devel
opments, — not falsified, but so belittled as practically
to be counted for nothing.   In this respect, agriculture
is exceptional.   The old story is always the safe story
you must plough and plough again; and manure; and
sow good seed, and enough; and pull the weeds; and
as sure as the rain falls, the crop will come.

Many nice additions to this method of treatment,
which my fine-farming friends will suggest, are antici-
pated by the old Roman, if we look far enough into his
book.   Thus, he knew the uses of a harrow; he knew
the wisdom of ploughing in a green crop; he had
steeps for his seed; he knew how to drain off the
surface-water, — nay, there is very much in his account
of the proper preparation of ground for olive-trees, or
vine-setting, which looks like a mastery of the principles that govern the modern system of drainage.*

Of what particular service recent investigations in
science have been to the practical farmer, and what
positive and available aid, beyond what could be derived from a careful study of the Roman masters, they
put into the hands of an intelligent worker, who is till-
ing ground simply for pecuniary advantage, I shall hope
to inquire and discourse upon some other day: when
that day comes, we will fling out the banner of the

* XLIII. "Sulcos, si locus aquosus erit, alveatos esse oportet," etc.

nineteenth century, and give a gun to Liebig, and John son, and the rest.

Meantime, as a farmer who endeavors to keep posted in all the devices for pushing lands which have an awkward habit of yielding poor crops into the better habit of yielding large ones, I will not attempt to conceal the chagrin with which I find this curmudgeon of a Roman Senator, living two centuries before Christ, and northward of Monte Gennaro, who never heard of " Hovey's Root-Cutter," or of the law of primaries, laying down rules* of culture so clear, so apt, so full, that I, who have the advantages of two thousand years, find nothing in them to laugh at, unless it be a few oblations to the gods ; † and this, considering that I am just now burning a little incense (Havana) to the nymph Volutia, is uncalled for.

And if Senator Cato were to wake up to-morrow, in the white house that stares through the rain yonder, and were to open his little musty vellum of slipshod maxims, and, in faith of it, start a rival farm in the bean-line, or in vine-growing, — keeping clear of the newspapers, — I make no doubt but he would prove as thrifty a neighbor as my good friend the Deacon.

We nineteenth-century men, at work among our cabbages, clipping off the purslane and the twitch-grass,

* This mention, of course, excludes the Senator's *formulæ* for unguents, aperients, cattle-nostrums, and pickled pork.

† CXXXIV. Cato, *De Re Rusticâ.*

are disposed to assume a very complacent attitude, as we lean upon our hoe-handles, — as if we were doing tall things in the way of illustrating physiology and the cognate sciences. But the truth is, old Laertes, near three thousand years ago, in his slouch cap and greasy beard, was hoeing up in the same way his purslane and twitch-grass, in his bean-patch on the hills of Ithaca. The difference between us, so far as the crop and the tools go, is, after all, ignominiously small. *He* dreaded the weevil in his beans, and *we* the club-foot in our cabbages ; *we* have the " Herald," and *he* had none ; *we* have " Plantation-Bitters," and *he* had his jug of the Biblian wine.

Varro.

M. VARRO, another Roman farmer, lies between the same covers " De Re Rusticâ " with Cato, and seems to have had more literary tact, though less of blunt sagacity. Yet he challenges at once our confidence by telling us so frankly the occasion of his writing upon such a subject. Life, he says, is a bubble, — and the life of an old man a bubble about to break. He is eighty, and must pack his luggage to go out of this world. (*"Annus octogesimus admonet me, ut sarcinas colligam antequam proficiscar e vitâ."*) Therefore he writes down for his wife, Fundania, the rules by which she may manage the farm.

And a very respectably old lady she must have been, to deal with the *villici* and the *coloni*, if her age bore suitable relation to that of her husband. The ripe maturity of many of the rural writers I have introduced cannot fail to arrest attention. Thus, Xenophon gained a strength in his Elian fields that carried him into the nineties; Cato lived to be over eighty; and now we have Varro, writing his book out by Tusculum at the same age, and surviving to counsel with Fundania ten years more. Pliny, too, (the elder,) who, if not a farmer, had his country-seats, and left very much to establish our acquaintance with the Roman rural life, was a hale, much-enduring man, of such soldierly habits and large abstemiousness as to warrant a good fourscore, — if he had not fallen under that murderous cloud of ashes from Mount Vesuvius, in the year 79.

The poets, doubtless, burnt out earlier, as they usually do. Virgil, whom I shall come to speak of presently, certainly did: he died at fifty-one. Tibullus, whose opening Idyl is as pretty a bit of gasconade about living in a cottage in the country, upon love and a few vege-tables, as a maiden could wish for, did not reach the fifties; and Martial, whose "Faustine Villa," if noth-ing else, entitles him to rural oblation, fell short of the sixties. Varro himself alludes with pride to the greater longevity of those who live in the country, and alleges as a reason, "*quod Divina natura dedit agros, ars*

humana ædificavit urbes." Is not this the possible
original of Cowper's " God made the country, and man
made the town "?

The old man is very full in his rules for Fundania,
not only as regards general management, but in respect
to the choice of land, the determination of its qualities, the building of the country-houses, the arrangement of the offices, the regimen of the servants, and
the treatment of the various manures and crops. He
clearly urges rotation, has faith in a very large influence of the moon, counts the droppings of pigeons
the best of all manures, and gives the sea-birds very
little credit for their contributions to the same office.*
I even find this octogenarian waxing jocose at times.
On a certain occasion he says, (it is mentioned in his
book of poultry and birds,†) " I paid a visit with a
friend to Appius Claudius, the Augur, and found him
seated, with Cornelius Merula [blackbird] and Fircel-
lius Pavo [peacock] on his left, while Minutius Pica
[magpie] and Petronius Passer [sparrow] were on his
right; whereupon my friend says, ' My good sir, you
receive us in your aviary, seated among your birds.' "
The jokelet is not indeed over-racy, but it has a quaint
twang, coming as it does in musty type over so many
centuries, from the pen of an old man of eighty, who

---

* Lib. ɪ cap. xxxviii. " Stercus optimum scribit Cassius esse volu-
crum, præter palustrium, ac nantium."

† Lib. III. cap. ii. *De Re Rustica.*

discussed guinea-fowl and geese, and who made morning calls at the house of Judge Appius Claudius.

Varro indulges in some sharp sneers at those who
had written on the same subject before him. This wai
natural enough in a man of his pursuits: he had written four hundred books.

Columella.

O F Columella we know scarcely more than that he
lived somewhere about the time of Tiberius, that
'he was a man of wealth, that he travelled extensively
through Gaul, Italy, and Greece, observing intelligently
different methods of culture, and that he has given the
fullest existing compend of ancient agriculture. In his
chapter upon Gardening he warms into hexameters;
but the rest is stately and euphonious prose. In his
opening chapter, he does not forego such praises of the
farmer's life as sound like a lawyer's address before a
county - society on a fair - day. Cincinnatus and his
plough come in for it; and Fabricius and Curius Dentatus ; with which names, luckily, our orators cannot
whet their periods, since Columella's mention of them
is about all we know of their farming.

He falls into the way, moreover, of lamenting, as
people obstinately continue to do, the "good old times,"
when men were better than "now," and when the rea-
sonable delights of the garden and the fields engrossed

3

them to the neglect of the circus and the theatres. But when he opens upon his subject proper, it is in grandiose Spanish style, (he was a native of Cadiz,) with a maxim broad enough to cover all possible conditions: — "Whoever would devote himself to the pursuit of agriculture should understand that he must summon to his aid — prudence in business, a faculty of spending, and a determination to work."* Or, as Tremellius says, — "That man will master the craft, who knows how to cultivate, *et poterit, et volet.*"

This is comprehensive, if not encouraging. It would be hard to say, indeed, in what particular this summation of Columella would not apply to the pursuit of almost any man. That "faculty of spending" is a tremendous bolster to a great many other things as well as farming. Neither parsons nor politicians can ignore it wholly. It is only another shape of the *poterit,* and the *poterit* only a scholarly rendering of pounds and pence. As if Tremellius had said, — That man will make his way at farming who understands the business, who has the money to apply to it, and who is willing to bleed freely. There are a great many people who have said the same thing since.

With a kindred sagacity this shrewd Roman advises a man to slip upon his farm often, in order that his stew

---

* 'Qui studium agricolationi dederit, sciat hæc sibi advocanda prudentiam rei, facultatem impendendi, voluntatem agendi."

ard may keep sharply at his work ; he even suggests
that the landlord make a feint of coming, when he has
no intention thereto, that he may gain a day's alertness
from the bailiff. The book is of course a measure of
the advances made in farming during the two hundred
years elapsed since Cato's time ; but those advances
were not great. There was advance in power to sys-
tematize facts, advance in literary aptitude, but no very
noticeable gain in methods of culture. Columella gives
the results of wider observation, and of more persistent
study ; but, for aught I can see, a man could get a crop
of lentils as well with Cato as with Columella ; a man
would house his flocks and servants as well out of the
one as the other ; in short, a man would grow into the
" faculty of spending " as swiftly under the teachings
of the Senator as of the later writer of the reign of
Tiberius.

It is to be observed, however, that, so far as one can
judge from the work of Columella, farming was now
conducted upon a grander scale. The days when Cincinnatus dug among his own cabbages, and Curius
Dentatus bent his own back to the *sarculum*, were long
gone by, and were looked back upon, I dare say, by the
first readers of the elegant Columella, as we look back
to the days of Captain Smith, Pocahontas, and corn-cakes
baked in the ashes. The details of a Roman farmery
which are entered upon by this author are of an extent
and of a nicety which would compare with an East-

Lothian steading. He divides the entire establishmenı into three distinct parts: the villa *urbana*, the villa *rustica*, and the *fructuaria*; or, as we might say, the mansion-house, the laborers' cottages, and the out-buildings. I give a reduced drawing of such a design from Castell's "Villas of the Ancients." * A huge kitchen, it

* The following letters and numbers indicate the several parts: —

A. THE VILLA URBANA.

a. Inner court.	*h.* Servants' hall.
b. Summer dining-room.	*i.* Dressing-room of baths.
c. Winter dining-room.	*k.* Bathing-room.
d. Withdrawing-rooms.	*l.* Warm cell.
e. Winter apartments.	*m.* Sweating-room.
f. Summer apartments.	*n.* Furnace.
g. Library.	*o.* Porters' lodges.

B. VILLA RUSTICA AND FRUCTUARIA.

1. Inner farm-yard.	23. Sheepfold.
2. Pond.	24. Shepherds.
3. Outer yard.	25. Goat-pens.
4. Kitchen.	26. Goatherds.
5. New wine.	27. Dog-kennels.
6. Old wine.	28. Cart-houses.
7. Housekeeper.	29. Hog-sties.
8. Spinning-room.	30. Hog-keepers.
9. To sick-room.	31. Bakehouse.
10. Lodges.	32. Mill.
11. Stairs to bailiff's room.	33. Outer pond.
12. Keeper of stoves.	34. Dunghills.
13. Stairs to work-house.	35. Wood and fodder.
14. Wine-press.	36. Hen-yard.
15. Oil-press.	37, 38. Dove-houses
16. Granaries.	39. Thrushes.
17. Fruit-room.	40. Poultry.
18. Master of cattle.	41. Poulterers.
19. Ox-stalls.	42. Porter.
20. Herdsmen.	43. Dog-kennels.
21. Stables.	44. Orchard.
22. Grooms	45. Kitchen-garden

A ROMAN FARMERY.

will be seen, forms a prominent feature of the " rustic • part of the establishment, and opening directly upon the kitchen are the ox-stalls. Behind these is a court flanked by the herdsmen's quarters, and by the wine-cellars; and still farther in the rear, a larger court with goat-pens, cells for the goatherds, and kennels for dogs. In short, it is an establishment which would have amazed old Hesiod with his couplet of ploughs and his " sharp-toothed cur."

Columella urges, like Cato, frequent ploughings, — suggesting that they be repeated until no trace of the furrows can be detected, by which we may infer that the ploughs carried but a scanty mould-board. He advises that manures be turned under immediately after their application, and shows himself up to the best practice of our time in directing that the manure-heap be protected from the weather. He commends the lucern and the cytisus, is full in the matter of all field-crops, and his garden-poem shows gleams of sunny fruit, from the apple to the pomegranate. His instructions in respect of poultry are of the amplest, and, bating a little heathen wickedness of treatment, are better than the majority of poulterers could give us now

It is but dull work to follow all these teachings ; here and there I warm into a little sympathy, as I catch sight, in his Latin dress, of our old friend *Curculio;* here and there I sniff a fruit that seems famil

lar, — as the *fraga*, or a *morum ;* and here and there
comes blushing into the crabbed text the sweet name
of some home-flower, — a lily, a narcissus, or a rose.
The chief value of the work of Columella, however,
lies in its clear showing-forth of the relative importance
given to different crops, under Roman culture, and to
the raising of cattle, poultry, fish, etc., as compared with
crops. Knowing this, we know very much that will
help us toward an estimate of the domestic life of the
Romans. We learn, with surprise, how little they regarded their oxen, save as working-animals, — whether
the milk-white steers of Clitumnus, or the dun Campanian cattle, whose descendants show their long-
horned stateliness to this day in the Roman forum.
The sheep, too, whether of Tarentum or of Canusium,
were regarded as of value chiefly for their wool and
milk ; and it is surely amazing, that men who could
appreciate the iambics of Horace and the eloquence of
Cicero should have shown so little fancy for a fat
saddle of mutton or for a mottled sirloin of beef.

A Roman Dream.

I CHANGE from Columella to Virgil, and from Virgil
back to some pleasant Idyl of Tibullus, and from
Tibullus to the pretty prate of Horace about the Sabine Hills ; I stroll through Pliny's villa, eying the

clipped box-trees ; I hear the rattle in the tennis-court,
I watch the tall Roman girls —

" Grandes virgines proborum colonorum " —

marching along with their wicker-baskets filled with
curds and fresh-plucked thrushes, until there comes
over me a confusion of times and places.

— The sound of the battle of to-day dies ; the fresh
blood-stains fade ; and I seem to wake upon the heights
of Tusculum, in the days of Tiberius.   The farm-flat
below is a miniature Campagna, along which I see
s*retching straight to the city the shining pavement of
the Via Tusculana.   The spires yonder melt into mist,
and in place of them I see the marble house-walls of
which Augustus boasted.   As yet the grander monuments of the Empire are not built ; but there is a
blotch of cliff which may be the Tarpeian Rock, and
beside it a huge hulk of building on the Capitoline
Hill, where sat the Roman Senate.   A little hitherward
are the gay turrets of the villa of Mæcenas, and of the
princely houses on the Palatine Hill, and in the foreground the stately tomb of Cæcilia Metella.   I see the
barriers of a hippodrome (where now howling jockeys
make the twilight hideous) ; a *gestatio*, with its lines of
trees, is before me, and the velvety lavender-green of
olive-orchards covers the hills behind.   Vines grow
upon the slope eastward, —

"Neve tibi ad solem vergant vineta cadenten.,"-

twining around, and flinging off a great wealth of ten drils from their supporting-poles (*pedamenta*). The figs begin to show the purple bloom of fruitage, and the *villicus*, who has just now come in from the *atriolum*, reports a good crop, and asks if it would not be well to apply a few loads of marl (*tofacea*) to the summer fallow, which Cato is just now breaking up with the Campanian steers, for barley.

Scipio, a stanch Numidian, has gone to market with three asses loaded with cabbages and asparagus. Villicus tells me that the poultry in the fattening-coops (as close-shut as the Strasburg geese) * are doing well, and he has added a *soupçon* of sweetening to their barley-gruel. The young doves have their legs faithfully broken, ("*obteras crura*,") and are placidly fattening on their stumps. The thrush-house is properly darkened, only enough light entering to show the food to some three or four thousand birds, which are in course of cramming for the market. The *cochlearium* has a good stock of snails and mussels; and the little dormice are growing into fine condition for an approaching Imperial banquet.

Villicus reports the clip of the Tarentine sheep un-

* "Locus ad hanc rem desideratur maxime calidus, et minimi lt mi-nis, in quo singulæ caveis angustioribus vel sportis inclusæ pendeant aves, sed ita coarctatæ, *ne versari possint.*" — Columella, Lib. VIII. cap. vii

usually fine, and free from burrs. The new must is all a-foam in the *vinaria;* and around the inner cellar (*gaudendum est!*) there is a tier of urns, as large as school-boys, brimming with ripe Falernian.

If it were not stormy, I might order out the farm-chariot, or *curriculum*, which is, after all, but a low, dumpy kind of horse-cart, and take a drive over the lava pavement of the Via Tusculana, to learn what news is astir, and what the citizens talk of in the forum. Is all quiet upon the Rhine? How is it possibly with Germanicus? And what of that story of the arrest of Seneca? It could hardly have happened, they say, in the good old days of the Republic.

And with this mention, as with the sound of a gun, the Roman pastoral dream is broken. The Campagna, the olive-orchards, the *columbarium*, fall back to their old places in the blurred type of Columella. The Campanian steers are unyoked, and stabled in the text of Varro. The turrets of the villa of Mæcenas, and of the palaces of Sylla and the Cæsars, give place to the spires of a New-England town, — southward of which I see through the mist a solitary flag flying over a soldiers' hospital. It reminds of nearer and deadlier perils than ever environed the Roman Republic, — perils out of which, if the wisdom and courage of the people do not find a way, some new Cæsar will point it with the sword.

Looking northward, I see there is a bight of blue in the sky ; and a lee set of dark-gray and purple clouds is folding down over the eastern horizon, — against which the spires and the flag show clearer than ever. It means that the rain has stopped ; and the rain hav ing stopped, my in-door work is done.

SECOND DAY.

Virgil.

SNOWING: the checkered fields below are trace-able now only by the brown lines of fences and the sparse trees that mark the hedge-rows. The white of the houses and of the spires of the town is seen dimly through the snow, and seems to waver and shift position like the sails and spars of ships seen through fog. And straightway upon this image of ships and swaying spars I go sailing back to the farm-land of the past, and sharpen my pen for another day's work among the old farm-writers.

I suspect Virgil was never a serious farmer. I am confident he never had one of those callosities upon the inner side of his right thumb which come of the lower thole of a scythe-snath, after a week's mowing. But he had that quick poet's eye which sees at a glance what other men see only in a day. Not a shrub or a tree, not a bit of fallow ground or of nodding lentil

escaped his observation ; not a bird or a bee ; not even
the mosquitoes, which to this day hover pestiferously
about the low-lying sedge-lands of Mantua. His first
pastoral, little known now, and rarely printed with his
works, is inscribed *Culex.**

Young Virgil appears to have been of a delicate constitution, and probably left the fever-bearing regions of
the Mincio for the higher plain of Milan for sanitary
reasons, as much as the other, — of studying, as men
of his parts did study, Greek and philosophy. There is
a story, indeed, that he studied and practised farriery,
as his father had done before him ; and Jethro Tull, in
his crude onslaught upon what he calls the Virgilian
husbandry, (chap. ix.,) intimates that a farrier could be
no way fit to lay down the rules for good farm-practice.
But this story of his having been a horse-doctor rests,
so far as I can discover, only on this flimsy tradition, —
that the young poet, on his way to the South of Italy,
after leaving Milan and Mantua, fell in at Rome with
the master-of-horse to Octavianus, and gave such shrewd
hints to that official in regard to the points and failings
of certain favorite horses of the Roman Triumvir (for
Octavianus had not as yet assumed the purple) as to
gain a presentation to the future Augustus, and rich
marks of his favor.

It is certain that the poet journeyed to the South

* " *Lusimus :* hæc ·ropter *Culicis* sint carmina dicta."

and that thenceforward the glorious sunshine of Baiæ
and of the Neapolitan shores gave a color to his poems
and to his life.

Yet his agricultural method was derived almost
wholly from his observation in the North of Italy. He
never forgot the marshy borders of the Mincio, nor the
shores of beautiful Benacus (Lago di Garda); who
knows but he may some time have driven his flocks
a-field on the very battle-ground of Solferino?

But the ruralities of Virgil take a special interest
from the period in which they were written. He followed upon the heel of long and desolating intestine
wars, — a singing-bird in the wake of vultures. No
wonder the voice seemed strangely sweet.

The eloquence of the Senate had long ago lost its
traditionary power ; the sword was every way keener.
Who should listen to the best of speakers, when Pom-
pey was in the forum, covered with the spoils of the
East? Who should care for Cicero's periods, when the
magnificent conqueror of Gaul is skirting the Umbrian
Marshes, making straight for the Rubicon and Rome?

Then came Pharsalia, with its bloody trail, from
which Cæsar rises only to be slaughtered in the Senate-
Chamber. Next comes the long duel between the
Triumvirate and the palsied representatives of the
Republican party. Philippi closes that interlude; and
there is a new duel between Octavianus and Antony

(Lepidus counting for nothing). The gallant lover of
Cleopatra is pitted against a gallant general who is
a nephew to the first Cæsar. The fight comes off at
Actium, and the lover is the loser ; the pretty Egyptian
Jezebel, with her golden-prowed galleys, goes sweeping
down, under a full press of wind, to swell the squadron
of the conqueror. The winds will always carry the
Jezebels to the conquering side.

Such, then, was the condition of Italy, — its families
divided, its grain-fields trampled down by the Volscian
cavalry, its houses red with fresh blood-stains, its homes
beyond the Po parcelled out to lawless returning soldiers, its public security poised on the point of the
sword of Augustus, — when Virgil's Bucolics appear : a
pastoral thanksgiving for the patrimony that had been
spared him, through court-favor.

There is a show of gross adulation that makes one
blush for his manhood ; but withal he is a most lithe-
some poet, whose words are like honeyed blossoms, and
whose graceful measure is like a hedge of bloom that
sways with spring breezes, and spends perfume as it
sways.

The Georgics were said to have been written at the
suggestion of Mæcenas, a cultivated friend of Augustus,
who, like many another friend of the party in power,
had made a great fortune out of the wars that desolated
Italy. He made good use of it, however. in patronizing

Viigil, and in bestowing a snug farm in the Sabine country upon Horace; where I had the pleasure of drinking goats' milk — " *dulci digne mero* " — in the spring
of 1846.

There can be no doubt but Virgil had been an attentive reader of Xenophon, of Hesiod, of Cato, and of
Varro; otherwise he certainly would have been unwor-
thy of the task he had undertaken, — that of laying
down the rules of good husbandry in a way that should
insure the reading of them, and kindle a love for the
pursuit.

I suspect that Virgil was not only a reader of all that
had been written on the subject, but that he was also an
insistant questioner of every sagacious landholder and
every sturdy farmer that he fell in with, whether on the
Campanian hills or at the house of Mæcenas. How
else does a man accomplish himself for a didactic work
relating to matters of fact? I suspect, moreover,
that Virgil, during those half dozen years in which he
was engaged upon this task, lost no opportunity of in-
specting every beehive that fell in his way, of measur-
ing the points and graces of every pretty heifer he saw
in the fields, and of noting with the eye of an artist
the color of every furrow that glided from the plough.
It is inconceivable that a man of his intellectual address
should have given so much of literary toil to a work
that was not in every essential fully up to the best

practice of the day. Five years, it is said, were given
to the accomplishment of this short poem. What say
our poetasters to this? Fifteen hundred days, we will
suppose, to less than twice as many lines; blocking out
four or five for his morning's task, and all the evening
— for he was a late worker — licking them into shape,
as a bear licks her cubs.

But what good is in it all? Simply as a work of
art, it will be cherished through all time, — an earlier
Titian, whose color can never fade. It was, besides, a
most beguiling peace-note, following upon the rude blasts
of war. It gave a new charm to forsaken homesteads.
Under the Virgilian leadership, Monte Gennaro and the
heights of Tusculum beckon the Romans to the fields;
the meadows by reedy Thrasymene are made golden
with doubled crops. The Tarentine sheep multiply
around Benacus, and crop close those dark bits of
herbage which have been fed by the blood of Roman
citizens.

Thus much for the magic of the verse; but there is
also sound farm-talk in Virgil. I am aware that Seneca,
living a few years after him, invidiously objects that
he was more careful of his language than of his doctrine, and that Columella quotes him charily, — that
the collector of the " Geoponics" ignores him, and that
Tull gives him clumsy raillery; but I have yet to see in
what respect his system falls short of Columella, or how

5

it differs materially, except in fulness, from the teachings of Crescenzi, who wrote a thousand years and more later. There is little in the poem, save its superstitions, from which a modern farmer can dissent.*

We are hardly launched upon the first Georgic before we find a pretty suggestion of the theory of rotation, —

"Sic quoque mutatis requiescunt fœtĭbuε γrra."

Rolling and irrigation both glide into the verse a few lines later. He insists upon the choice of the best seed, advises to keep the drains clear, even upon holy-days, (268,) and urges, in common with a great many shrewd New-England farmers, to cut light meadows while the dew is on, (288–9,) even though it involve night-work. Some, too, he says, whittle their torches by fire-light, of a winter's night; and the good wife, meantime, lifting a song of cheer, plies the shuttle merrily.

In the opening of the second book, Virgil insists, very wisely, upon proper adaptation of plantations of fruit-trees to different localities and exposures, — a mat ter which is far too little considered by farmers of our day. His views in regard to propagation, whether by cuttings, layers, or seed, are in agreement with those

* Of course, I reckon the

"Exceptantque leves auras; et sæɼe sine allis," etc.,

(Lib III. 274,) as among the superstitions.

of the best Scotch nurserymen; and in the matter of
grafting or inoculation, he errs (?) only in declaring
certain results possible, which even modern gardening
has not accomplished. Dryden shall help us to the
pretty falsehood : —

> " The thin-leaved arbute hazel-grafts receives,
> And planes huge apples bear, that bore but leaves.
> Thus mastful beech the bristly chestnut bears,
> And the wild ash is white with blooming pears,
> And greedy swine from grafted elms are fed
> With falling acorns, that on oaks are bred."

It is curious how generally this belief in something
like promiscuous grafting was entertained by the old
writers. Palladius repeats it with great unction in his
poem " De Insitione," two or three centuries later ; *
and in the tenth book of the " Geoponics," a certain
Damogerontis (whoever he may have been) says, (cap.
lxv.,) " Some rustic writers allege that nut-trees and
resinous trees (τὰ ῥητίνην ἔχοντα) cannot be successfully grafted; but," he continues, "this is a mistake ; I
have myself grafted the pistache-nut into the terebin-
thine."

Is it remotely possible that these old gentlemen understood the physiology of plants better than we ?

As I return to Virgil, and slip along the dulcet lines,

---

* The same writer, under Februarius, Ti.. XVII., gives a very curious method of grafting the willow, so that it may bear peaches.

I come upon this cracking laconism, in which is compacted as much wholesome advice as a loose farm-writer
would spread over a page: —

> " Laudato ingentia rura,
> Exiguum colito ":

"Praise big farms ; stick by little ones." The wisdom
of the advice for these days of steam-engines, reapers,
and high wages, is more than questionable; but it is in
perfect agreement with the notions of a great many old-
fashioned farmers who live nearer to the heathen past
than they imagine.

The cattle of Virgil are certainly no prize-animals.
Any good committee would vote them down incontinently : —

> ——— " Cui turpe caput, cui plurima cervix,"

(iii. 52,) would not pass muster at any fair of the last
century, whatever Professor Daubeny may say.

The horses are better; there is the dash of high
venture in them ; they have snuffed battle; their limbs
are suppled to a bounding gallop, — as where in the
Æneid every resounding hoof-beat upon the dusty
plain is repeated in the pauses of the poem.*

The fourth book of the Georgics is full of the murmur of bees, showing how the poet had listened, and
had loved to listen. After describing minutely how

* " Qua lrupedante putrem sonitu quatit ungula campum."

and where the homes of the honey-makers are to be placed, he offers them this delicate attention: —

> " Then o'er the running stream or standing lake
> A passage for thy weary people make;
> With osier floats the standing water strew;
> Of massy stones make bridges, if it flow;
> That basking in the sun thy bees may lie,
> And, resting there, their flaggy pinions dry."
>
> DRYDEN.

Who cannot see from this how tenderly the man had watched the buzzing yellow-jackets, as they circled and stooped in broad noon about some little pool in the rills that flow into the Lago di Garda? For hereabout, of a surety, the poet once sauntered through the noon-tides, while his flock cropped the "milk-giving cytisus,"* upon the hills.

And charming hills they are, as my own eyes can witness: nay, my little note-book of travel shall itself tell the story. (The third shelf, upon the right, my boy.)

---

* This plant, so often mentioned and commended by classic writers, Prof. Daubeny believes to be identical with the *Medicago arborea* of the Greek Archipelago: p. 170, *Roman Husbandry.* Heresbach (translation of Barnaby Googe) describes it as " a plant all hairy & whytish, as Rhamnus is, having branches halfe a yard long & more, whereupon groweth leavis like unto Fenigreke or clover. but something lesse, having a rising crest in the midst of them ' — *Art of Husbandry,* Book I.

An Episode.

NO matter how many years ago, — I was going from Milan, (to which place I had come by Piacenza and Lodi,) on my way to Verona by Brescia and Peschiera. At Desenzano, or thereabout, the blue lake of Benaco first appeared. A few of the higher mountains that bounded the view were still capped with snow, though it was latter May. Through fragrant locusts and mulberry-trees, and between irregular hedges, we dashed down across the isthmus of Sermione, where the ruins of a Roman castle flout the sky.

Hedges and orchards and fragrant locusts still hem the way, as we touch the lake. and, rounding its southern skirt, come in sight of the grim bastions of Peschiera. A Hungarian sentinel, lithe and tall, I see pacing the rampart, against the blue of the sky. Women and girls come trooping into the narrow road, — for it is near sunset, — with their aprons full of mul berry-leaves. A bugle sounds somewhere within the fortress, and the mellow music swims the water, and beats with melodious echo — boom on boom — against Sermione and the farther shores.

The sun just dipping behind the western mountains, with a disk all golden, pours down a flood of yellow light, tinting the mulberry-orchards, the edges of the Roman castle, the edges of the waves where the lake stirs, and spreading out into a bay of gold where the lake lies still.

Virgil never saw a prettier sight there ; and I was thinking of him, and of my old master beating off spondees and dactyls with a red ruler on his thread-bare knee, when the sun sunk utterly, and the purple shadows dipped us all in twilight.

" *È arrivato, Signore!* " said the *vetturino.* True enough, I was at the door of the inn of Peschiera, and snuffed the stew of an Italian supper.

Virgil closes the first book of the Georgics with a poetic forecast of the time when ploughmen should touch upon rusted war-weapons in their work, and turn out helmets empty, and bones of dead soldiers, — as indeed they might, and did. But how unlike a poem it will sound, when the schools are opened on the Rappahannock again, and the boy scans, — choking down his sobs, —

"Aut gravibus rastris galeas pulsabit iuanes,
Grandiaque effossis mirabitur ossa sepulcris,"

and the master veils his eyes!

I fear that Virgil was harmed by the Georgican success, and became more than ever an adulator of the ruling powers. I can fancy him at a palace tea-drinking, where pretty court-lips give some witty turn to his " *Sic Vos, non Vobis,*" and pretty court-eyes glance tenderly at Master Maro, who blushes, and asks some

Sabina (not Poppæa) after Tibullus and his Delia
But a great deal is to be forgiven to a man who can
turn compliments as Virgil turned them. What can be
more exquisite than that allusion to the dead boy Marcellus, in the Sixth Book of the Æneid? He is reading
it aloud before Augustus, at Rome. Mæcenas is
there from his tall house upon the Esquiline; possibly
Horace has driven over from the Sabine country, — for,
alone of poets, he was jolly enough to listen to the
reading of a poem not his own. Above all, the calm-
faced Octavia, Cæsar's sister, and the rival of Cleopatra, is present. A sad match she has made of it
with Antony; and her boy Marcellus is just now dead,
— dying down at Baiæ, notwithstanding the care of
that famous doctor, Antonius Musa, first of hydropaths.

Virgil had read of the Sibyl, — of the entrance to
Hades, — of the magic metallic bough that made
Charon submissive, — of the dog Cerberus, and his sop,
— of the Greeks who welcomed Æneas, — then of the
father Anchises, who told the son what brave fate
should belong to him and his, — warning him, meantime, with alliterative beauty, against the worst of
wars, —

> " Ne, pueri, ne tanta animis assuescite bella,
>   Neu patriæ validas in viscera vertite vires," —

too late, alas! There were those about Augustus who
could sigh over this.

Virgil reads on : Anchises is pointing out to Æneas tnat old Marcellus who fought Hannibal ; and beside him, full of beauty, strides a young hero about whom the attendants throng.

"And who is ti.e young hero," demands Æneas, "over whose brow a dark fate is brooding?"

(The bereaved Octavia is listening with a yearning heart.)

And Anchises, the tears starting to his eyes, says, —

"Seek not, O son, to fathom the sorrows of thy kindred. The Fates, that lend him, shall claim him ; a jealous Heaven cannot spare such gifts to Rome. Then, what outcry of manly grief shall shake the battlements of the city ! what a wealth of mourning shall Father Tiber see, as he sweeps past his new-made grave ! Never a Trojan who carried hopes so high, nor ever the land of Romulus so gloried in a son."

(Octavia is listening.)

"Ah, piety ! alas for the ancient faith ! alas for the right hand so stanch in battle ! None, none could meet him, whether afoot or with reeking charger he pressed the foe. Ah, unhappy youth ! If by any means thou canst break the harsh decrees of Fate, thou wilt be — Marcellus !"

It is Octavia's lost boy ; and she is carried out fainting.

But Virgil receives a matter of ten thousand sesterces

a line, — which, allowing for difference in exchange and value of gold, may (or may not) have been a matter of ten thousand dollars. With this bouncing bag of sesterces, Virgil shall go upon the shelf for to-day.

Tibullus and Horace.

TIBULLUS was the son of a Roman gentleman who had been proscribed in the fierce civil wars of the Republic, and who probably lost his head, while his estates were ravaged by pillaging soldiers. Such a record gave the poet a wholesome horror of war, which he emphasizes with a vengeance up and down throughout his elegies. Yet he had his own experience of battles, — at Philippi and in Aquitania; but he loved better a quiet country-home which he possessed on the edge of the Campagna, midway between the heights of Tibur and of Tusculum. Horace, I dare say, made him passing visits there, on his way to the "*frigidum Præneste*" it lay upon the direct road thither from Rome, and I suspect that they two made many a jolly night of it together. Certain it is that Tibullus was not inveterate in his prejudices against a social glass. I quote a little testimony thereto from the opening elegy of his second book : —

> " Now quaff Falernian, let my Chian wine,
>   Poured from the cask, in massy goblets shine !

Drink deep, my friends, all, all, be madly gay;
'T were sacrilegious not to reel to-day."

The poet loved the country only less than his Delia
and Nemesis. And when the latter gives him the slip
in Rome, and retires to her farm-villa, he vows that he
will follow her, (III. Book 2,) and if necessary, disguise
himself as one of her henchmen of the fields.

" Cupid joys to learn the ploughman's phrase,
And, clad a peasant, o'er the fallows strays.
Oh how the weighty prong I'll busy wield,
Should the fair wander to the labored field!
A farmer then the crooked ploughshare hold,
Whilst the dull ox throws up the unctuous mould:
I'd not complain though Phœbus burnt the lands,
And painful blisters swelled my tender hands."

Over and over he weaves into his elegies some tender
rural scene which shows not only his own taste, but
what beauties were relished by his admirers — of whom
he counted so many — in Rome.

I must name Horace for the reason of his " *Procul
beatus*," etc., if I had no other; but the truth is, that
though he rarely wrote intentionally of country-matters,
yet there was in him that fulness of rural taste which
bubbled over — in grape-clusters, in images of rivers,
in snowy Soracte, in shade of plane-trees; nay, he
could not so much as touch an *amphora* but the purple
juices of the hill-side stained his verse as they stained
his lip. See, too, what a charming rural spirit there is

in his ode to Septimius, (VI. 2); and the opening to
Torquatus * (VII. 4) is the limning of one who has
followed the changes of the bursting spring with his
whole heart in his eyes: —

> The snow is gone, the grass is seen,
> The woods wear waving robes of green;
> 'T is spring again, — she wakes, she wakes,
> The icy fetters all she breaks;
> And every brooklet, wanton, free,
> Goes singing sweetly down the lea.

Pliny's Country-Places.

ON my last wet day I spoke of the elder Pliny, and
now the younger Pliny shall tell us something of
one or two of his country-places. Pliny was a govern-

* " Diffugere nives, redeunt jam gramina campis," —
every school-boy knows it: but what every school-boy does not know,
and but few of the masters, is this charming, jingling rendering of it
into the Venetian dialect: —

> " La neve xè andàda,
>   Su i pràl torna i fiori
>   De cento colori,
>   E a dosso de i àlbori
>   La fogia è tornada
>   A farli vestir.

> " Che gusto e dilèto
>   Che dà quèla tèra
>   Cambiàda de cièra,
>   E i fiumi che placidi
>   Sbassài nel so' lèto
>   Va zòzo in te 'l mar! "

This, with other odes, is prettily turned by Sig. Pietro Bussolino
and given as an appendix to the *Serie degli Scritti in Dialetto Vene-
siano*, by Bart. Gamba.

ment-official, and was rich : whether these facts had any bearing on each other I know no more than I should know if he had lived in our times.

I know that he had a charming place down by the sea, near to Ostia. Two roads led thither : " both of them," he says, " in some parts sandy, which makes it heavy and tedious, if you travel in a coach ; but easy enough for those who ride. My villa " (he is writing to his friend Gallus, Lib. II. Epist. 20) " is large enough for all convenience, and not expensive."

He describes the portico as affording a capital retreat in bad weather, not only for the reason that it is pro· tected by windows, but because there is an extraordinary projection of the roof. " From the middle of this por- tico you pass into a charming inner court, and thence into a large hall which extends towards the sea, — so near, indeed, that under a west wind the waves ripple on the steps. On the left of this hall is a large loung- ing-room (*cubiculum*), and a lesser one beyond, with windows to the east and west. The angle which this lounging-room forms with the hall makes a pleasant lee, and a loitering-place for my family in the winter. Near this again is a crescent-shaped apartment, with windows which receive the sun all day, where I keep my favorite authors. From this, one passes to a bedchamber by a raised passage, under which is a stove that commu· nicates an agreeable warmth to the whole apartment

The other rooms in this portion of the villa are for the freedmen and slaves ; but still are sufficiently well ordered (*tam mundis*) for my guests."

And he goes on to describe the bath-rooms, the cooling-rooms, the sweating-rooms, the tennis-court, "which lies open to the warmth of the afternoon sun." Adjoining this is a tower, with two apartments below and two above, — besides a supper-room, which commands a wide lookout along the sea, and over the villas that stud the shores. At the opposite end of the tennis-court is another tower, with its apartments opening upon a museum, — and below this the great dining-hall, whose windows look upon gardens, where are box-tree hedges, and rosemary, and bowers of vines. Figs and mulberries grow profusely in the garden ; and walking under them, one approaches still another banqueting-hall, remote from the sea, and adjoining the kitchen-garden. Thence a grand portico (*cryptoporticus*) extends with a range of windows on either side, and before the portico is a terrace perfumed with violets. His favorite apartment, however, is a detached building, which he has himself erected in a retired part of the grounds. It has a warm winter-room, looking one way on the terrace, and another on the ocean ; through its folding-doors may be seen an inner chamber, and within this again a sanctum, whose windows command three views totally separate and distinct, — the sea, the woods, or

the villas along the shore. "Tell me," he says, "if all
this is not very charming, and if I shall not have the
honor of your company, to enjoy it with me?"

If Pliny regarded the seat at Ostia as only a con
venient and inexpensive place, we may form some notion
of his Tuscan property, which, as he says in his letter
to his friend Apollinaris, (Lib. V. Epist. 6,) he prefers
to all his others, whether of Tivoli, Tusculum, or Pales-
trina. There, at a distance of a hundred and fifty miles
from Rome, in the midst of the richest corn-bearing and
olive-bearing regions of Tuscany, he can enjoy country
quietude. There is no need to be slipping on his toga ;
ceremony is left behind. The air is healthful ; the scene
is quiet. " *Studiis animum, venatu corpus exerceo.*"

" If you were to come here and see the numbers of
old men who have lived to be grandfathers, and great
grandfathers, and hear the stories they can entertain you
with of their ancestors, you would fancy yourself born
in some former age. The disposition of the country
is the most beautiful that can be imagined: figure to
yourself an immense amphitheatre, but such as only the
hand of Nature could form. Before you lies a vast
extended plain, bounded by a range of mountains
whose summits are crowned with lofty and venerable
woods, which supply variety of game ; from hence, as
the mountains decline, they are adorned with underwood. Intermixed with these are little hills of se

strong and fat a soil that it would be difficult to find a
single stone upon them : their fertility is nothing inferior to that of the lowest grounds ; and though their
harvest, indeed, is something later, their crops are as
well ripened. At the foot of these hills the eye is
presented, wherever it turns, with one unbroken view of
numberless vineyards, which are terminated by a border, as it were, of shrubs. From thence you have a
prospect of adjoining fields and meadows below. The
soil of the former is so extremely stiff, and upon the
first ploughing *it rises in such vast clods, that it is neces*
sary to go over it nine several times with the largest
oxen and the strongest ploughs, before they can be thor-
oughly broken ; whilst the enamelled meadows produce
trefoil, and other kinds of herbage as fine and tender
as if it were but just sprung up, being continually
refreshed by never-failing rills."

I will not follow him through the particularity of the
description which he gives to his friend Apollinaris.
There are the wide-reaching views of fruitful valleys
and of empurpled hill-sides ; there are the fresh winds
sweeping from the distant Apennines ; there is the
gestatio with its clipped boxes, the embowered walks,
the colonnades, the marble banquet-rooms, the baths,
the Carystian columns, the soft, embracing air, and the
violet sky. I leave Pliny seated upon a bench in a
marble alcove of his Tuscan garden. From this bench,

the water, gushing through several little pipes, as if it were pressed out by the weight of the persons reposing upon it, falls into a stone cistern underneath, whence it is received into a polished marble basin, so artfully contrived that it is always full, without ever overflowing. " When I sup here," he writes, " this basin serves for a table, — the larger dishes being placed round the margin, while the smaller ones swim about in the form of little vessels and water-fowl." Such *al fresco* suppers the country-gentlemen of Italy ate in the first century of our era! Pliny was always a friend of the ruling powers, and knew how to praise them.

One more illustration of his country-estates I venture to give, on the following page, in a drawing from Castell. It will be observed that there are indications of an approach, in some portions of the grounds, to what is called the natural style, which is currently supposed to be a modern suggestion. There are reasons, however, to believe the contrary; not the least of which may be found in a certain passage in the " Annals of Tacitus," * cited by Horace Walpole, (Vol. II. p. 523,) which shows as great irreverence for the stately formalities of gardening as either Repton or Price could have desired.

* " Ceterum Nero usus est patriæ ruinis, extruxitque domum, in qua haud perinde gemmæ et aurum miraculo essent, solita pridem et luxu vulgata; quam arva, et stagna, et, *in modum solitudinum, hinc silvæ*, *inde aperta spatia, et prospectus*, magistris et machinatoribus severe et celero quibus ingenium et audacia erat etiam quæ natura denega visset per artem tentare." — Lib. XV.

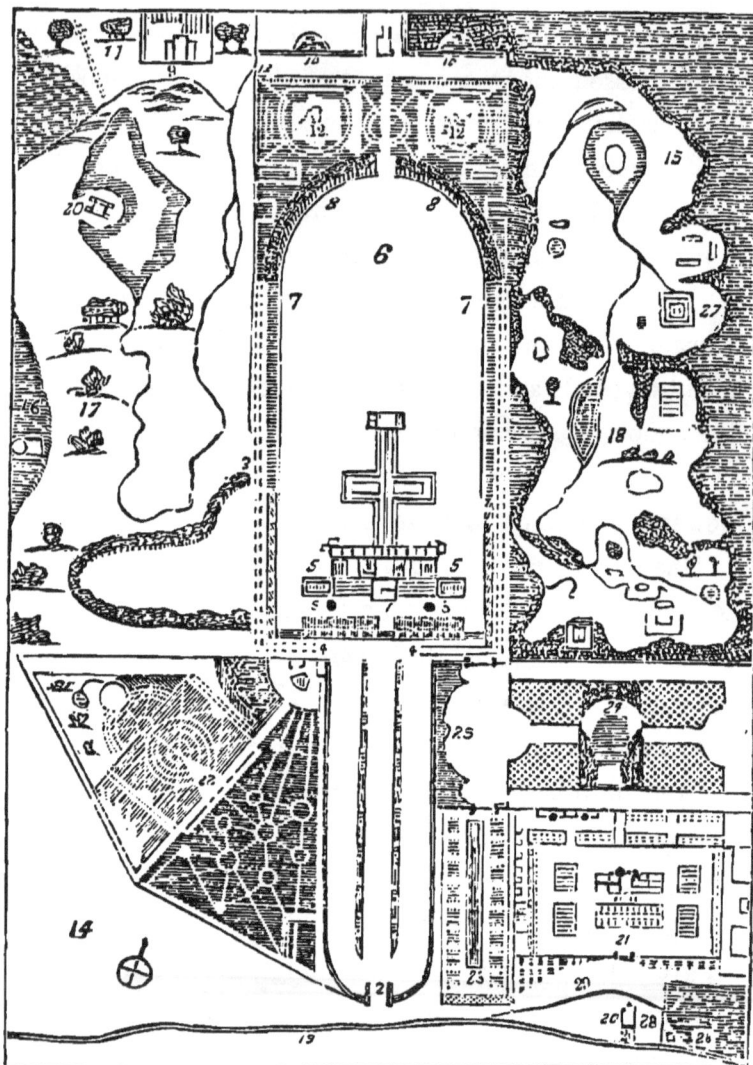

PLINY'S VILLA.*

* Explanation of references: —

1. Villa.
2. Gestatio.
3. Walk around terrace.

4, 4. Slopes with forms of beasts in boxwood.
5, 5. Terraces.

Palladius.

PALLADIUS wrote somewhere about the middle of the fourth century. A large part of his work is arranged in the form of a calendar for the months, and it closes with a poem which is as inferior to the poems of the time of Augustus as the later emperors were inferior to the Cæsars.* There is in his book no notable advance upon the teachings of Columella, whom he frequently quotes, — as well as certain Greek authorities of the Lower Empire. I find in his treatise a somewhat fuller list of vegetables, fruits, and field-crops

6. Hippodrome.
7. Plane-trees around hippodrome.
8. Cypress - trees forming wall of green.
9. Garden-alcoves.
10. Wall of box.
11. Little meadow of garden.
12, 12. Circles within which were landscapes in miniature, with mountains, brooks, trees, etc.
13. Walks diverging, shrouded in moss.
14. Meadow.
15. Hills covered with heavy wood.
16. Underwood on declivities of hill.
17. Vineyards.
18. Grain-fields.
19. River.
20. Temple of Ceres.
21. Farmery.
22. Vivarium or Park.
23. Kitchen-garden.
24. Orchard.
25. Apiary.
26. Snailery.
27. Hutch for dormice.
28. Osiers.
29. Aqueduct.

* I drop in a note a little confirmatory stanza *De Prunis :* —

> "Pruna suis addunt felicia germina memoris,
> Donaque cognato corpore læta ferunt.
> Exarinat fœtus, sed brachia roboris armat
> Castaneæ prunus jussa tenere larem."

The botany is as bad as the poetry.

than belongs to the earlier writers. I find more variety
of treatment. I see a waning faith in the superstitions
of the past: Bacchus and the Lares are less jubilant
than they were; but the Christian civilization has no:
yet vivified the art of culture. The magnificent gardens of Nero and the horticultural experiences of the
great Adrian at Tivoli have left no traces in the
method or inspiration of Palladius.

Professor Daubeny.

I WILL not pass wholly from the classic period
without allusion to the recent book of Professor
Daubeny on Roman husbandry. It is charming, and
yet disappointing, — not for failure, on his part, to trace
the traditions to their sources, not for lack of learning
or skill, but for lack of that *afflatus* which should pour
over and fill both subject and talker, where the talker
is lover as well as master.

Daubeny's husbandry lacks the odor of fresh-turned
ground, — lacks the imprint of loving familiarity. He
is clearly no farmer: every man who has put his hand
to the plough (*aratori crede*) sees it. Your blood does
not tingle at his story of Boreas, nor a dreamy languor
creep over you when he talks of sunny south-winds.

Had he written exclusively of bees, or trees, or
flowers, there would have been a charming murmur,

like the *susurrus* of the poets, — and a fragrance as of crushed heaps of lilies and jonquils. But Daubeny approaches farming as a good surgeon approaches a *cadaver.* He disarticulates the joints superbly; but there is no tremulous intensity. The bystanders do not feel the thrill with which they see a man bare his arm for a capital operation upon a live and palpitating body.

The Dark Age.

FROM the time of Palladius to the time of Pietro Crescenzi is a period of a thousand years, a period as dreary and impenetrable as the snow-cloud through which I see faintly a few spires staggering : so along the pages of Muratori's interminable annals gaunt figures come and go ; but they are not the figures of farmers.

Goths, wars, famines, and plague succeed each other in ghastly procession. Boëthius lifts, indeed, a little rural plaint from out of the gloom, —

> " Felix nimium prior ætas,
> Contenta fidelibus arvis," * —

but the dungeon closes over him ; and there are outstanding orders of Charlemagne which look as if he had an eye to the crops of Italy, and to a good vegeta

* *De Consol. Phil.*, Lib. II.

ble stew with his Transalpine dinners, — but for the
most part the land is waste. Dreary and tangled
marsh-lands, with fevers brooding over them, are around
Ferrara and Mantua, and along all the upper valley of
the Arno. Starveling peasants are preyed upon by
priests and seigneurs. No man, powerful or humble,
could be sure of reaping what he sowed. I see some
such monster as Eccelino reaping a harvest of blood.
I see Lombards pouring down from the mountain-
gates with falcons on their thumbs, ready to pounce
upon the purple *columbæ* that trace back their lineage
to the doves Virgil may have fed in the streets of Mantua. I see torrents of people, the third of them women,
driven mad by some fanatical outcry, sweeping over
the whole breadth of Italy, and consuming all green
things as a fire consumes stubble. Think of what the
fine villa of Pliny would have been, with its boxwood
bowers and floating dishes, under the press of such
crusaders! It was a precarious time for agricultural
investments : I know nothing that could match it, unless it may have been the later summers' harvests in
the valley of the Shenandoah.

Upon a parchment (*strumento*) of Ferrara, bearing
date A. D. 1113, (Annals of Muratori,) I find a memo-
randum of contract which looks like reviving civilization. "*Terram autem illam quam roncabo, frui debeo
per annos tres; postea reddam se-raticum.*" The Latin

is stiff, but the sense is sound. "If I grub up wild land, I shall hold it three years for pay."

I also find, in the same invaluable storehouse of medi æval history, numerous memoranda of agreements, in virtue of which the tenant was to deliver to the land- lord, or other feudal master, a third or a fourth part of all the grain raised, duly threshed, besides a third por- tion of the wine, and, in some instances, a special return for the cottage, of a young chicken, five sheep, three days' work with oxen, and as many of personal labor (*cum manibus*). From the exceeding moderation of this apportionment of shares, at a period when the working-farmer or rent-payer (*livellario*) was reckoned little better than a brute, we may reasonably infer the poverty of the harvests, and the difficulties of culti- vation.

Geoponica Geoponicorum.

I SHALL make no apology for introducing next to the reader the " Geoponica Geoponicorum," — a somewhat extraordinary collection of agricultural opin- ions, usually attributed, in a loose way, to the Emperor Constantine Porphyrogenitus, who held the Byzantine throne about the middle of the tenth century. It was undoubtedly under the order of Constantine that the collection took its present shape ; but whether a body of manuscripts under the same name had not previ ously existed, and, if so, to whom is to be credited the authorship, are questions which have been discussed through a wilderness of Greek and Roman type, by the various editors.

The edition before me (that of Niclas, Leipsic) gives no less than a hundred pages of prolegomena, prefaces, introductory observations, with notes to each and all, interlacing the pages into a motley of patchwork ; the whole preceded by two, and followed by five stately dedications. The weight of authority points to Cassianus Bassus, a Bithynian, as the real compiler, — notwithstanding his name is attached to particular chapters of the book, and notwithstanding he lived as early as the fifth century. Other critics attribute the collection to Dionysius Uticensis, who is cited by both Varro and Columella. The question is unsettled, and is not worth the settling.*

My own opinion — in which, however, Niclas and Needham do not share — is, that the Emperor Porphyrogenitus, in addition to his historical and judicial labors,† wishing to mass together the best agricultural

---

* The work was translated by the Rev. T. Owen of Queen's College, Oxford, and published in 1805. I have not, however, been able to see a copy of this translation. From a contemporary notice in the *Monthly Review*, (Oct. 1806,) I am led to believe that it met with very little favor. Arthur Young also speaks of the work with ill-founded contempt, in his introduction to *A Course of Experiments* etc.

† See Gibbon. — opening of Chapter LIII.

opinions of the day, expressed that wish to some trusted Byzantine official (we may say his Commissioner of Patents). Whereupon the Byzantine official (commis- sioner) goes to some hungry agricultural friend, of the Chersonesus, and lays before him the plan, with promise of a round Byzantine stipend. The agricul- tural friend goes lovingly to the work, and discovers some old compilation of Bassus or of Dionysius, into which he whips a few modern phrases, attributes a few chapters to the virtual compiler of the whole, makes one or two adroit allusions to local scenes, and carries the result to the Byzantine official (commissioner). The official (commissioner) has confidence in tne opin- ions and virtues of his agricultural friend, and indorses the book, paying over the stipend, which it is found necessary to double, by reason of the unexpected cost of execution. The official (commissioner) presents the report to the Emperor, who receives it gratefully, — at the same time approving the bill of costs, which has grown into a quadruple of the original estimates.

This hypothesis will explain the paragraphs which so puzzle Niclas and Needham ; it explains the evi- dent interpolations, and the local allusions. The only extravagance in the hypothesis is its assumption that the officials of Byzantium were as rapacious as our own.

Thus far, I have imagined a certain analogy between

the work in view and the "Patent Office Agricultural Reports." * The analogy stops here : the " Geoponica " is a good book. It is in no sense to be regarded as a work of the tenth century, or as one strictly Byzantine : nearly half the authors named are of Western origin, and I find none dating later than the fifth century, — while many, as Apuleius, Fiorentinus, Africanus, and the poor brothers Quintilii, who died under the stab of Commodus, belong to a period preceding that of Palladius. Aratus and Democritus (of Abdera) again, who are cited, are veterans of the old Greek school, who might have contributed as well to the agriculture of Thrace or Macedonia in the days of Philip as in the days of the Porphyrogenitus.

The first book, of meteorologic phenomena, is nearly identical in its teachings with those of Aratus, Varro, and Virgil. The subject of field-culture is opened with the standard maxim, repeated by all the old writers, that the master's eye is invaluable.† The doctrine of

---

* I am glad to say that the Report of the Department of Agriculture for 1862 shows a great gain — in arrangement, in width of discussion and in practical value. *Macte virtute, Dom. Newton!*

† As a curious illustration of the rhetoric of the different agronomes, I give the various wordings of this universal maxim.

The " Geoponica" has, — " Πολλῷ τὸν ἀγρὸν ἀμείνω ποιεῖ δεσπότου συνεχὴς παρουσία." Lib. II. cap. i.

Columella says, — " Ne ista quidem præsidia tantum pollent, quantum vel una præsentia domini." I. i. 18.

Cato says, — " Frons occipitio prior est." Cap. ɪᴠ.

Palladius puts it, — " Præsent'a domini provectus est agri." I. ᴠɪ

rotation, or frequent change of crops, is laid down with unmistakable precision. A steep for seed (hellebore) is recommended, to guard against the depredations of birds or mice.

In the second book, in certain chapters credited to Fiorentinus, I find, among other valuable manures mentioned, sea-weed and tide-drift, (Τὰ ἐκ τῆς θαλάσσης δὲ ἐκβρασσόμενα βρυώδη,) which I do not recall in any other of the old writers. He also recommends the refuse of leather-dressers, and a mode of promoting putrefaction in the compost-heap, which would almost seem to be stolen from "Bommer's Method." He further urges the diversion of turbid rills, after rains, over grass lands, and altogether makes a better compend of this branch of the subject than can be found in the Roman writers proper. Grain should be cut before it is fully ripe, as the meal is the sweeter. What correspondent of our agricultural papers, suggesting this as a novelty, could believe that it stood in Greek type as early as ever Greek types were set? A farm foreman should be apt to rise early, should win the respect of his men, should fear to tell an untruth, regard religious observances, and not drink too hard.

The elder Pliny writes, — "Majores fertilissimum in agro oculum domini esse dixerunt." Hist. Nat., Lib. XVIII. cap. ii.

And Crescenzi, more than a thousand years later, rounds it into Ital ian thus: — "La presentia del signore utilita e del campo; e chi t ban dona la vigna sara abandonato da lei da lavoratori." Lib. II. cap. ix.

Three or four books are devoted to a very full discussion of the vine, and of wines, — not differing materially, however, from the Columellan advice. In discussing the moral aspects of the matter, this Geoponic author enumerates other things which will intoxicate as well as wine, — even some waters; also the wine made from barley and wheat, which barbarians drink. Old men, he says, are easily made drunk; women not easily, by reason of temperament; but by drinking enough they may come to it.

Where the discourse turns upon pears, (Lib. X. cap. xxiii.,) it is urged, that, if you wish specially good fruit, you should bore a hole through the trunk at the ground, and drive in a plug of either oak or beech, and draw the earth over it. If it does not heal well, wash for a fortnight with the lees of old wine: in any event, the wine-lees will help the flavor of the fruit. Almost identical directions are to be found in Palladius, (Tit. XXV.,) but the above is credited to Diophanes, who lived in Asia Minor a full century before Christ.

Book XI. opens with flowers and evergreens, introduced (by a Latin translation) in a mellifluous roll of genitives : — "*plantationem rosarum, et liliorum, et violarum, et reliquorum florum odoratorum.*" Thereafter is given the pretty tradition, that red roses came of nectar spilled from heaven. Love, who bore the celestial vintage, tripped a wing, and overset the vase; and the nectar, spilling on the valleys of the earth, bubbled up in roses. Next we have this kindred story of the lilies. Jupiter wished to make his boy Hercules (born of a mortal) one of the gods: so he snatches him from the bosom of his earthly mother, Alcmena, and bears him to the bosom of the godlike Juno. The milk is spilled from the full-mouthed boy, as he traverses the sky, (making the Milky Way,) and what drops below stars and clouds, and touches earth, stains the ground with — lilies.

In the chapter upon pot-herbs are some of those allusions to the climate of Constantinople which may have served to accredit the work in the Byzantine court. I find no extraordinary methods of kitchen-garden culture, — unless I except the treatment of muskmelon-seeds to a steep of milk and honey, in order to improve the flavor of the fruit. (Cap. xx.) The remaining chapters relate to ordinary domestic animals, with diversions to stags, camels, hare, poisons, scorpions, and serpents. I can cheerfully commend the work to those who have a snowy day on their hands, good eyesight, and a love for the subject.

Crescenzi.

A ND now, while the snow lasts, let us take one look at Messer Pietro Crescenzi, a Bolognese of the fourteenth century. My copy of him is a little, fat, unctuous, parchment-bound book of 1534, bought upon a street-stall under the walls of the University of Bologna.

Through whose hands may it not have passed since its printing! Sometimes I seem to snuff in it the taint of a dirty-handed friar, who loved his pot-herbs better than his breviary, and plotted his yearly garden on some shelf of the hills that look down on Castagnolo : other times I scent only the mould and the damp of some monastery shelf, that guarded it quietly and cleanly while red-handed war raged around the walls.

Crescenzi was a man of good family in Bologna, being nephew of Crescenzi di Crescenzo, who died in 1268, an ambassador in Venice. Pietro was educated to the law, and, wearying of the civil commotions in his native town, accepted judicial positions in the independent cities of Italy, — Pisa and Asti among others; and after thirty years of absence, in which, as he says, he had read many authors,* and seen many sorts of farming, he gives his book to the world.

Its arrangement is very similar to that of Palladius, to which he makes frequent reference. Indeed, he does something more and worse than to refer to him : he steals from him by the page. To be sure he had some

---

* "E molti libri d' antichi e de' novelli savi lessi e studiai, e diverse e varie operazioni de' coltivatori delle terre vidi e conobbi."

nine hundred years of margin, since Palladius lived, in the course of which the stock of papyrus had been cut off; vellum was dear, and rag-paper was hardly yet in vogue. It is not probable, therefore, that those for whose benefit Crescenzi wrote would detect his plagiarisms. Palladius stole from the Greeks far and near; and in repeating the theft Crescenzi only restored to the Italians what was theirs by inheritance.

But it must not be supposed that he is wholly dependent upon Palladius. He writes upon the arrangement of farmeries like one who had built them, and of horses like one who loved them: he tells us of their good points and of their bad points, and how they should be tested. He is more sensitive than were the Roman writers to the disadvantages of a wet soil, and advises how it may be treated. He gives rules for mortar-making, and suggests that the timber for house-building be cut in November or December, in the old of the moon. Both Palladius and himself urge the use of earthen pipes for conducting water, and give a cement (quick-lime mixed with oil) for making water-tight their junction.*

In matters of physiology he shows a near approach

---

* Lib. I. cap. ix. The pipes named — *doccioni di terra* — could not have differed materially from our draining-tile, which we are accustomed to regard as a modern invention.

to modern views : he insists that food for plants must be in a liquid form.*

He quotes Columella's rule for twenty-four loads (*carrette*) of manure to hill-lands per acre, and eighteen to level land; and adds, — "Our people put the double of this," — "*I nostri mettano più chel doppio.*"

But the book of our friend Crescenzi is interesting not so much for its maxims of agronomic wisdom as for its association with one of the most eventful periods of Italian history. The new language of the Peninsula † was just now crystallizing into shape, and was presently to receive the stamp of currency from the hands of Dante and Boccaccio. A thriving commerce through the ports of Venice and Amalfi demanded all the products of the hill-sides. Milan, then having a population of two hundred thousand, had turned a great river into the fields, which to this day irrigates thousands of acres of rice-lands. Wheat was grown in profusion, at that time, on fields which are now desolated by the malaria, or by indolence. In the days of Crescenzi, gunpowder was burned for the first time in battle; and for the first time crops of grain were paid for in bills of exchange. All the Peninsula was vibrating with the throbs of a new and more splendid life. The art that

* "Il proprio cibo delle piante sara alcuno humido ben mischiato." Cap. xiii.

† Crescenzi's book was written in Latin, but was very shortly after (perhaps by himself) rendered into the street-tongue of Italy.

had cropped out of the fashionable schools of Byzan·
tium was fast putting them in eclipse ; and before Cres·
cenzi died, if he loved art in fresco as he loved art
in gardens, he must have heard admiringly of Cimabue,
and Giotto, and Orcagna.

A Florentine Farm.

IN 1360 a certain Paganino Bonafede composed a
poem called " Il Tesoro de' Rustici "; but I believe
it was never published; and Tiraboschi calls it rather
dull, — "*poco felice.*" If we could only bar publicity to
all the *poco felice* verses !

In the middle of the fifteenth century the Florentine
Poggio * says some good things in a rural way ; and still
later, that whimsical, disagreeable Politiano, † who was a
pet of Lorenzo de' Medici, published his " Rusticus."
Roscoe says, with his usual strained hyperbole, that it
is inferior in kind only to the Georgics.   The fact is, it
compares with the Georgics as the vilest of the Medici
compare with the grandest of the Cæsars.

The young Michele Verini, of the same period, has
given, in one of his few remaining letters, an eloquent
description of the Cajano farm of Lorenzo de' Medici.
It lay between Florence and Pistoia.   The river Om·

* *Epistola de Laude Ruris.*
† See Roscoe, *Life of Lorenzo de' Medici*, Chap. VIII

6

brone skirted its fields.   It was so successfully irrigated
that three crops of grain grew in a year.   Its barns had
stone floors, walls with moat, and towers like a castle.
The cows he kept there (for ewes were now superseded)
were equal to the supply of the entire city of Florence.
Hogs were fed upon the whey ; and peacocks and pheasants innumerable roamed through the woods.

Politiano also touches upon the same theme in stiff
hexameters.   They occur in his poem of " Sylva," which
was written in praise of Homer, but which closes with
a descriptive dash at the farm of the great Florentine.
The reader shall have it, as Englished by Mr. Roscoe : —

> " Go on, Lorenzo, thou, the Muses' pride,
> Pierce the hard rock and scoop the mountain's side;
> The distant streams shall hear thy potent call,
> And the proud arch receive them as they fall,
> Thence o'er thy fields the genial waters lead,
> That with luxuriant verdure crown the mead.
> There rise thy mounds th' opposing flood that ward;
> There thy domains thy faithful mastiffs guard:
> Tarentum there her hornèd cattle sends,
> Whose swelling teats the milky rill distends;
> There India's breeds of various colors range,
> Pleased with the novel scene and pastures strange,
> Whilst nightly closed within their sheltered stall
> For the due treat their lowing offspring call.
> Meantime the milk in spacious coppers boils,
> With arms upstript the elder rustic toils,
> The young assist the curdled mass to squeeze

And place in cooling shades the new-made cheese.
Where mulberry-groves their length of shadow spread
Secure the silk-worm spins his lustrous thread;
And, culled from every flower the plunderer meets,
The bee regales thee with her rifled sweets;
There birds of various plume and various note
Flutter their captive wings: with cackling throat
The Paduan fowl betrays her future breed,
And there the geese, once Rome's preservers, feed,
And ducks amusive sport amidst thy floods,
And doves, the pride of Venus, throng thy woods."

While I write, wandering in fancy to that fair plain where Florence sits a queen, with her girdle of shining rivers, and her garland of olive-bearing hills, — the snow is passing. The spires have staggered plainly and stiffly into sight. Again I can count them, one by one. I have brought as many authors to the front as there are spires staring at me from the snow.

Let me marshal them once more : — Verini, the young Florentine ; Politiano, who cannot live in peace with the wife of his patron ; Crescenzi, the magistrate and farmer joined ; the half-score of dead men who lie between the covers of the " Geoponica " ; the martyr Boëthius, who, under the consolations of a serene, perhaps Christian philosophy, cannot forget the charm of the fields ; Palladius, who is more full than original ; Pliny the Consul, and the friend of Tacitus ; Tibullus, the elegiac lover ; Horace, whose very laugh is brim-

ming with the buxom cheer of the country ; and .ast, —
Virgil.

I hear no such sweet bugle note as his along all the
line.   Hark ! —

"Claudite jam rivos, pueri, sat prata biberunt."

Even so : *Claudite jam libros, parvuli !* — Shut up the
books, my little ones !   Enough for to-day.

THIRD DAY.

A Picture of Rain.

WILL any of our artists ever give us, on canvas, a good, rattling, saucy shower? There is room in it for a rare handling of the brush: — the vague, indistinguishable line of hills, (as I see them to-day,) — the wild scud of gray, with fine gray lines, slanted by the wind, and trending eagerly downward, — the swift, petulant dash into the little pools of the highway, making fairy bubbles that break as soon as they form, — the land smoking with excess of moisture, — and the pelted leaves all wincing and shining and adrip.

I know no painter who has so well succeeded in putting a wet sky into his pictures as Turner; and in this I judge him by the literal *chiaroscuro* of engraving. In proof of it, I take down from my shelf his " Rivers of France ": a book over which I have spent a great many pleasant hours, and idle ones too, — if it be idle to travel leagues at the turning of a page, and to see hill sides spotty with vineyards, and great bridges wallow

ing through the Loire, and to watch the fishermen of
Honfleur putting to sea. There are skies, as I said, in
some of these pictures which make a man instinctively
think of his umbrella, or of his distance from home : no
actual rain-drift stretching from them, but such unmistakable promise of a rainy afternoon, in their little par-
allel wisps of dark-bottomed clouds, as would make a
provident farmer order every scythe out of the field.

In the "Chair of Gargantua," on which my eye falls,
as I turn over the pages, an actual thunder-storm is
breaking. The scene is somewhere upon the Lower
Seine. From the middle of the right of the picture the
lofty river-bank stretches far across, forming all the
background ; — its extreme distance hidden by a bold
thrust of the left bank, which juts into the picture just
far enough to shelter a village, whose spire stands gleaming upon the edge of the water. On all the foreground
lies the river, broad as a bay. The storm is coming
down the stream. Over the left spur of the bank, and
over the meeting of the banks, it broods black as night.
Through a little rift there is a glimpse of serene sky,
from which a mellow light streams down upon the edges
and angles of a few cliffs upon the farther shore. All
the rest is heavily shadowed. The edges of the coming
tempest are tortuous and convulsed, and you know that
a fierce wind is driving the black billows on ; yet all
the water under the lee of the shores is as tranquil as

a dream ; a white sail, near to the white village, hangs slouchingly to the mast: but in the foreground the tempest has already caught the water ; a tall lugger is scudding and careening under it as if mad ; the crews of three fishermen's boats, that toss on the vexed water, are making a confused rush to shorten sail, and you may almost fancy that you hear their outcries sweeping down the wind. In the middle scene, a little steamer is floating tranquilly on water which is yet calm ; and a column of smoke piling up from its tall chimney rises for a space placidly enough, until the wind catches and whisks it before the storm. I would wager ten to one, upon the mere proof in the picture, that the fishermen and the washerwomen in the foreground will be drenched within an hour.

When I have once opened the covers of Turner, — especially upon such a wet day as this, — it is hard for me to leave him until I have wandered all up and down the Loire, revisited Tours and its quiet cathedral, and Blois with its stately chateau, and Amboise with its statelier, and coquetted again with memories of the Maid of Orléans.

Southern France and Troubadours.

FROM the Upper Loire it is easy to slip into the branching valleys which sidle away from it far down into the country of the Auvergne. Turner does not go there, indeed; the more's the pity; but I do, since it is the most attractive region rurally (Brittany perhaps excepted) in all France. The valleys are green, the brooks are frequent, the rivers are tortuous, the mountains are high, and luxuriant walnut-trees embower the roads. It was near to Moulins, on the way hither, through the pleasant Bourbonnois, that Tristram Shandy met with the poor, half-crazed Maria, piping her evening service to the Virgin.

And at that thought I must do no less than pull down my "Tristram Shandy," (on which the dust of years has accumulated,) and read again that tender story of the lorn maiden, with her attendant goat, and her hair caught up in a silken fillet, and her shepherd's pipe, from which she pours out a low, plaintive wail upon the evening air.

It is not a little singular that a British author should have supplied the only Arcadian resident of all this Arcadian region. The Abbé Delille was, indeed, born hereabout, within sight of the bold Puy de Dome, and within marketing-distance of the beautiful Clermont. But there is very little that is Arcadian, in freshness or simplicity, in either the " Gardens " or the other verse of Delille.

Out of his own mouth (the little green-backed book, my boy) I will condemn him : —

" Ce n'est plus cette simple et rustique déesse
Qui suit ses vieilles lois; c'est une enchanteresse
Qui, la baguette en main, par les hardis travaux
Fait naître des aspects et des trésors nouveaux,
Compose un sol plus riche et des races plus belles,
Fertilise les monts, dompte les rocs rebelles."

The *baguette* of Delille is no shepherd's crook ; it has more the fashion of a drumstick, — *baguette de tambour.* If I follow on southward to Provence, whither I am borne upon the scuds of rain over Turner's pictures, and the pretty Bourbonnois, and the green mountains of Auvergne, I find all the characteristic literature of that land of olives is only of love or war: the vines, the olive-orchards, and the yellow hill-sides pass for nothing. And if I read an old *Sirvente* of the Troubadours, beginning with a certain redolence of the fields, all this yields presently to knights, and steeds caparisoned, —

" Cavalliers ab cavals armatz."

The poem from which I quote has a smooth sound and a certain promise of ruralities. It is attributed to Bertrand de Born,* who lived in the time when even the lion-hearted King Richard turned his brawny fingers to the luting of a song. Let us listen : —

" The beautiful spring delights me well,
When flowers and leaves are growing;
And it pleases my heart to hear the swell
Of the birds' sweet chorus flowing

* M. Raynouard, *Poésies des Troubadours*, II. 200.

In the echoing wood;
And I love to see, all scattered around,
Pavilions and tents on the martial ground,
And my spirit finds it good
To see, on the level plains beyond,
Gay knights and steeds caparisoned."

But as the Troubadour nestles more warmly into the rhythm of his verse, the birds are all forgotten, and the beautiful spring, and there is a sturdy clang of battle, that would not discredit our own times : —

" I tell you that nothing my soul can cheer,
Or banqueting or reposing,
Like the onset cry of 'Charge them!' rung
From each side, as in battle closing;
Where the horses neigh,
And the call to 'aid' is echoing loud,
And there, on the earth, the lowly and proud
In the foss together lie,
And yonder is piled the mingled heap
Of the brave that scaled the trenches steep.

" Barons! your castles in safety place,
Your cities and villages, too,
Before ye haste to the battle-scene:
And Papiol! quickly go,
And tell the lord of 'Yes and No'
That peace already too long hath been!" •

• I cannot forbear taking a bit of margin to print the closing stanzas of the original, which carry the clash of sabres in their very sound.

" Ie us dic que tan no m' a sabor
Manjars ni beure ni dormir,
Cum a quant aug cridar: A lor!

I am on my way to Italy, (it may as well be con-
fessed,) where I had fully intended to open my rainy
day's work ; but Turner has kept me, and then Auvergne, and then the brisk battle-song of a Troubadour.

Among the Italians.

WHEN I was upon the Cajano farm of Lorenzo
the Magnificent, during my last "spell of wet,"
it was uncourteous not to refer to the pleasant com-
memorative poem of " Ambra," which Lorenzo himself
wrote, and which, whatever may be said against the
conception and conduct of it, shows in its opening
stanzas that the great Medici was as appreciative of
rural images — fir-boughs with loaded snows, thick cypresses in which late birds lurked, sharp-leaved juni-
pers, and sturdy pines fighting the wind — as ever he

> D' ambas las partz; et aug agnir
>   Cavals voitz per l' ombratge,
> Et aug cridar : Aidatz ! Aidatz !
> E vei cazer per los fossatz
>   Paues e graus per l' erbatge,
> E vei los mortz que pels costatz
> An los trousons outre passatz.
>
> " Baros, metetz en gatge
> Castels e vilas e clutatz,
> Enans q' usquecs no us guerrelaҳ
>
> " Papiol. d' ogradatge
> Ad *Oc e No* t' en vai viatz,
> Dic li que trop estan en pats."

had been of antique jewels, or of the verse of such as Politiano. And if I have spoken slightingly of this latter poet, it was only in contrast with Virgil, and in view of his strained Latinity. When he is himself, and wraps his fancies only in his own sparkling Tuscan, we forget his classic frigidities, and his quarrels with Madonna Clarice, and are willing to confess that no pen of his time was dipped with such a relishing *gusto* into the colors of the hyacinths and trembling pansies, and into all the blandishments of a gushing and wanton spring. I may particularly designate a charming little rural poem of his, entitled " Le Montanine," charmingly translated by Parr Greswell.*

But classical affectation was the fashion of that day A certain Bolognese noble, Berò by name, wrote ten Latin books on rural affairs ; yet they are little known, and never had any considerable reputation. Another scholar, Pietro da Barga, who astonished his teachers by his wonderful proficiency at the age of twelve, and who was afterward guest of the French ambassador in Venice, wrote a poem on rural matters, to which, with an exaggerated classicism, he gave the Greek name of " Cynegeticon" ; and about the same time Giuseppe Voltolina composed three books on kitchen-gardening. I name these writers only out of sympathy with their

* See Wm. Parr Greswell's *Memoirs of Politiano*, with transla-
tions.

topics : I would not advise the reading of them : it
would involve a long journey and scrupulous search to
find them, through I know not what out-of-the-way
libraries ; and if found, no essentially new facts or theories could be counted on which are not covered by the
treatise of Crescenzi. The Pisans or Venetians may
possibly have introduced a few new plants from the
East; the example of the Medici may have suggested
some improvements in the arrangement of forcing-
houses, or the outlay of villas ; but in all that regarded
general husbandry, Crescenzi was still the man.

I linger about this period, and the writers of this
time, because I snuff here and there among them the
perfume of a country bouquet, which carries the odor
of the fields with it, and transports me to the "empurpled hill-sides" of Tuscany. Shall I name Sanna-
zaro, with his "Arcadia"? — a dead book now, — or
"Amyntas," who, before he is tall enough to steal apples
from the lowest boughs, (so sings Tasso,) plunges head
and ears in love with Sylvia, the fine daughter of
Montano, who has a store of cattle, "*richissimo d'*
armenti"?

Then there is Rucellai, who, under the pontificate of
Leo X., came to be Governor of the Castle of Sant'
Angelo, and yet has left a poem of fifteen hundred lines
devoted to Bees. In his suggestions for the allaying
of a civil war among these winged people, he is quite

beyond either Virgil or Mr. Lincoln. "Pluck some
leafy branch," he says, "and with it sprinkle the con-
tending factions with either honey or sweet grape-juice,
and you shall see them instantly forego their strife " : —

> " The two warring bands joyful unite,
> And foe embraces foe: each with its lips
> Licking the others' wings, feet, arms, and breast,
> Whereon the luscious mixture hath been shed,
> And all inebriate with delight."

So the Swiss,* he continues, when they fall out among
themselves, are appeased by some grave old gentleman,
who says a few pleasant words, and orders up a good
stoop of sweet wine, in which all parties presently dip
their beards, and laugh and embrace and make peace,
and so forget outrage.

Guarini, with all his affectations, has little prettinesses
which charm like the chirping of a bird; — as where he
paints (in the very first scene of the " Pastor Fido ")
the little sparrow flitting from fir to beech, and from
beech to myrtle, and twittering, "How I love! how I

---

* " Come quando nei Suizzeri si muove
Sedizione, e che si grida a l' arme;
Se qualche nom grave allor si leva in piede
E comincia a parlar con dolce lingua,
Mitiga i petti barbari e feroci;
E intanto fa portare ondanti vasi
Pieni di dolci ed odorati vini:
Allora ognun le labbra e 'l mento imrierge
Ne' le spumanti tazze," etc.

love!'· And the bird-mate (" *il suo dolce desio* ") twit-
ters in reply, " How I love, how I love, too!" " *Ardo d'*
amore anch' io."

Messer Pietro Bembo was a different man from Guarini. I cannot imagine him listening to the sparrows;
I cannot imagine him plucking a flower, except he
have some courtly gallantry in hand, — perhaps toward
the Borgia. He was one of those pompous, stiff, scho-
lastic prigs who wrote by rules of syntax; and of syntax he is dead. He was clever and learned; he wrote
in Latin, Italian, Castilian: but nobody reads him; he
has only a little crypt in the "Autori Diversi." I think
of him as I think of fine women who must always
rustle in brocade embossed with hard jewels, and who
never win the triumphs that belong to a charming morning *déshabillé* with only the added improvisation of a
rose.

In his " Asolani" Bembo gives a very full and minute
description of the gardens at Asolo, which relieved the
royal retirement of Caterina, the Queen of Cyprus.
Nothing could be more admirable than the situation:
here were skirts of mountains which were covered, and
are still covered, with oaks; there were grottos in the
sides of cliffs, and water so disposed — in jets, in pools
enclosed by marble, and among rocks — as to counterfeit all the wildness of Nature; there was the same
stately array of cypresses, and of clipped hedges, which

had belonged to the villas of Pliny; temples were deo orated with blazing frescos, to which, I dare say, Car paccio may have lent a hand, if not that wild rake, Giorgione. Here the pretty Queen, with eight thousand gold ducats a year, (whatever that amount may have been,) and some seventy odd retainers, held her court; and here Bembo, a dashing young fellow at that time of seven or eight and twenty, became a party to those disquisitions on Love, and to those recitations of song, part of which he has recorded in the "Asolani." I am sorry to say, the beauty of the place, so far as regards its artificial features, is now all gone. The hall, which may have served as the presence-chamber of the Queen was only a few years since doing service as a farmer's barn; and the traces of a Diana and an Apollo were still coloring the wall under which a few cows were crunching their clover-hay.

All the gardening of Italy at that period, as, indeed, at almost all times, depended very much upon architec tural accessories: colonnades and wall-veil with frescos make a large part of Italian gardening to this day. The Isola Bella in the Lago Maggiore, and the Bor ghese Garden at Rome, are fair types. And as I recall the sunny vistas of this last, and the noontide loungings upon the marble seats, counting white flecks of statues amid the green of cypresses, and watching the shadow which some dense-topped pine flings upon a marble

flight of steps or a marble balustrade, I cannot sneer at
the Italian gardening, or wish it were other than it is.
The art-life of Italy is the crowning and the overlap-
ping life. The Campagna seems only a bit of foreground
to carry the leaping arches of the aqueducts, and to throw
the hills of Tivoli and Albano to a purple distance.
The farmers (*fattori*) who gallop across the fields, in
rough sheepskin wrappers, and upon scurvy-looking
ponies, are more picturesque than thrifty; and if I gallop in company with one of them to his home upon the
farther edge of the Campagna, (which is an allowable
wet-day fancy,) I shall find a tall stone house smeared
over roughly with plaster, and its ground-floor devoted
to a crazy cart, a pony, a brace of cows, and a few goats;
a rude court is walled in adjoining the house, where a
few pigs are grunting. Ascending an oaken stair-way
within the door, I come upon the living-room of the
fattore; the beams overhead are begrimed with smoke,
and garnished here and there with flitches of bacon; a
scant fire of fagots is struggling into blaze upon an open
hearth; and on a low table, bare of either cloth or
cleanliness, there waits him his supper of *polenta*, which
is nothing more or less than our plain boiled Indian-
pudding. Add to this a red-eyed dog, that seems to be
a savage representative of a Scotch colley, — a lean,
wrinkled, dark-faced woman, who is unwinding the ban-
dages from a squalling *bambino*, — a mixed odor of

7

garlic and of goats, that is quickened with an ammo-
niacal pungency,—and you may form some idea of
the home of a small Roman farmer in our day. It
falls away from the standard of Cato; and so does
the man.

He takes his twenty or thirty acres, upon shares, from
some wealthy proprietor of Rome, whose estate may
possibly cover a square mile or two of territory. He
sells vegetables, poultry, a little grain, a few curds, and
possibly a butt or two of sour wine. He is a type of a
great many who lived within the limits of the old
Papal territory: whether he and they have dropped
their musty skeepskins and shaken off their unthrift
under the new government, I cannot say.

Around Bologna, indeed, there was a better race of
farmers: the intervening thrift of Tuscany had always
its influence. The meadows of Terni, too, which are
watered by the Velino, bear three full crops of grass in
the season ; the valley of the Clitumnus is like a miniature of the Genesee ; and around Perugia the crimson-
tasselled clovers, in the season of their bloom, give to
the fields the beauty of a garden.

The old Duke of Tuscany, before he became soured
by his political mishaps, was a great patron of agricul·
tural improvements. He had princely farms in the
neighborhood both of his capital and of Pisa. Of the
latter I cannot speak from personal observation ; but

the dairy-farm, *Cascina*, near to Florence, can hardly
have been much inferior to the Cajano property of the
great Lorenzo. The stables were admirably arranged,
and of permanent character; the neatness was equal to
that of the dairies of Holland. The Swiss cows, of a
pretty dun-color, were kept stalled, and luxuriously fed
upon freshly cut ray-grass, clover, or vetches, with an
occasional sprinkling of meal; the calves were invari-
ably reared by hand; and the average *per diem* of milk,
throughout the season, was stated at fourteen quarts;
and I think Madonna Clarice never strained more than
this into the cheese-tubs of Ambra. I trust the burgh-
ers of Florence, and the new *Gonfaloniere*, whoever he
may be, will not forget the dun cows of the Cascina, or
their baitings with the tender vetches.

The redemption of the waste marsh-lands in the Val
di Chiana by the engineering skill of Fossombroni, and
the consequent restoration of many thousands of acres
which seemed hopelessly lost to fertility, is a result of
which the Medici would hardly have dreamed, and
which would do credit to any age or country.

About the better-cultivated portions of Lombardy
there is an almost regal look. The roads are straight,
and of most admirable construction. Lines of trees lift
their stateliness on either side, and carry trailing festoons of vines. On both sides streams of water are
flowing in artificial canals, interrupted here and there

by cross sluices and gates, by means of which any or all of the fields can be laid under water at pleasure, so that old meadows return three and four cuttings of grass in the year. There are patches of Indian-corn which are equal to any that can be seen on the Miami; hemp and flax appear at intervals, and upon the lower lands rice. The barns are huge in size, and are raised from the ground upon columns of masonry.

I have a dapper little note-book of travel, from which these facts are mainly taken; and at the head of one of its pages I observe an old ink‑sketch of a few trees, with festoons of vines between. It is yellowed now, and poor always; for I am but a dabbler at such things. Yet it brings back, clearly and briskly, the broad stretch of Lombard meadows, the smooth Mac-adam, the gleaming canals of water, the white finials of Milan Cathedral shining somewhere in the distance, the thrushes, as in the "Pastor Fido," filling all the morning air with their sweet

> "Ardo d' amore! ardo d' amore!"

the dewy clover-lots, looking like wavy silken plush, the green glitter of mulberry-leaves, and the beggar in steeple-crowned hat, who says, "*Grazia*," and "*A rivedervi!*" as I drop him a few kreutzers, and rattle away to the North, and out of Italy.

Conrad Heresbach.

A BOUT the year 1570, Conrad Heresbach, who wa§
Councillor to the Duke of Clèves, (brother to that
unfortunate Anne of Clèves, a wife-victim of Henry
VIII.,) wrote four Latin books on rustic affairs, which
were translated by Barnaby Googe, a Lincolnshire
farmer and poet, who was in his day gentleman-pen-
sioner to Queen Elizabeth. Our friend Barnaby introduces his translation in this style : — " I haue thought
it meet (good Reader) for thy further profit & pleasure,
to put into English these foure Bookes of Husbandry,
collected & set forth by Master Conrade Heresbatch,
a great & a learned Counceller of the Duke of Cleues :
not thinking it reason, though I haue altered & increased his worke, *with mine owne readings & obserua-*
tions, ioined with the experience of sundry my friends,
to take from him (as diuers in the like case haue done)
the honour & glory of his owne trauaile : Neither is it
my minde, that this either his doings or mine, should
deface, or any wayes darken the good enterprise, or
painfull trauailes of such our countrymen of England, as haue plentifully written of this matter : but
always haue, & do giue them the reuerence & honour due to so vertuous, & well disposed Gentlemen,
namely, *Master Fitz herbert,* & *Master Tusser :* whose
workes may, in my fancie, without any presumption,

compare with any, either *Varro*, *Colamella*, or *Palla-*
dius of *Rome.*"

There is a delightful simplicity of manner about the
conduct of this old " Book of Husbandry," of which, I
doubt not, a large measure is to be attributed to the
Lincolnshire farmer.   It is, like the greater part of
Xenophon's " Œconomicus," in the form of dialogue,
and its quaintness, its *naïveté*, its Christian unction, give
good reason for the suggestion of Sir Harris Nicolas,
— that we are indebted to it for Walton's cast of the
" Angler."   The parties to the first conversation, " Of
Earable-ground and Tillage," are Cono, a country-gentleman, Metella, his wife, Rigo, a citizen, and Hermes,
a servant.

" Ah maister Cono (says Rigo,) I am glad I haue
found you in the midst of your country pleasures :
surely you are a happy man, that shifting yourselfe from
the turmoiles of the court, can picke out so quiet a
life, & giving over all, can secretly lie hid in the pleasant Countries, suffering us in the meane time to be tost
with the cares & businesse of the common weale."

And thereupon the discourse opens concerning the
pleasures and duties of a country-life, and the reconcile-
ment of them with a due regard for the public welfare.
And as they push on good-naturedly in the discussion,
Rigo says, "Tell me I beseech you, how you bestow
your time, & how you are occupied all the day."

With which request Cono most willingly complies, and gives us this unique picture of the occupations of a well-to-do country-gentleman of the Continent, about the middle of the sixteenth century : —

" I use commonly to rise, first of all myselfe. specially in Sommer, when we lose the healthfullest & sweetest time with sluggishnesse. In the Winter, if I be loathe, if either the unreasonablenesse of the weather or sicknesse cause me to keepe my bed, I commit all to my Steward, whose faith & diligence I am sure of, whom I haue so well instructed, that I may safely make him my deputie: I haue also Euriclia my maid, so skilful in huswifery. that shee may well be my wives suffragan ; these twaine we appoint to supply our places : but if the weather & time serve, I play the workemaster myselfe. And though I haue a Baylife as skilfull as may be, yet remembering the old saying, that the best doung for the field is the master's foot, & the best provender for the Horse the Masters eye, I play the overseer myselfe.

" When my servants are all set to worke, & everie man as busie as may be, I get me into my closet to serve God, & to reade the holy Scriptures: (for this order I always keepe to appoint myselfe everie day my taske, in reading some part either of the old Testament or of the new ;) that done, I write or read such things as I thinke most needfull, or dispatch what businesse

soever I have in my house, or with sutors abroad. A
little before dinner I walke out, if it be faire, either it
my garden, or in the fields; if it be foule, in my gal-
lerie: when I come in, I find an egge, a chicke, a peece
of kid, or a peece of veale, fish, butter, & such like,
as my foldes, my yarde, or my dairie & fishponds will
yeeld: sometimes a Sallat, or such fruits as the garden
or orchard doth beare: which victuals without aney
charges my wife provideth me, wherewith I content myselfe as well as if I had the daintiest dish in Europe: I
never lightly sit above one houre at my meate: after
dinner I passe the time with talking with my wife, my
servants, or if I have any, with my ghests: I rise &
walke about my ground, where I view my workemen,
my Pastures, my Meddowes, my Corne, & my Cattel.
. . . . In the meanwhile I behold the wonderfull wise-
dome of Nature & the incomprehensible working of the
most Mighty God in his creatures. Here waigh I with
myselfe, the benefits & wonderfull workes of His, who
bringeth forth grasse for the Cattel, & greene hearbe
for the use of man. With these sights do I recreate
my minde, & give thanks unto God the creator & con-
server of all things, singing the song ' Praise thou the
Lord ol. my soule ! '

"Then returning home, I go to writing or reading, or
such other businesse as I have: but with study or invention, I never meddle n three houres after I have dined.

I suppe with a small pittance, & after supper I either
seldome or never write or reade, but rather passe the
time seeing my sheepe come home from the Fielde, &
my Oxen dragging home the plow with weary neckes,
in beholding the pleasant pastures sweetly smelling
about my house, & my heards of Cattel lowing hard
by mee : sometimes I list to rest mee under an old
Holme, sometimes upon the greene grasse; in the
meantime passeth by mee the pleasant River, the
streames falling from the springs with a comfortable
noise; or else walking by the River-side, or in my garden or neerest pastures, I confer with my wife or servants of husbandry, appointing what things I will have
done : if my Baylife have any thing to say, if any thing
be to be bought or sold : for a good husband, as Cato
saith, must rather bee a seller than a buyer. Sometimes,
(specially in winter) after supper, I make my minister
to tell something out of the holy Scripture, or else some
pleasant story, so that it be honest & godly, & such
as may edifie. Two or three hours after supper I get
me to bed, & commonly as I said before, the last in
the house except my Chamberlaine & my Steward."

Heresbach cites familiarly and very frequently the
elder authors, particularly Cato and Varro; he accepts
with an easy conscience too many of the old fables of
the Latinists; he has abiding faith in " the moon being
aloft " in time of sowing; he assures us that " if you

graffe your peare upon a Mulbery, you shall have red
Peares; the Medlar being graffed upon the Thorne, the
graffe groweth to great bignesse; Upon the Pine tree it
bringeth a sweet fruit but not lasting." Again he tells
us, " If you break to powder the horne of a Ram &
sowe it watering it well, it is thought it will come to be
good Sperage " (asparagus).

Yet he holds in proper discredit the heathen galaxy
of gods, and when Thrasybulus (one of the parties to
his talk upon orcharding) asks who first planted the
vine, and says " the common sort doe attribute the first
invention of it to Bacchus," the good Heresbach (in the
person of Marius) puts him down in this style: " We
that are taught by God's holy worde, doe know that it
was first found out by the Patriarke Noah, immediately
after the drowning of the world: It may be, the Wine
was before that time, though the planting & the use
thereof was not then knowne. The heathen both most
falsely & very fondly, as in many other things, doe
give the invention of the same unto the God Bacchus.
But Noah lived many yeeres before either Bacchus, Sa-
turnus, or Uranius were borne."

Of butter, upon which the elder Latinists * do not
descant, he gives us this primitive account; and I know

---

* The word *butyrum* occurs once in Columella, as an application to a
wound in a sheep. Even Crescenzi makes no mention of butter and
talks in an apologetic strain of the cheese made from the milk of cows,
— " ii loro latte e cascio assai si confa alluso de l' hucmo, advenga che
non sia cosi buono come quello de la pecora." Lib. IX. cap. lxvi.

.no earlier one : — " Of milke is made Butter, whose use (though chiefely at this day among the Flemings) is yet a good & profitable foode in other countries, & much used of our old Fathers, yea even of the very Patriarches (as the Scriptures witnesseth). The commoditie thereof besides many other, is the asswaging of hunger, & the preserving of strength : it is made in this sorte. The Milke, as soone as it is milked, is put out of the Paile into Bowles or Pannes, the best are earthen Pannes, & those rather broad than deepe : this done, the second or the third day, the creame that swimmes aloft is fleeted off, & put into a vessel rather deepe than big, round & cilinder fashion : although in other places they have other kind of Charmes, low & flat, wherein with often beating & moving up & downe, they so shake the milke, as they sever the thinnest part off from the thicke, which at the first, gathers together in little crombles, & after with the continuance of the violent moving, commeth to a whole wedge or cake : thus it is taken out & either eaten fresh, or barrelled with salt."

I have before me two editions of this old work : the first of Barnaby Googe, published in 1614, and the second newly compiled with additions by Captaine Garvase Markhame, and bearing date of 1631. From this we may infer that the book had considerable popularity in England ; and it is curious to observe how the gallant Captain has filed away many of the religious reflections of Heresbach or of Googe, and introduced such addenda as show him to have been a high liver and an ardent sportsman. Thus when Barnaby has brought to an end his pleasant talk about the vine, the Captain adds this rule for giving an aromatic flavor to the grape. " You shall take," he says, " Damask rose water & boyle therein the powder of cloaves, cin-amon, three graines of Amber & one of Muske, & when it is come to be somewhat thicke, take a round gouge & make an hole on the maine stocke of the Vine, full as deepe as the heart, & then put therein the medicine, stopping the hole with Cypress or Juniper, & the next Grapes which shall spring out of the vine will taste as if they were perfumed."

Again, Barnaby closes his discourse of " Hennes " with a pleasant allusion to that " Christian Gentlewom-an of milde & sweet disposition, the Ladie Hales of Kent," who used to make capons of her turkey-cocks: the ungallant Captain drops the compliment to the Ladie Hales, and gives us three or four pages upon cock-fighting; " for my owne part," says he, " I doe not finde (in this Kingdome of ours) any monument of pleasure whatsoever more ancient than the cock-pit."

Upon the last page of the book are some rules for purchasing land, which I suspect are to be attributed to the poet of Lincolnshire, rather than to Heresbach.

They are as good as they were then ; and the poetry
none the worse : —

> " First see that the land be clear
> In title of the seller;
> And that it stand in danger
> Of no woman's dowrie;
> See whether the tenure be bond or free,
> And release of every fee of fee;
> See that the seller be of age,
> And that it lie not in mortgage;
> Whether ataile be thereof found,
> And whether it stand in statute bound;
> Consider what service longeth thereto,
> And what quit rent thereout must goe;
> And if it become of a wedded woman,
> Think thou then on covert baron;
> And if thou may in any wise,
> Make thy charter in warrantise,
> To thee, thine heyres, assignes also;
> Thus should a wise purchaser doe."

The learned Lipsius was a contemporary and a not
far-off neighbor of Councillor Heresbach ; and although
his orthodoxy was somewhat questionable, and his Calvinism somewhat stretchy, there can be no doubt of the
honest rural love which belongs to some of his letters,
and especially to this smack of verse (I dare not say
poetry) with which he closes his *Eighth* (*Cent. I.*) : —

> " Vitam si liceat mihi
> Formare arbitriis meis:
> Non fasces cupiam aut opes,
> Non clarus niveis equis

Captiva agmina traxerim.
  In solis habitem locis,
Hortos possideam atque **agros,**
Illic ad strepitus aquæ
Musarum studiis fruar.
  Sic cum fata mihi ultima
Pernerit Lachesis mea;
Tranquillus moriar senex."

I have ventured to English it in this way: —

Were it given to me to choose
The life that I would live,
No honors I 'd ask, no gold,
No car with snowy steeds
Trailing its captive bands.
In lonely places I 'd live
With gardens and fields my own.
There, to the murmur of streams,
Of poets I 'd drink my fill.
So, when at the last Lachesis
Should clip the fateful thread,
She 'd find me waiting and willing,
An old man tranquilly dead.

La Maison Rustique.

I PASS over the Rhine — using books for stepping-stones — into the French territory. In the pleasant country of the Ardèche, at the little town of Villeneuve-le-Berg, — a half-day's ride away from the Rhone bank and but a little farther from the famous vineyard of the Hermitage, — there is a monument to the memory of

Olivier de Serres, who is fondly called the Father of
French agriculture, and who is specially honored because he first introduced the culture of the mulberry
and the rearing of silk-worms. Every peasant of that
region feels a debt of gratitude to him, which he ac-
knowledges by the pride he entertains in his monument
of Villeneuve-le-Berg. The French have a delightfully open-hearted way of declaring their allegiance to
their benefactors, and of setting up memorials to them.
It is true they take on a frenzy every century or two of
ripping open the tombs of kings, or emperors, — even
of such as their darling Henri Quatre, — and sowing
their ashes broadcast. But there are some memories
they cherish unflinchingly, and some monuments they
will always guard : that of Olivier de Serres is one of
them. He enjoyed in his latter years the special patronage of Henri IV., and his great work, "Théâtre
d'Agriculture," may be reckoned the first considerable
contribution to the literature of the subject in France.

At about the same period, Charles Estienne, brother
of the famous printer, and himself a printer and physician, wrote largely on rural subjects, collecting his vari
ous treatises finally under the name of "Prædium Rus-
ticum," which he afterward translated into French, and
called "La Maison Rustique." The work was largely
added to by Liebault, his son-in-law ; and, with such
successive improvements and emendations, year after

year, as have almost buried the origina., it has come fairly down to our own day, and is thought a neces-sary purchase by every country-gentleman in France.

I have before me now an old English edition of the book, dated 1616, translated by Richard Surflet and " newly Reviewed, Corrected and Augmented, with di-vers large additions," by our friend Garvase Markham. A great many absurd fables are told in it with a curious air of gravity; thus if a farmer would know the price of corn, he says, " Let him chuse out at adventure twelve graines of Corne the first day of Januarie, let him make cleane the fire-Harth, and kindle a fire there-upon; afterward let him call some boy or girle of his neighbors, or of his owne house, let him command the partie to put one of these graines upon the Harth, made verie cleane and hot: then hee shall marke if the said graine do leape or lye still : if it leape a little, then corne shall be reasonably cheape; but if it leape verie much it shall be verie cheape; if it leape toward the fire more or lesse, corne shall be more or lesse deare; if it lye still and leape not, then Corne shall stand at one price for this first moneth."

I wish that our modern speculators in bread-stuffs were capable of formularies as innocent; but I fear their motives of sale or purchase are warmed by a hotter fire than belongs to any earthly hearth-stone. Liebault, being a physician, mingles a great deal of medical ad-

vice with the agricultural. Thus he suggests to us a
certain familiar remedy for an old style of headache, in
this fashion : — " If the Head complaine itselfe of too
much Drinke, there may be made a Frontlet with wild
Time, Maiden-haire, and Roses ; or else to drinke of
the shavings of Hartshorne, with Fountaine or River
water : or if you see that your stomacke be not sicke,
thou mayst take of the haire of the Beast that hath
made thee ill, and drinke off a good glasse of Wine."

Again, where he talks of pine-trees he says, (and
modern practitioners will agree with him in this also,)
" such as have weake lungs, must goe a taking of the
ayre into the pine Forests." He tells us that an apple
grafted upon the pear will produce the fruit called
" pearmains," and if they be grafted on quinces, " you
shall have Paradise apples." But on the other hand,
he questions the old stories of promiscuous grafting,
and insists that rosin-bearing trees cannot be grafted.
To have great cherries, he says, " you must often break
the cherry tree," — a notion which has its confirmation
in the modern practice of heading in old trees for the
sake of producing fresh-bearing wood. He advises
mulching, and constant tillage of both orcharding and
vines. He urges the winter foddering of cattle from
stacks about the meadows, in order to secure a proper
distribution of the manure, — a slovenly practice for
which too many New-England farmers wil' be glad to

find a respectable authority, although it be some three centuries old. Any distribution is, it is true, better than none; but the waste on the score of food, of fat, and of manure, is by far too great to warrant any encouragement of the system.

The reader may be interested in seeing some names of esteemed apples in that time, — such as Ruddocke, Rambur, Fairewife, Gastlet, Great-eye, Greening, Barbarian, and among special favorites were Shortstart, Honiemeale, and Garden-globe. Liebault is moreover the first, I believe, to introduce to the European public some of the mysteries of the tobacco-plant. It was quite new in his day, and had been brought, he tells us, by the captain of a ship trading with the Floridas. Out of respect to Master John Nicot, he urges that it be called Nicotiana ; and he enumerates some dozen or more of diseases and aches which it will infallibly cure, while he sums up the testimony thereto with as pretty a grace and as loud assurance as Dr. Brandreth could command. I venture to introduce his description of one curative method which is entertained kindly by a few old-fashioned persons even now : —

"If you take of the best Tabacco or Nicotiana, and twine it very hard as you can together, then with a knife shred it very small and spreading it upon a cleane sheet of paper, drie it over a gentle fire made of charcoale, then when it is cold you shall put it into a Tabacco pipe

that is verie cleane or new burnt (the figure thereof is
needless to relate, because the world is so much en-
chanted therewith, that not anything whatever is halfe
so common as this is now a daies) and having stopt it
hard into the pipe, you shall with a Wax candle, or other
sweet flame, set it on fire, and then sucking and drawing
the Smoake into your mouth, you shall force the fume
forth at your nostrills, which fume will (if the head be
well covered) make that you shall avoid at the mouth
such quantitie of slimy and flegmatick water, as that
your body will thereby become leane, as if you had
fasted long: by which one may conjecture that the
dropsie not confirmed may be holpen by taking the
same fume : the same fume taken at the mouth is singular good for them that have a short breath, old cough,
or rheumes."

Had Dr. Liebault been a nurseryman and lived at
Brooklyn or Rochester, I should have suspected him
of having a "limited number of fine stocky plants" of
this valuable herb for sale.

French Ruralisms.

I DO not find much among the older French writers
to stimulate one who is agriculturally, or even pas-
torally inclined.   They hold their places on the shelves
of a country-library, like city-guests at a country-table.

They overbear one with the grand air they carry. No
homely sounds chime with the chatter of them. The
truth is, the French do not love the country ; a mouldy
château with extinguisher-turrets lifting above a copse
of poplars, which is set all astir in October witk a little
coterie of Parisians who bang at the birds, (without
much harming them,) and play piquet, and talk of
Paris, — this is their measure of country-delights. Or
if a little more of sentiment is grafted upon the fancy,
there must be bright copper *casseroles* in the kitchen,
maids in short skirts, a dance under the trees, peasant
hats and sashes, a tame lamb in ribbons, pictures by
Watelet in the *salon*, — all which is met and enjoyed
as they sit out a play at the theatre, which being over,
— " *allons donc !* " — they flock home to the city.

A great Frenchman will sometimes go to the country to die, but never to live. Voltaire would have been
miserable at Ferney without his little court of admirers
trailing out from Geneva ; he planted himself there on
the verge of two States only that he might escape the
possible persecution of either ; he contrived his château
for the best housing of his adulators and of his gilt
coach, rather than for any views it might give of Lake
Leman and Mont Blanc : his favorite walk was a *ber-
ceau* - avenue of clipped hornbeams, still vigorous in
their ugliness, and allowing only rare glimpses of the
wonderful vision of lake and mountain toward Geneva.

I am sure that he loved the patter of the little feet of his feminine idolaters upon the gravel-path better than any bird-song, or any echo of thunder from the wooded heights of the Jura. There is no trace of natural scenery in the " Henriade " ; and as for the " Pucelle," there is not in all its weary length so much as a fig-leaf to cover its indecencies.

If he plants the borders of his fields, it is with a view to revenue ; his keen eye never lost sight of that. He ridicules a French author who had talked of a gain in agriculture of one hundred per cent. : " five hundred," says Voltaire, " would not be too much"; and then, with a sardonic grin, — " *Heureux Parisiens, jouissez de nos travaux, et jugez de l' Opéra Comique !* "

He speaks on one occasion of the restoration of sterile lands, and says the only feasible way is " to trans-port good earth to them ; this, repeated year after year, added to manure, may make them fertile " ; and he adds, " none but a rich man could undertake this," — an ob-servation which is entirely sound.

Again he says if cavalry are camped on such ground a sufficient length of time, it may be redeemed.* The English indeed hurdle sheep for purposes of fertiliza-tion, but could any save a Frenchman ever have sug-gested the idea of hurdling a squadron of cavalry?

* He adds to this extraordinary suggestion a no less extraordinary comment, — " *Cette dépense se fesant dans le royaume, il n'y aurait pas un denier de perdu.*"

If any ripe outburst of rural feeling were to be counted upon for a surety in any of the older French authors, one might, it would seem, reasonably look for it in the books of the many-sided, jovial, philosophic, indolent Montaigne. He was born and lived in Périgord, with a fine, flowing landscape under his eye; he hated cities; he hated crowds; he hated politics; he hated war. He travelled widely and wherever his humor led him; his eye was as keen as a falcon's; he reported upon all possible relations of man to man; he wrote of Fear, and Custom, and Death, and Idleness, and Cannibals, and I know not what besides: but of trees or rivers or vineyards or mountains he is as silent as if he had never seen them.

He neither wishes to build, nor loves field-sports nor gardens, nor " other such pleasures " * of a country-life. He has no special attachment for his paternal castle: "If I feared much to die away from it," he says, "I should never go abroad; for I feel death always pressing at my reins. It is all one to me where I die. If I could choose, I think it would be rather on horseback than in my bed."

Boileau, whose name — Despreaux — is suggestive of the meadows, is utterly incapable of any touch that quickens one's memory of either fields or stream. He

* " N'y ce plaisir de bastir, qu'on dit estre si attrayant, n'y la chasse, n'y les jardins, n'y ces autres plaisirs de la vie retirée, ne me peuvent beaucoup amuser." — Liv. III. cap. 9.

wrote, indeed, a poetic epistle to his gardener, (XI.);
but with the substitution of a curry-comb for the spade
it might have been addressed to his hostler. The epistle may very likely have been suggested by one of
Horace, *Ad Suum Villicum ;* but they are widely unlike. Under all of the Roman poet's pleasant banter
of his bailiff, you see a yearning for the freshness and
freedom of his farm-life. He admits his old dissipation
and the long nights he has made of it with the "covet-
ous Cynara"; but now he only asks short suppers, and
long sleep on some grassy river-bank, —

"Cena brevis juvat, et prope rivum somnus in berba."

Boileau, on the other hand, has no loves to confess, but
muddles and confounds his gardener with a story of
the immense strain upon the mind which his poetic
labors involve.

Madame de Sévigné wrote most charmingly ; and one
would have supposed that on her visits to her old and
beautiful home in Brittany her epistles would have
caught something of the color of the country, and
that she would delight in conveying to her daughter in
Provence glimpses of the Breton peasants, and some of
the perfume of the Breton .gardens and of the Breton
pine woods . but no ; her letters from her château of
Les Rochers are as flashingly Parisian and as *salon-*
bound as if they had been written under the shadow
of Notre Dame. Lady Wortley Montagu would have

written a different style of letter from a country-house
in Brittany ; but—*que voulez-vous?*—the Sévigné was a
Frenchwoman.

Felton in his " Portraits," * a pleasant, but slipshod
book, takes occasion in his opening chapter to claim
both Sévigné and Boileau as intense lovers of gardening, of which he says their writings give proof. I cannot find the evidence. The Lamoignon letter of Boileau (Epist. VI.) has no unction in its rural allusions ;
its peasant cottages are dug out of a cliff of sandstone,
and the poet regales himself with the delights of Au-
teuil chiefly because he escapes there the abusive talk
of the city.   Mme. de Sévigné's warmest picture of a garden is of one where she passed an evening, at the
Hotel de Condé, (16th July, 1677) : — " There were
iets-d'eaux, cabinets, terraced walks, six *hautbois* in
one corner, six violins in another, a little nearer six
delightful flutes, a supper that appeared by enchant-
ment, an admirable bass-viol, and over all — the moon-
light."   A true French garden !

Boileau made pretensions, it is true, in his Lamoignon
epistle ; but Bossuet was honester, — so honest that his
gardener said to him, " Si je plantais des St. Augus-
tins et des St. Chrysostomes, vous les viendriez voir ;
mais pour vos arbres, vous ne vous en souciez guère."

* *On the Portraits of English Authors on Gardening*   By S. Felton.
London, 1830. 8vo

If Rousseau be any exception to what I have said, he is at the least a Swiss exception. An exceptional man, indeed, he was in every way, — so full of genius, so imbruted by vanity, so ignobly selfish, so masterful in the inthralment of all sensitive minds by the binding, glittering meshes of his talk. Keenly apprehensive of beauty, whatever form it might take, this man must have enjoyed the garden-experience near to Chambery, under the tutelage of Mme. de Warens; yet he tells us very little about it. The lady was disposed to be a *farmeress;* but Jean Jacques was looking at the heavens, or busying himself with vain study of music. He had no practical talent, except for language. In his "Rêveries du Promeneur Solitaire" there are scattered little bits of rurality, quickened by his botanizing; I may specially designate his descriptions of scenes upon the isle of St. Pierre, in the Lake of Bienne. And in the "Nouvelle Héloise" (Part 4, Let. XI.) there is a most charming picture of a garden-wilderness, which those gentlemen who have lands upon their hand, and who are fettered by the ordinary rules of the gardeners, might read to their profit. It is a sweet sylvan tangle of beauties, amid which birds are singing and rills are flowing. I will not venture upon any translation.*

* "Dans les lieux plus découverts je voyais çà et là, sans ordre et sans symétrie, des broussailles de roses, de framboisiers, de groseilles, des fourrés de lilas, de noisetier, de sureau, de seringat, de genêt, de trifolium, qui paraient la terre en lui donnant l'air d'être en friche

In his " Confessions " he says, — " It was in the midst
of the Park of Montmorenci, in that profound and
delicious solitude, with woods around me, and waters,
and the songs of all birds, and the perfume of orange-
blossoms, that I composed, in a continued ecstasy, the
fifth book of ' Émile ' ; and its fresh coloring is due in a
large degree to the locality where I wrote."

It is a frank admission from one in whom frank-
ness was perhaps the largest virtue. In that same
fifth book there is a pleasant picture of Émile teaching the peasantry ; by way of diversion he shows them
how to make a new sort of farm-wagon, and he surprises
them all by taking in hand the plough and laying a
straighter furrow than any of them could do. Whereupon Rousseau says, (and I have heard kindred talk in
the mouths of my neighbors,) — " *Ils ne se moquent pas*

Je suivais des allées tortueuses et irrégulières bordées de ces bocages
fleuris, et couvertes de mille guirlandes de vigne de Judée, de vigne-
vierge, de houblon, de liseron, de couleuvrée, de clématite, et d'autres
plantes de cette espèce, parmi lesquelles le chèvre-feuille et le jasmin
daignaient se confondre. Ces guirlandes semblaient jetées négligem-
ment d'un arbre à l'autre, comme j'en avais remarqué quelquefois
dans les forêts, et formaient sur nous des espèces de draperies qui nous
garantissaient du soleil, tandis que nous avions sous nos pieds un mar-
cher doux, commode, et sec, sur une mousse fine, sans sable, sans herbe,
et sans rejetons raboteux. Alors seulement je découvrais, non sans
surprise, que ces ombrages verds et touffus, qui m'en avaient tant im-
posé de loin, n'étaient formés que de ces plantes rampantes et parasites,
qui, guidées le long des arbres, environnaient leur têtes du plus épais
feuillage, et leurs pieds d'ombre et de fraîcheur." I give a glimpse
only at a scene which fills four full pages of Rousseau's best descriptive language.

de lui comme d'un beau diseur d'agriculture; *ils voient qu'il la sait en effet.*"

I do not think it could ever have been said of Rousseau. I can hardly imagine a man more poorly qualified for the masculine employments that belong to a continued and devoted country - life. His period of novitiate at the Chaumettes, where he lived in the silken leash of Mme. de Warens, was no test. His botanizing was a casual habit; and throughout all his seclusion, he was more occupied with the wonders of his own brain and his own passions, than with the wonders of Nature. Yet he painted Nature well, and wantoned in his power; but his power was dearer to him than his subject. He never loved the forest, as Bernardin de St. Pierre loved the lusty verdure of the tropics.

This latter, — Frenchman though he was, — when so poor that he could command only a garret in the *faubourg*, equipped his little window always with a pot of flowers; and in " Paul and Virginia " he left a bouquet whose perfume is dear to all boys and girls, even now.

Of the hundred and odd plays of Saintine we remember, and care to remember, nothing; but his Picciola, struggling through the crevice of a prison pavement, has, under his love and art, made its tender leaflets to flutter winningly in the eyes of all the world.

A Minnesinger.

THE clouds are breaking. I began my day among the Troubadours; why not close it with a blithe song of a "Minnesinger"? It is full of the forest-freshness of the North; there is in it no Southern clang of battle. It clears the air; it mocks at gloom; it beckons to a ramble upon the green shores of England.

> "May, sweet May, again is come, —
> May, that frees the land from gloom.
> Children, children, up and see
> All her stores of jollity!
> O'er the laughing hedge-rows' side
> She hath spread her treasures wide;
> She is in the greenwood shade,
> Where the nightingale hath made
> Every branch and every tree
> Ring with her sweet melody:
> Hill and dale are May's own treasures,
> Youth, rejoice in sportive measures;
> Sing ye! join the chorus gay!
> Hail this merry, merry May!
>
> "Up, then, children, we will go
> Where the blooming roses grow;
> In a joyful company
> We the bursting flowers will see;
> Up! your festal dress prepare!
> Where gay hearts are meeting, there
> May hath pleasures most inviting,
> Heart and sight and ear delighting:

Listen to the birds' sweet song,
Hark! how soft it floats along!
Courtly dames our pleasures share,
Never saw I May so fair;
Therefore dancing will we go;
Youths, rejoice, the flowrets blow;
Sing ye! join the chorus gay!
Hail this merry, merry May! " *

* Attributed to Earl Conrad of Kirchberg, and cited by Roscoe in
his notes to Sismondi's *Literature of Europe.*

FOURTH DAY.

Piers Plowman.

A SMART little couplet of volumes from Soho Square, London, bears me away from the murky November sky that confronts me out-of-doors, to

> " a May morwenynge
> On Malverne hilles." *

And there Piers Plowman shall lay open for me the first farm-furrow upon English soil. For want of better, we may count him the type of a British farmer in the reign of Edward III., — those famous days of Crecy and of Poictiers. It is true that the allusions to field-culture in the book are only incidental; but it is something that the author of the old verse made a ploughman his preacher, by which we may infer that the craft was held in respect by the people; there are also certain indications of the modes of country-life and of farm-fare which I hope to bring into view.

---

* *The Vision and Creed of Piers Plowman:* (edited by Thomas Wright:) an allegorical poem of about the middle of the fourteenth century, by Langlande (?) an English monk.

Piers one day falls asleep on Malvern Hills, and has a vision. The whole world is gathered in a meadow. Piers looks on at King, knights, ladies, and hirelings, and sees by-and-by Lady Church come among them with her godly talk ; but Lady Mammon (Mede) finds more listeners, and, at the instigation of the lawyers, a marriage is set on foot between Mammon and Falsehood. Conscience breaks up the match, whereupon the King, who has a regard for Mammon, advises that she marry Conscience. But Conscience objects that the lady's reputation is bad ; whereat they fall into a wrangle, and the King commands them to kiss and be friends. Conscience says he "would die first," and appeals to Reason, who comes and brings Peace. This delights the King, and Reason is in great favor and commences preaching ; and the " field full of folk," all listening, want to find their way to the Tower of Truth. But they boggle on the road. Piers Plowman knows it, and says if they will wait till he has ploughed a half-acre on the highway, he will guide them.

> " Now is Perkyn and his pilgrim *
> To the plow faren:
> Dikers and delvers
> Digged up the ridges:
> Other workmen there were
> That wroughten full well;

* I have ventured to modernize the language somewhat, though preserving so far as possible the peculiar alliterative construction, and the rhythm.

Each man in his manner
Made up his task,
And some to please Perkyn
Piked up the weeds.
At high prime Piers
Let the plow stand
To oversee for himself,
Whoso had best wrought,
And whom he should hire
When harvesting came.
And some were a-sitting
A-singing at the ale,
Helping till the half land
With ' High, trolly-lolly ! ' "

And Piers swears at them, — as later farmers have done, — " by the peril of his soul." But the lazy folk are full of all manner of excuses, to which Piers will not listen, but berates them the more. Whereat one called the " Waster" grows wrathy, and bids Perkyn " ' go hang ' with his plow."

" Will you or won't you,
We 'll have our will
Of your flour and your flesh,
Fish when we like ;
And make merry therewith,
Mauger your cheeks."

Piers in a stout passion summons Hunger to his aid, who straightway pinches Waster by the stomach till nis eyes water, (" *bothe hise eighen watrede,*") and buffets him about the cheeks so that he looked like a lantern "all his life after." At this all his brother-sluggards rushed into the barn, and " flapped on with flails " from morning till night.

The Plowman prays Hunger, who has served him so good a turn, to go home with him; and Hunger discourses on the way from Bible texts, improvingly, counselling moderation in eating and drinking, and giving a pleasant rap at the doctors: —

> " For murderous are many Leeches
> Lord, amend their ways!
> With all their drugs, they bring men death
> Ere Destiny would do 't."

At last Piers asks Hunger to leave him ; but Hunger must have his dinner before he goes, and this gives us a hint of farmers' fare in 1370 : —

> " I have no penny, quoth Piers
> Pullets to buy;
> I have no geese nor grunters,
> But green cheeses two,
> A few small curds and cream,
> Cake of oaten meal,
> I have two loaves of bean and bran
> Bakéd for my folk,
> And I have parseley and porettes,
> And plants eno' of cole,
> And eke a cow and a calf,
> And a cart mare
> To draw a-field my dung,
> The while the drought lasteth."

9

The Farmer of Chaucer's Time.

SITTING thus, with the poem of Piers Plowman in my hand, and the dashing Lady Mede making rainbows in my thought, (as she does for us poor mortals alway,) I wonder what a country-life would have been in those royal days of England which just preceded the bloody times of the " Roses," — when the gallantry of the Black Prince was a toast with gallant men everywhere, — when the Gloucestershire monks made the "touchingest" wine in England, — when Venetian ships brought silks for wives who could wear them, — when ploughmen wore serge and blankets, and drank the "nattiest" of ale, — and when Chaucer made tales like honey.

I suppose that a country - gentleman of moderate means in those times would have lived in a cumbrous, low house, built of oaken timber filled in with mortar, or flint stones, (if they were near him,) with a great hall for its principal apartment, hung around with flitches of venison, and with a rude chimney-place where half a sheep was roasted at a time upon a wooden spit.

I suppose that he would have taught his boys prac- tice with the strong-bow, and that his girls would tease him for some bit of jewelry brought over by the Genoese ships. I am sure that wheaten bread was a ‑arity, and that his hirelings got only that made from

barley, or, what was cheaper, peas and beans. I suspect
a cask of ale was always on tap, and that the farmer
was sometimes drunken — of the forenoon. If he
lived in Cornwall, he would send his " doung carts " to
the shore for sea-sand to dress his wheat-crop; and if
he were near some monastery, the monks might send
him now and then a stoop of their wine, or come from
time to time to read to his women-folk, out of Piers
Plowman, (if they were radical,) or out of Chaucer,
(if they were conservative); but I suspect that the
country-gentleman would listen to neither, — leaving
that bit of hospitality to the girls, — and would fall
asleep upon his oaken settle, and dream, and make
sounds through his nose, —

" As though he saidest aye — Sampsoun ! Sampsoun ! "

He must have had great stock of colewort and
parsley and leeks * in his garden, and, if an epicure,
may have boasted a bed of cucumbers. He would
have a drove of hogs, of course, which wandered very
much where it willed, under the guidance of some
hireling, who, if he had dropped the neck-collar of
Wamba, wore a jerkin every way as rough, a staff
with a sharp pike in its end, and his hair "yshorne
round by his eres."

* Hume says it was not until the end of the reign of Henry VIII.
that ary " edible roots " were produced in England; but this is abun.
dantly disproved by Piers Plowman's talk.

And if such a country-gentleman boasted a bailiff
to oversee his farm-lands, he was very likely such
another as Chaucer has painted in the Reve: —

> " a slendre colerike man,
> His berd was shave as nigh as ever he can.
> Ful long were his legges, and ful lene,
> Ylike a staff there was no calf ysene.
> Wel coulde he kape a garner and a binne;
> There was not auditour coude on him winne.
> Wel wiste he by the drought and by the rain,
> The yelding of his seed and of his grain."

Of all things, such a landholder must have dreaded
most the visit of some distinguished dignitary of the
Church, who travelled with some four hundred in his
train, treading down all his grain-crops, and his home-
close, robbing his larder, and killing off the fattest of
his bucks and of his wethers ; and whatever promises
an archbishop might make of the new " graffes " he
would send him, or some manuscript copy of Crescenzi,
or of Columella, I think he must have been glad to see
the palfrey of his Reverence go ambling out of his farm-
yard.*   The farm-implements of such a landholder
must have been very cumbrous ; I doubt if the ploughs
had improved much upon that ill-shapen affair with one
wheel, whose picture has come down to us in the Cal

* I have endeavored to make this portrait historically true, and
am indebted for its several particulars to Malmesbury, Langlande,
Chaucer, Mathew Paris, Holinshed, Latimer, and Macpherson's "An
nals of Commerce."

endar of the Cotton MSS.* Quick-witted men, even
if they were dwellers in the country, took more pride in
a good pack of hounds than in a good array of farm-
tools; and we inherit much of the same barbarism in
these days, when some runt of a fast trotter is sure to
carry away all the honors and all the applause from our
best cattle-shows.

I do not suppose that a British farmer of the fourteenth century would have cared much for gardening,
beyond his patch of colewort, parsley, and onions; and
the larger landholders, who boasted baronial titles, would
hardly have ventured to place any rare things of fruit
or flower outside their battlemented walls or moat.
The priors and the abbots were the men most successful with the vineyards and orcharding: *they* reaped the
good things of life in those days: town-boys did not
venture over the walls of a priory to steal pippins; and
in the herbary of the " Nonnes Priestes Tale " there is
enumeration of such a stock of herbs that the very reading of it is savory with tincture of rhubarb.

Henry II. long before this had his park and his labyrinth at Woodstock, of which the deepest trace left is
the tragic memory of Fair Rosamond. And if parks,
then surely flowers, — if not in gardens, at least in the
pages of the poets, where henceforth I may gather
them as I list, to garnish this wet-day talk. At the

* Stratt.

bare thought of them, I seem to hear the royal captive James pouring madrigals through the window of his
Windsor prison, —

> " the hymnis consecrat
> Of Iovis use, now soft, now loud among,
> That all the gardens and the wallis rung."

And through the " Dreme " of Chaucer I seem to see
the great plain of Woodstock stretching away under
my view, all white and green, — "green y-powdered
with daisy." Upon the half-ploughed land, lying yonder
veiled so tenderly with the mist and the rain, I could
take oath to the very spot where five hundred years
ago the ploughman of Chaucer, all " forswat,"

> " plucked up his plowe
> Whan midsomer mone was comen in
> And shoke off shear, and coulter off drowe,
> And honged his harnis on a pinne,
> And said his beasts should ete enowe
> And lie in grasse up to the chin."

With due respect for the poet, it would be bad husbandry to allow cattle steaming from the plough to lie
down in grass of that height.

Sir Anthony Fitz-herbert.

SIR ANTHONY FITZ-HERBERT, who died in
1538, is the first duly accredited writer on British
husbandry. There are some few earlier ones, it is true,

— a certain " Mayster Groshede, Bysshop of Lyncoln,"
and a Henri Calcoensis, among them. Indeed, Mr.
Donaldson, who has compiled a bibliography of British farm-writers, and who once threatened a poem on
kindred subjects, has the effrontery to include Judge
Littleton. I have a respect for Judge Littleton, and for
Coke on Littleton, but it is tempered with some early
experiences in a lawyer's office, and some later experiences of the legal profession ; and however well he
may have written upon " Tenures," I do not feel disposed to admit him to the present galaxy.

It is worthy of remark, in view of the mixed complexion which I have given to these wet-day studies,
that the oldest printed copy of that sweet ballad of the
" Nut Browne Mayde " has come to us in a Chronicle of
1503, which contains also a chapter upon " the crafte
of graffynge & plantynge & alterynge of fruyts." What
could be happier than the conjunction of the knight of
' the grenwode tree " with a good chapter on " graffynge " ?

Fitz-herbert's work is entitled a " Boke of Husbandrie," and counts, among other headings of discourse,
the following : —

" Whether is better a plough of horses or a plough
of oxen."

" To cary out dounge & mucke, & to spreade it."

" The fyrste furryng of the falowes."

"To make a ewe to love hir lambe."

" To bye lean cattel."

" A shorte information for a young gentylemaι ιιιαι entendeth to thryve."

" What the wyfe oughte to dooe generally."

(*seq.*) "To kepe measure in spendynge."

" What be God's commandments."

" What joyes & pleasures are in heaven."

" A meane to put away ydle thoughts in praing."

At the close of his book he says, — " Thus endeth the ryghte profytable Boke of Husbandrye, compyled sometyme by Mayster Fitzherbarde, of charitee and good zele that he have to the weale of this most noble realme, which he did not in his youth, but after he had exercised husbandrye, with greate experience, forty years."

By all this it may be seen that Sir Anthony took as broad a view of husbandry as did Xenophon.

Among other advices to the " young gentyleman that entendeth to thryve" he counsels him to rise betime in the morning, and if " he fynde any horses, mares, swyne, shepe, beastes in his pastures that be not his own ; or fynde a gap in his hedge, or any water standynge in his pasture uppon his grasse, whereby he may take double herte, bothe losse of his grasse, & rotting of his shepe, & calves; or if he fyndeth or seeth anything that ιs amisse, & wold be amended, let him take out his tables

& wryte the defautes ; & when he commeth home to
dinner, supper, or at nyght, then let him call his bayley,
& soo shewe him the defautes. For this," says he,
" used I to doo x or xi yeres or more ; & yf he cannot
wryte, lette him nycke the defautes uppon a stycke."

Sir Anthony is gracious to the wife, but he is not
tender ; and it may be encouraging to country-house-
wives nowadays to see what service was expected of
their mothers in the days of Henry VIII.

"It is a wives occupacion to winow al maner of
cornes, to make malte, wash & wring, to make hey, to
shere corne, & in time of neede to helpe her husbande
to fyll the mucke wayne or donge carte, dryve the
plough, to lode hay corne & such other. Also to go or
ride to the market to sell butter, chese, mylke, egges,
chekens, kapons, hennes, pygges, gees & al maner
of corne. And also to bye al maner of necessary
thinges belonging to a household, & to make a true
rekening & accompt to her husband what she hath
receyved & what she hathe payed. And yf the husband
go to market to bye or sell as they ofte do, he then to
shew his wife in lyke maner. For if one of them should
use to disceive the other, he disceyveth himselfe, & he
is not lyke to thryve, & therfore they must be true
ether to other.

" I could peradventure shew the husbande of divers
pointes that the wives disceve their husbandes in, &

in like maner howe husbandes disceve their wives. But
yf I should do so, I shuld shew mo subtil pointes of
discceite then either of them knew of before ; & therefore me semeth best to holde my peace."

His knowledge on these latter points will be ex-
plained when I say that this old agricultural worthy
was also a lawyer and in large practice. It is not common for one of his profession to discuss " What be God's
commandments." He was buried where he was born,—
upon the banks of the River Dove, at the little town of
Norbury in Derbyshire.

Thomas Tusser.

I COME next to Master Tusser,—poet, farmer,
chorister, vagabond, happily dead at last, and with
a tomb whereon some wag wrote this : —

> " Tusser, they tell me, when thou wert alive,
> Thou teaching thrift, thyself could never thrive;
> So, like the whetstone, many men are wont
> To sharpen others when themselves are blunt."

I cannot help considering poor Tusser's example one
of warning to all poetically inclined farmers.

He was born at a little village in the County of
Essex. Having a good voice, he came early in life to
be installed as singer at Wallingford College; and
showing here a great proficiency, he was shortly after
impressed for the choir of St. Paul's Cathedral. After-

ward he was for some time at Eton, where he had the
ill-luck to receive some fifty-four stripes for his shortcomings in Latin; thence he goes to Trinity College,
Cambridge, where he lives " in clover." It appears
that he had some connections at Court, through whose
influence he was induced to go up to London, where he
remained some ten years, — possibly as singer, — but
finally left in great disgust at the vices of the town, and
commenced as farmer in Suffolk, —

> " To moil and to toil
> With loss and pain, to little gain,
> To cram Sir Knave "; —

from which I fancy that he had a hard landlord, and
but little sturdy resolution. Thence he goes to Ips-
wich, or its neighborhood, with no better experience.
Afterward we hear of him with a second wife at Dere-
ham Abbey; but his wife is young and sharp-tempered,
and his landlord a screw: so he does not thrive here,
but goes to Norwich and commences chorister again;
but presently takes another farm in Fairstead, Essex,
where it would seem he eked out a support by collecting tithes for the parson. But he says, —

> " I spyed, if parson died,
> (All hope in vain,) to hope for gain
> I might go dance."

Possibly he did go dance : he certainly left the tithe-
business, and after settling in one more home, from

which he ran to escape the plague, we find him return
ed to London, to die, — where he was buried in the
Poultry.

What is specially remarkable about Tusser is his air
of entire resignation amid all manner of vicissitudes:
he does not seem to count his hardships either wonderful or intolerable or unmerited.   He tells us of the
thrashing he had at Eton, (fifty-four licks,) without
greatly impugning the head-master; and his shiftless-
ness in life makes us strongly suspect that he deserved
it all.

There are good points in his poem, showing close
observation, good sense, and excellent judgment.   His
rules of farm-practice are entirely safe and judicious,
and make one wonder how the man who could give
such capital advice could make so capital a failure.   In
the secret lies all the philosophy of the difference between knowledge and practice.   The instance is not
without its modern support: I have the honor of acquaintance with several gentlemen who lay down
charming rules for successful husbandry, every time
they pay the country a visit; and yet even their poultry-
account is always largely against the constipated hens.

I give one or two specimens of Tusser's mode of
preachment; the first from his March's husbandry: —

"Sow barley in March, in April, and May,
The later in sand, and the sooner in clay.

What worser for barley than wetness and cold?
What better to skilful than time to be bold?

"Let barley be harrowed finely as dust,
　Then workmanly trench it, and fence it ye must.
　This season well plied, set sowing an end,
　And praise and pray God a good harvest to send.

" Some rolleth their barley straight after a rain,
　When first it appeareth, to level it plain;
　The barley so used the better doth grow,
　And handsome ye make it, at harvest to mow.

" At spring (for the summer) sow garden ye shall,
　At harvest (for winter) or sow not at all.
　Oft digging, removing, and weeding, ye see,
　Makes herb the more wholesome and greater to be."

Again in his teaching for February he says, very
shrewdly : —

" Who slacketh his tillage a carter to be,
　For groat got abroad, at home lose shall three;
　And so by his doing, he brings out of heart
　Both land for the corn and horse for the cart.

" Who abuseth his cattle, and starves them for meat,
　By carting or ploughing his gain is not great:
　Where he that with labor can use them aright,
　Hath gain to his comfort, and cattle in plight."

Fuller, in his " Worthies," says Tusser "spread his
bread with all sorts of butter, yet none would stick
thereon." In short, though the poet wrote well on

farm-practice, he certainly was not a good exemplar of
farm-successes.   With all his excellent notions about
sowing and reaping, and rising with the lark, I should
look for a little more of stirring mettle and of dogged
resolution in a man to be recommended as a tenant.
I cannot help thinking less of him as a farmer than as
a kind-hearted poet; too soft of the edge to cut very
deeply into hard-pan, and too porous and flimsy of
character for any compacted resolve: yet taking life
tenderly, withal; good to those poorer than himself
making a rattling appeal for Christmas charities; hospitable, cheerful, and looking always to the end with an
honest clearness of vision : —

> " To death we must stoop, be we high, be we low,
>   But how, and how suddenly, few be that know;
>   What carry we, then, but a sheet to the grave,
>   (To cover this carcass,) of all that we have? "

Sir Hugh Platt.

SIR HUGH PLATT, who lived in the latter part of
the sixteenth century, is called by Mr. Weston in
his catalogue of English authors, " the most ingenious
husbandman of his age."   He is elsewhere described as
a gentleman of Lincoln's Inn, who had two estates in
the country, besides a garden in St. Martin's Lane.   He
was an enthusiast in agricultural, as well as horticul

tural inquiries, corresponding largely with leading farmers, and conducting careful experiments within his own grounds. In speaking of that " rare and peerless plant. the grape," he insists upon the wholesomeness of the wines he made from his Bednall-Greene garden : " And if," he says, " any exception shold be taken against the race and delicacie of them, I am content to submit them to the censure of the best mouthes, that professe any true skill in the judgement of high country wines : although for their better credit herein, I could bring in the French Ambassador, who (now almost two yeeres since, comming to my house of purpose to tast these wines) gaue this sentence upon them : that he neuer drank any better new wine in France."

I must confess to more doubt of the goodness of the wine than of the speech of the ambassador ; French ambassadors are always so complaisant !

Again he indulges us in the story of a pretty conceit whereby that "delicate Knight," Sir Francis Carew, proposed to astonish the Queen by a sight of a cherrytree in full bearing, a month after the fruit had gone by in England. This secret he performed, by " straining a Tent or couer of canuass ouer the whole tree, and wetting the same now and then with a scoope or horne, as the heat of the weather required : and so, by witholding the sunne beams from reflecting upon the ber ries, they grew both great, and were very long before they had gotten their perfect cherrie-colour: and when he was assured of her Majestie's comming, he remoued the Tent, and a few sunny daies brought them to their full maturities."

These notices are to be found in his " Flores Paradisæ." Another work, entitled " Dyuers Soyles for manuring pasture and arable land," enumerates, in addition to the usual odorous collection, such extraordinarily new matters (in that day) as "salt, street-dirt, clay, Fullers earth, moorish earth, fern, hair, calcination of all vegetables, malt dust, soap - boilers ashes, and marle." But what I think particularly commends him to notice, and makes him worthy to be enrolled among the pioneers, is his little tract upon " The Setting of Corne." *

In this he anticipates the system of " dibbling ' grain, which, notwithstanding, is spoken of by writers within half a century † as a new thing; and which, it is needless to say, still prevails extensively in many parts of England. If the tract alluded to be indeed the work of Sir Hugh Platt, it antedates very many of the suggestions and improvements which are usually

* This is not mentioned either by Felton in his *Portraits*, etc., by Johnson in his *History of Gardening*, or by Loudon. Donaldson gives the title, and the headings of the chapters. I also observe that it is alluded to by a late writer in the *London Quarterly.*

✢ See Young, *Annals of Agriculture*, Vol III. p. 219, *et seq.*

accorded to Tull. The latter, indeed, proposed the drill, and repeated tillage ; but certain advantages, before unconsidered, such as increased tillering of individual plants, economy of seed, and facility of culture, are common to both systems. Sir Hugh, in consecutive chapters, shows how the discovery came about; "why the corne shootes into so many eares"; how the ground is to be dug for the new practice ; and what are the several instruments for making the holes and covering the grain.

He further relates, with a simplicity which is almost suspicious, that the art of dibbling grain originated with a silly wench who had been put by her master to the setting of carrots and radishes; and having some seed-wheat in her bag, she dropped some kernels into the holes prepared for the carrots, and these few kernels shot up with such a wonderful luxuriance as had never been seen before.

I cannot take a more courteous leave of this worthy gentleman than by giving his own *envoi* to the most considerable of his books: — " Thus, gentle Reader, having acquainted thee with my long, costly, and laborious collections, not written at Adventure, or by an imaginary conceit in a Scholler's private studie, but wrung out of the earth, by the painfull hand of experience: and having also given thee a touch of Nature, whom no man as yet ever durst send naked into the

10

worlde without her veyle: and Expecting, by thy good
entertainement of these, some encouragement for higher
and deeper discoveries hereafter, I leave thee to the
God of Nature, from whom all the true light of Nature
proceedeth."

Gervase Markham.

GERVASE MARKHAM must have been a roistering gallant about the time that Sir Hugh was
conducting his experiments on " Soyles " ; for, in 1591,
he had the honor to be dangerously wounded in a duel
which he fought in behalf of the Countess of Shrews-
bury ; there are also some painful rumors current (in
old books) in regard to his habits in early life, which
weaken somewhat our trust in him as a quiet country-
counsellor. I suspect, that, up to mature life, at any
rate, he knew much more about the sparring of a
game-cock than the making of capons. Yet he wrote
books upon the proper care of beasts and fowls, as
well as upon almost every subject connected with husbandry. And that these were good books, or at least
in large demand, we have in evidence the memoran-
dum of a promise which some griping bookseller ex-
torted from him, under date of July, 1617 :—

" I, Gervase Markham, of London, Gent, do promise

hereafter never to write any more book or books to be printed of the diseases or cures of any cattle, as horse, oxe, cowe, sheepe, swine and goates, &c. In witness whereof, I have hereunto sett my hand, the 24ᵗʰ day of Julie. " GERVIS MARKHAM."

I have already alluded to his edition of the " Maison Rustique " of Liebault; and notwithstanding the religiously meditative air which belongs to some portions of his " Country Contentments," he had a hand in the concoction of one or two poems that kindled greatly the ire of the Puritan clergy.

From a book of his to which he gave the title of " The English Husbandman " I venture to copy on the next page a little plan of an English farm-house, which he assures us is given not to please men of dignity, but for the profit of the plain husbandman.

There is no doubt but he was an adroit book-maker; and the value of his labors, in respect to practical husbandry, was due chiefly to his art of arranging, compacting, and illustrating the maxims and practices already received. His observations upon diseases of cattle and upon horsemanship were doubtless based on experimental knowledge; for he was a rare and ardent sportsman, and possessed all a sportsman's keenness in the detection of infirmities.

In this connection I quote a little passage about the

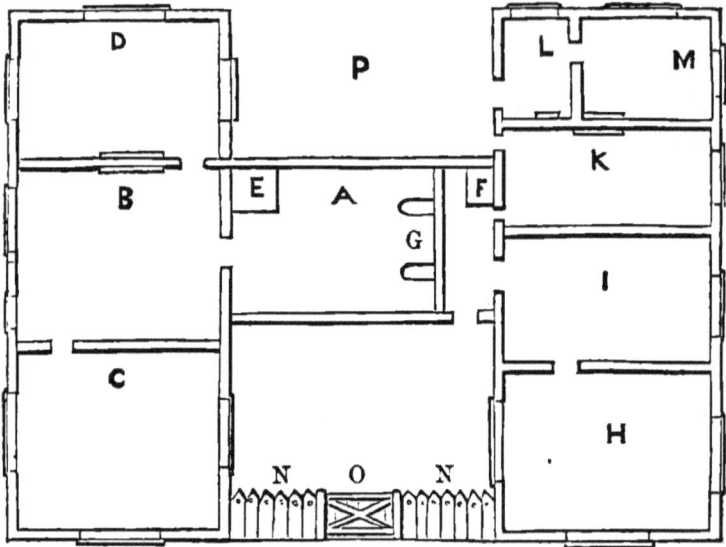

A MODEL ENGLISH FARM-HOUSE, A. D. 1600.*

manner of "putting a Cocke into battel," which he has
interpolated upon the grave work of the Councillor
Heresbach.

"When your cocke is equally matched, it is then
your part to give him all the naturall and lawfull advantages, which may availe for his conquest; as first to

* Explanation of references:—

"A. Signifies the great hall.
B. The dining-parlor for stran-
gers.
C. Closet for use of mistress.
D. Strangers' lodging.
E. Staircase to room over parlor.
F. Staircase to goodman's room.
G. The skrene in the hall.

H. Inner cellar to serve for larder.
I. Buttery.
K. Kitchen.
L. Dairy-house.
M. Milk-house.
N. A faire sawne pale.
O. Great gate to ride in to hall-dore
P. Place for pump."

disburden him of all things superfluous, as extravagant
feathers about his head, the long feathers of his Mane,   ν
even from the head to the Shoulders, and this must be
done as close to the necke as may be, for the least
feather his enemy can catch hould on, is a ladder by
which he will rise to destroy him; also the small
feathers about his rumpe and others of like nature.
As thus he takes away things superfluous, so you must
add to those which have anything wanting, as if his
Beake be rough, you must smooth it, but not weaken it;
if his Spurres be blunt and uneven, you must sharpen
them and make them so piercing that on the smallest
entrance, they may run up to the very beame of the
leg; and for his wings you must make them like the
wings of a Dragon, every feather like a ponyard, stab-
bing and wounding wheresoever they touch : this done
rub his head over with your own Spittel, and so leave
him to Fortune."

The advice may seem somewhat out of date, and yet
I cannot help being reminded by it of the way in which
our politicians prepare their Presidential candidates.
The last suggestion of Markham (as cited above) is
particularly descriptive.

It would be unfair to the good man's memory to leave
him pitting a cock ; so I will give the reader some of
his hints in regard to the appointments of the English
housewife.

"Let her garments," he says, (and it might be said in New England,) "be comely and strong, made as well to preserve health, as to adorn the person, altogether without toyish garnishes, or the gloss of light colors, and as far from the vanity of new and fantastick fashions, as near to the comely imitation of modest matrons. Let her dyet be wholsome and cleanly, prepared at due hours, and cooked with care and diligence; let it be rather to satisfie nature, than her affections, and apter to kill hunger, than revive new appetites. Let it proceed more from the provision of her own yard, than the furniture of the markets; and let it be rather esteemed for the familiar acquaintance she hath with it, than for the strangeness and rarity it bringeth from other countries.

"To conclude, our English Housewife must be of chaste thoughts, stout courage, patient, untired, watchful, diligent, witty, pleasant, constant in friendship, full of good neighborhood, wise in discourse, but not frequent therein, sharp and quick of speech, but not bitter or talkative, secret in her affairs, comfortable in her counsels, and generally skilfull in the worthy knowledges which do belong to her vocation."

Again he gives us the details of a " humble feast of a proportion which any good man may keep in his family."

"As thus : — first, a shield of brawn with mustard;

secondly, a boyl'd capon ; thirdly, a boyl'd piece of
beef ; fourthly, a chine of beef rosted ; fifthly, a neat's
tongue rosted ; sixthly, a pig rosted ; seventhly, chewits
baked ; eightly, a goose rosted ; ninthly, a swan rosted ;
tenthly, a turkey rosted ; eleventh, a haunch of venison
rosted ; twelfth, a pasty of venison ; thirteenth, a kid
with a pudding in the belly; fourteenth, an olive pye ;
the fifteenth, a couple of capons; the sixteenth, a
custard or dowsets."

This is what Master Gervase calls a frugal dinner, for
the entertainment of a worthy friend ; is it any wonder
that he wrote about " Country Contentments " ?

My chapter is nearly full ; and a burst of sunshine is
flaming over all the land under my eye ; and yet I am
but just entered upon the period of English literary
history which is most rich in rural illustration. The
mere backs of the books relating thereto, as my glance
ranges over them, where they stand in tidy platoon,
start a delightfully confused picture to my mind.

I think it possible that Sir Hugh Platt may some
day entertain at his Bednall-Greene garden the worshipful Francis Bacon, who is living down at Twickenham, and who is a thriving lawyer, and has written essays, which Sir Hugh must know, — in which he discourses shrewdly upon gardens, as well as many kindred
matters ; and through his wide correspondence, Sir

Hugh must probably have heard of certain new herbs which have been brought home from Virginia and the Roanoke, and very possibly he is making trial of a tobacco-plant in his garden, to be submitted some day to his friend, the French ambassador.

I can fancy Gervase Markham " making a night of it" with those rollicking bachelors, Beaumont and Fletcher, at the " Mermaid," or going with them to the Globe Theatre to see two Warwickshire brothers, Edmund and Will Shakspeare, who are on the boards there, — the latter taking the part of Old Knowell, in Ben Jonson's play of " Every Man in his Humour." His friends say that this Will has parts.

Then there is the fiery and dashing Sir Philip Sidney, who threatened to thrust a dagger into the heart of poor Molyneux, his father's steward, for opening private letters (which poor Molyneux never did) ; and Sir Philip knows all about poetry and the ancients; and in virtue of his knowledges, he writes a terribly magniloquent and tedious " Arcadia," which, when he comes to die gallantly in battle, is admired and read everywhere : nowadays it rests mostly on the shelf. But the memory of his generous and noble spirit is far livelier than his book. It was through him, and his friendship, probably, that the poet Spenser was gifted by the Queen with a fine farm of three thousand acres among the Bally-Howra hills of Ireland.

And it was here that Sir Walter Raleigh, that "shepherd of the sea," visited the poet, and found him seated

> " amongst the coolly shade
> Of the green alders, by the Mulla's shore."

Did the gallant privateer possibly talk with the farmer about the introduction of that new esculent, the
potato?* Did they talk tobacco? Did Colin Clout
have any observations to make upon the rot in sheep,
or upon the probable " clip " of the year?
Nothing of this; but

> "He pip'd, I sung; and when he sung, I pip'd:
> By chaunge of tunes each making other merry."

The lines would make a fair argument of the poet's
bucolic life. I have a strong faith that his farming was
of the higgledy-piggledy order; I do not believe that
he could have set a plough into the sod, or have made
a good "cast" of barley. It is certain, that, when

* Introduced probably by Sir Walter Raleigh about 1586. But the
vegetable was a delicacy (or at least a rarity) in James I.'s time; and
in 1619 a small number were bought for the Queen's use at one shilling per pound. In 1662 they were recommended by the Royal Society
for more extended cultivation.

Scott Burn, *Outlines of Modern Farming*, p. 43, gives (without authority) the year 1750 as the date of their final introduction as a field-
crop. Parkinson, in his *Theatrum Botanicum*, first published in 1640,
names among garden-vegetables, " Spanish potatoes, Virginia potatoes,
and Canada potatoes (Jerusalem artichoke)." See also Johnson, *History
of Gardening*, p. 103. John Mortimer, writing as late as 1707, (*Country
man's Kalendar*,) says of the potato, " The root is very near the nature
of the Jerusalem artichoke, but not so good or wholesome. These are
planted either of roots or seeds, and may probably be propagated in
great quantities, and prove good food for swine."

the Tyrone rebels burned him out of Kilcolman Castle,
he took no treasure with him but his Elizabeth and
the two babes ; and the only treasures he left were the
ashes of the dear child whose face shone on him there
for the last time, —

> " bright with many a curl
> That clustered round her head."

I wish I could love his " Shepherd's Calendar " ; but
I cannot.   Abounding art of language, exquisite fancies, delicacies innumerable there may be ; but there is
no exhilarating air from the mountains, no crisp breezes,
no songs that make the welkin ring, no river that
champs the bit, no sky-piercing falcon.

And as for the " Faëry Queene," if I must confess it,
I can never read far without a sense of suffocation from
the affluence of its beauties.   It is a marvellously fair
sea and broad, — with tender winds blowing over it,
and all the ripples are iris-hued; but you long for some
brave blast that shall scoop great hollows in it, and
shake out the briny beads from its lifted waters, and
drive wild scuds of spray among the screaming cur-
lews.

In short, I can never read far in Spenser without taking a rest, — as we farmers lean upon our spades, when
the digging is in unctuous fat soil that lifts heavily.

And so I leave the matter, — with the " Faëry
Queene " in my thought, and leaning on my spade.

FIFTH DAY.

English Weather.

WE are fairly on English ground now; of course,
it is wet weather. The phenomena of the British climate have not changed much since the time when
the rains "let fall their horrible pleasure" upon the
head of the poor, drenched outcast, Lear. Thunder
and lightning, however, which belonged to that particular war of the elements, are rare in England. The
rain is quiet, fine, insinuating, constant as a lover, — not
wasting its resources in sudden, explosive outbreaks.

During a foot-tramp of some four hundred miles,
which I once had the pleasure of making upon English
soil, and which led me from the mouth of the Thames
to its sources, and thence through Derbyshire, the West
Riding of Yorkshire, and all of the Lake counties, I do
not think that the violence of the rain kept me housed
for more than five days out of forty. Not to say that
the balance showed sunshine and a bonny sky; on the

contrary, a soft, lubricating mist is the normal condition
of the British atmosphere ; and a neutral tint of gray
sky, when no wet is falling, is almost sure to call out
from the country-landlord, if communicative, an explosive and authoritative, " Fine morning, this, Sir ! "

The really fine, sunny days — days you believed in
rashly, upon the sunny evidence of such blithe poets as
Herrick — are so rare, that, after a month of British
travel, you can count them on your fingers.   On such a
one, by a piece of good fortune, I saw all the parterres
of Hampton Court, — its great vine, its labyrinthine
walks, its stately alleys, its ruddy range of brick, its
clipped lindens, its rotund and low-necked beauties of
Sir Peter Lely, and the red geraniums flaming on the
window-sills of once royal apartments, where the pen-
sioned dowagers now dream away their lives.   On
another such day, Twickenham, and all its delights of
trees, bowers, and villas, were flashing in the sun as
brightly as ever in the best days of Horace Walpole or
of Pope.   And on yet another, after a weary tramp, I
toiled up to the inn-door of " The Bear," at Woodstock ;
and after a cut or two into a ripe haunch of Oxfordshire mutton, with certain "tiny kickshaws," I saw, for
the first time, under the light of a glorious sunset, that
exquisite velvety stretch of the park of Woodstock, —
dimpled with water, dotted with forest-clumps, — where
companies of sleek fallow-deer were grazing by the

hundred, where pheasants whirred away down the aisles of wood, where memories of Fair Rosamond and of Rochester and of Alice Lee lingered, — and all brought to a ringing close by Southey's ballad of " Blenheim," as the shadow of the gaunt Marlborough column slanted across the path.

There are other notable places, however, which seem — so dependent are we on first impressions — to be always bathed in a rain - cloud. It is quite impossible, for instance, for me to think of London Bridge save as a great reeking thoroughfare, slimy with thin mud, with piles of umbrellas crowding over it, like an army of turtles, and its balustrade streaming with wet. The charming little Dulwich Gallery, with its Berghems, Gainsboroughs, and Murillos, I remember as situated somewhere (for I could never find it again of my own head) at a very rainy distance from London, under the spout of an interminable waterfall. The guide-books talk of a pretty neighborhood, and of a thousand rural charms thereabout; I remember only one or two draggled policemen in oil-skin capes, and with heads slanted to the wind, and my cabby, in a four-caped coat, shaking himself like a water-dog, in the area. Exeter, Gloucester, and Glasgow are three great wet cities in my memory, — a damp cathedral in each, with a damp-coated usher to each, who shows damp tombs, and whose talk is dampening to the last degree. I suppose they have sunshine in these places, and in the light of the sun I am sure that marvellous gray tower of Gloucester must make a rare show; but all the reports in the world will not avail to dry up the image of those wet days of visit.

Considering how very much the fair days are over-balanced by the dirty, thick, dropping, misty weather of England, I think we take a too sunny aspect of her history: it has not been under the full-faced smiles of heaven that her battles, revolutions, executions, and pageants have held their august procession; the rain has wet many a May-day and many a harvesting, whose traditional color (through tender English verses) is gaudy with yellow sunshine. The revellers of the "Midsummer Night's Dream" would find a wet turf eight days out of ten to disport upon. We think of Bacon without an umbrella, and of Cromwell without a mackintosh; yet I suspect both of them carried these, or their equivalents, pretty constantly. Raleigh, indeed, threw his velvet cloak into the mud for the Virgin Queen to tread upon, — from which we infer a recent shower; but it is not often that an historical incident is so suggestive of the true state of the atmosphere.

History, however, does not mind the rain: agriculture must. More especially in any view of British agriculture, whether old or new, and in any estimate of its theories or progress, due consideration must be had for the generous dampness of the British atmosphere. To this cause is to be attributed primarily that wonderful velvety turf which is so unmatchable elsewhere; to the same cause, and to the accompanying even temperature, is to be credited very much of the success of the turnip-culture, which has within a century revolution- ized the agriculture of England; yet again, the mag- ical effects of a thorough system of drainage are no- where so demonstrable as in a soil constantly wetted, and giving a steady flow, however small, to the discharging tile. Measured by inches, the rain - fall is greater in most parts of America than in Great Britain; but this fall is so capricious with us, often so sudden and violent, that there must be inevitably a large surface-discharge, even though the tile, three feet below, is in working or- der. The true theory of skilful drainage is, not to carry away the quick flush of a shower, but to relieve a soil too heavily saturated by opening new outflows, setting new currents astir of both air and moisture, and thus giving new life and an enlarged capacity to lands that were dead with a stagnant over-soak.

Bearing in mind, then, the conditions of the British climate, which are so much in keeping with the "wet weather" of these studies, let us go back again to old Markham's day, and amble along — armed with our umbrellas — through the current of the seventeenth century.

Time of James the First.

JAMES I., that conceited old pedant, whose "Coun-
terblast to Tobacco" has worked the poorest of
results, seems to have had a nice taste for fruits; and
Sir Henry Wotton, his ambassador at Venice, writing
from that city in 1622, says, — "I have sent the choic-
est melon-seeds of all kinds, which His Majesty doth
expect, as I had order both from my Lord Holderness
and from Mr. Secretary Calvert." Sir Henry sent also
with the seeds very particular directions for the culture
of the plants, obtained probably from some head-gar-
dener of a Priuli or a Morosini, whose melons had the
full beat of Italian sunshine upon the south slopes of
the Vicentine mountains. The same ambassador sends
at that date to Lord Holderness "a double-flowering
yellow rose, of no ordinary nature";* and it would be
counted of no ordinary nature now, if what he avers
be true, — that "it flowreth every month from May till
almost Christmas."

King James took special interest in the establishment
of his garden at the Theobald Palace in Hertfordshire :
there were clipped hedges, neat array of linden-avenues,
fountains, and a Mount of Venus within a labyrinth ;
twelve miles of wall encircled the park, and the soldiers
of Cromwell foun1 fine foraging-ground in it, when they

* *Reliquiæ Wottonianæ*, p. 317, *et seq.*

entered upon the premises a few years later. The schoolmaster-king formed also a guild of gardeners in the city of London, at whose hands certificates of capa- city for garden-work were demanded, and these to be given only after proper examination of the applicants. Lord Bacon possessed a beautiful garden, if we may trust his own hints to that effect, and the added praises of Wotton. Cashiobury, Holland House, and Greenwich gardens were all noted in this time ; and the experi- ments and successes of the proprietor of Bednall-Greene garden I have already alluded to. But the country- gentleman, who lived upon his land and directed the cultivation of his property, was but a very savage type of the Bedford or Oxfordshire landholders of our day. It involved a muddy drag over bad roads, after a heavy Flemish mare, to bring either one's self or one's crops to market.

Sir Thomas Overbury, who draws such a tender pic- ture of a " Milke-Mayde," is severe, and, I dare say, truthful, upon the country-gentleman. " His conversa- tion," says he, " amongst his tenants is desperate : but amongst his equals full of doubt. His travel is seldome farther than the next market towne, and his inquisition is about the price of corne : when he travelleth, ʒe will goe ten mile out of the way to a cousins house of his to save charges ; and rewards servants by taking them by the hand when hee departs. Nothing under a

11

sub-pœna can draw him to *London :* and when he is there, he sticks fast upon every object, casts his eyes away upon gazing, and becomes the prey of every cut-purse. When he comes home, those wonders serve him for his holy-day talke. If he goe to court, it is in yellow stockings : and if it be in winter, in a slight tafety cloake, and pumps and pantofles."

The portrait of the smaller farmer, who, in this time, tilled his own ground, is even more severely sketched by Bishop Earle. " A plain country fellow is one that manures his ground well, but lets himself lye fallow and untilled. He has reason enough to do his business, and not enough to be idle or melancholy. . . . . His hand guides the plough, and the plough his thoughts, and his ditch and land-mark is the very mound of his medita-tions. He expostulates with his oxen very understand-ingly, and speaks *gee,* and *ree,* better than English. His mind is not much distracted with objects, but if a good fat cow come in his way, he stands dumb and astonished, and though his haste be never so great, will fix here half an hours contemplation. His habitation is some poor thatched roof, distinguished from his barn by the loop-holes that let out smoak, which the rain had long since washed through, but for the double ceiling of bacon on the inside, which has hung there from his grandsires time, and is yet to make rashers for pos-terity. He apprehends Gods blessings only in a good year, or a fat pasture, and never praises him but on *good ground.*"

Such were the men who were to be reached by the agricultural literature of the day! Yet, notwithstanding this unpromising audience, scarcely a year passed but some talker was found who felt himself competent to expound the whole art and mystery of husbandry.

Adam Speed, Gent., (from which title we may presume that he was no Puritan,) published a little book in the year 1626, which he wittily called " Adam out of Eden." In this he undertakes to show how Adam, under the embarrassing circumstance of being shut out of Paradise, may increase the product of a farm from two hundred pounds to two thousand pounds a year by the rearing of rabbits on furze and broom! It is all mathematically computed; there is nothing to disappoint in the figures; but I suspect there might be in the rabbits.

Gentleman Speed speaks of turnips, clover, and potatoes; he advises the boiling of " butchers' blood " for poultry, and mixing the " pudding " with bran and other condiments, which will " feed the beasts very fat."

The author of " Adam out of Eden " also indulges himself in verse, which is certainly not up to the measure of " Paradise Lost." This is its taste: —

" Each soyl hath no liking of every grain,
Nor barley nor wheat is for every vein;

Yet know I no country so barren of soyl
But some kind of corne may be gotten with toyL
Though husband at home be to count the cost what,
Yet thus huswife within is as needful as tnat:
What helpeth in store to have never so much,
Half lost by ill-usage, ill huswifes, and such? "

The papers of Bacon upon subjects connected with rural life are so familiar that I need not recur to them. His particular suggestions, however sound in themselves, (and they generally are sound,) did by no means meas-ure the extent of his contribution to the growth of good husbandry. But the more thorough methods of investigation which he instituted and encouraged gave a new and healthier direction to inquiries connected not only with agriculture, but with every experimental art.

Thus, Gabriel Platte, publishing his "Observations and Improvements in Husbandry," about the year 1638, thinks it necessary to sustain and illustrate them with a record of "twenty experiments."

Sir Richard Weston, too, a sensible up - country knight, has travelled through Flanders about the same time, and has seen such success attending upon the turnip and the clover culture there, that he urges the same upon his fellow-landholders, in a "Discourse of Husbandrie."

Samuel Hartlib.

THE book last named was published under the au-
spices of Hartlib,— the same Master Samuel Hartlib
to whom Milton addressed his tractate " Of Education,"
and of whom the great poet speaks as "a person sen*
hither [to England] by some good Providence from a
far country, to be the occasion and incitement of great
good to this island."

This mention makes us curious to know something
more of Master Samuel Hartlib. I find that he was
the son of a Polish merchant, of Lithuania, was himself engaged for a time in commercial transactions, and
came to England about the year 1640. He wrote several theological tracts, edited sundry agricultural works,
including, among others, those of Sir Richard Weston,
and published his own observations upon the shortcomings of British husbandry. He also proposed a grandiose
scheme for an agricultural college, in order to teach
youths " the theorick and practick parts of this most
ancient, noble, and honestly gainfull art, trade, or mystery." Another work published by him, entitled " The
Legacy," besides notices of the Brabant husbandry, em-
braces epistles from various farmers, who may be supposed to represent the progressive agriculture of England. Among these letters I note one upon " Snag-
greet," (shelly earth from river-beds) ; another upon

" Seaweeds " ; a third upon " Sea-sand " , and a fourth
uʲᵒᴸ " Woollen-rags."

I also excerpt from the same book a diagram of a
farm-outlay which some ingenious correspondent contributed, and which — however well it may appear on
paper — I would by no means advise an amateur farmer to adopt. I give it only as a curious relic of the
agricultural whims of that day. It is signed Coressey
Dymock. The contributor observes that it may form
the plot of an entire " Lordship," or may serve for a
farm of two or three hundred acres.

Hartlib was in good odor during the days of the
Commonwealth ; for he lived long enough to see that
bitter tragedy of the executed king before Whitehall
Palace, and to hold over to the early years of the Restoration. But he was not in favor with the people
about Charles II. ; the small pension that Cromwell
had bestowed fell into sad arrearages ; and the story is,
that he died miserably poor.

It is noticeable that Hartlib, and a great many sensible old gentlemen of his date, spoke of the art of husbandry as a mystery. And so it is ; a mystery then,
and a mystery now. Nothing tries my patience more
than to meet one of those billet-headed farmers who —
whether in print or in talk — pretend to have solved
the mystery and mastered it.

Take my own crop of corn yonder upon the flat

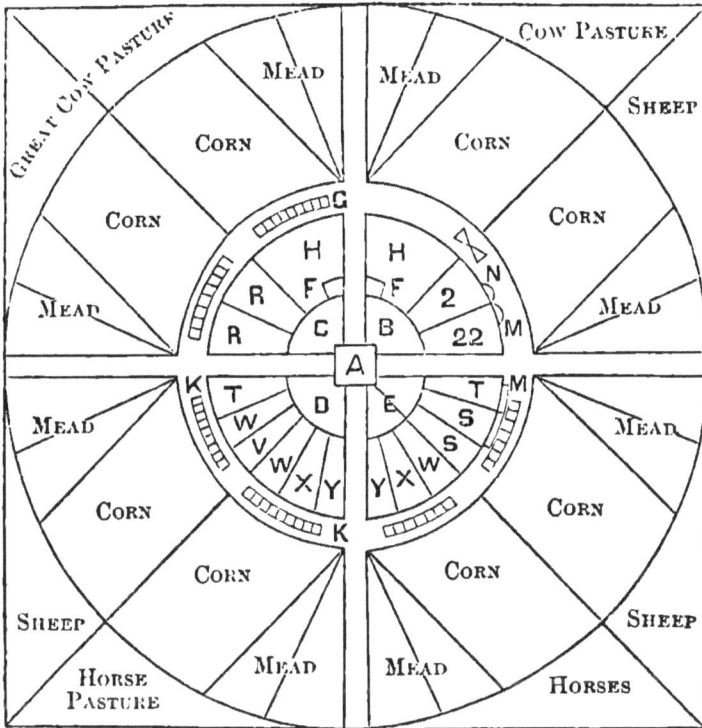

DIAGRAM OF FARM-OUTLAY.*

* Explanation of references: —

A. Dwelling-house in centre.
B. Kitchen-garden.
C. Orchard.
D. Choice garden.
E. Physicall garden.
F, F. Dairy and laundry.
G. Sheep-cotes.
H, H. Closes for swine.
K, K. Great corn-barns
L. Stables and swine-styes.

M, M. Little houses for poultry.
N. Standing racks.
Q, Q. Closes for single animals.
R. R. Closes for mares and foal.
S. S. Pastures for sheep.
T, T. Closes for work-purposes.
V. Pasture for fat beeves.
W. Close for diseased beasts.
X. Close for saddle-horse.
Y. Close for weaning calves.

which I have watched since the day when it first shot
up its little dainty spears of green, until now its spin-
dles are waving like banners: the land has been faithfully ploughed and fed and tilled; but how gross appliances all these, to the fine fibrous feeders that nave
been searching, day by day, every cranny of the soil, —
to the broad leaflets that, week by week, have stolen out
from their green sheaths to wanton with the wind and
caress the dews! Is there any quick-witted farmer who
shall tell us with anything like definiteness what the
phosphates have contributed to all this, and how much
the nitrogenous manures, and to what degree the de
posits of *humus?* He may establish the conditions of
a sure crop, thirty, forty, or sixty bushels to the acre,
(seasons favoring); but how short a reach is this
toward determining the final capacity of either soil or
plant! How often the most petted experiments laugh
us in the face! The great miracle of the vital labora-
tory in the plant remains to mock us. We test it; we
humor it; we fondly believe that we have detected its
secret: but the mystery stays.

A bumpkin may rear a crop that shall keep him
from starvation; but to develop the *utmost* capacity of
a given soil by fertilizing appliances, or by those of
tillage, is the work, I suspect, of a wiser man than belongs to our day. And when I find one who fancies
he has resolved all the conditions which contribute to

this miracle of God's, and can control and fructify
at his will, I have less respect for his head than for a
good one — of Savoy cabbage. The great problem of
Adam's curse is not worked out so easily. The sweat-
ing is not over yet.

If, however, we are confronted with mystery, it is not
blank, hopeless, fathomless mystery. It is a lively
mystery, that piques and tempts and rewards endeavor.
It unfolds with an appetizing delay. If our plummet-
lines do not reach the bottom, it is only because they
are too short; but they are growing longer. Every
year a new secret is laid bare, which, in the flush of
triumph, seems a crowning development; whereas it
presently appears that we have only opened a new door
upon some further labyrinth.

Period of the Commonwealth and Restoration.

THROUGHOUT the seventeenth century, the progress in husbandry, without being at any one
period very brilliant, was decided and constant. If
there was anything like a relapse, and neglect of
good culture, it was most marked shortly after the
Restoration. The country-gentlemen, who had entertained a wholesome horror of Cromwell and his troop-
ers, had, during the Commonwealth, devoted them
selves to a quiet life upon their estates, repairing the

damages which the Civil War had wrought in their fortunes and in their lands. The high price of farm-products stimulated their efforts, and their country-isolation permitted a harmless show of the chivalrous contempt they entertained for the new men of the Commonwealth. With the return of Charles they abandoned their estates once more to the bailiffs, and made a rush for the town and for their share of the "leeks and onions."

But the earnest men had been constantly at work. Sainfoin and turnips were growing every year into credit. The potato was becoming a crop of value; and in the year 1664 John Foster devoted a treatise to it, entitled, "England's Happiness increased, or a Sure Remedy against all Succeeding Dear Years, by a Plantation of Roots called Potatoes."

For a long time the crop had been known, and Sir Thomas Overbury had made it the vehicle of one of his sharp witticisms against people who were forever boasting of their ancestry,— their best part being below ground. But Foster anticipates the full value of what had before been counted a novelty and a curiosity. He advises how custards, paste, puddings, and even bread, may be made from the flour of potatoes.

John Worlidge in 1669 gave to the public a "System of Husbandry" very full in its suggestions, — advising green fallows, and even recommending and describing a drill for the putting in of seed, and for distributing with it a fine fertilizer.

Evelyn, also, about this time, gave a dignity to rural pursuits by his " Sylva " and " Terra," both these treatises having been recited before the Royal Society The " Terra " is something muddy,* and is by no means exhaustive ; but the " Sylva " for more than a century was the British planter's hand-book, being a judicious, sensible, and eloquent treatise upon a subject as wide and as beautiful as its title. Even Walter Scott, — himself a capital woodman, — when he tells (in " Kenilworth ") of the approach of Tressilian and his Doctor companion to the neighborhood of Say's Court, cannot forego his tribute to the worthy and cultivated author who once lived there, and who in his " Sylva " gave a manual to every British planter, and in his life an exemplar to every British gentleman.

Evelyn was educated at Oxford, travelled widely upon the Continent, was a firm adherent of the royal party, and at one time a member of Prince Rupert's famous troop. He married the daughter of the British ambassador in Paris, through whom he came into possession of Say's Court, which he made a gem of beauty. But in his later years he had the annoyance of seeing his fine parterres and shrubbery trampled

* Of clay he says, " It is a cursed step-dame to almost all vegetation, as having few or no meatuses for the percolation of alimenta showers.''

down by that Northern boor, Peter the Great, who made his residence there while studying the mysteries of ship-building at Deptford, and who had as little reverence for a parterre of flowers as for any other of the tenderer graces of life.

The British monarchs have always been more regardful of those interests which were the object of Evelyn's tender devotion. I have already alluded to the horticultural fancies of James I. His son Charles was an extreme lover of flowers, as well as of a great many luxuries which hedged him against all Puritan sympathy. "Who knows not," says Milton, in his reply to the ΕΙΚΩΝ ΒΑΣΙΛΙΚΗ, "the licentious remissness of his Sunday's theatre, accompanied with that reverend statute for dominical jigs and May-poles, published in his own name," etc. ?

But the poor king was fated to have little enjoyment of either jigs or May-poles; harsher work belonged to his reign; and all his garden-delights came to be limited finally to a little pot of flowers upon his prison-window. And I can easily believe that the elegant, wrong-headed, courteous gentleman tended these poor flowers daintily to the very last, and snuffed their fragrance with a Christian gratitude.

Charles was an appreciative lover of poetry, too, as well as of Nature. I wonder if it ever happened to him, in his prison-hours at Carisbrooke, to come upon

Milton's " L' Allegro," (first printed in the very year of the Battle of Naseby,) and to read, —

> " In thy right hand lead with thee
> The mountain nymph, sweet Liberty;
> And if I give thee honor due,
> Mirth, admit me of thy crew
> To live with her, and live with thee,
> In unreprovèd pleasures free;
> To hear the lark begin his flight,
> And, singing, startle the dull night,
> From his watch-tower in the skies,
> Till the dappled dawn doth rise;
> Then to come, in spite of sorrow,
> And at my window bid good-morrow,
> Through the sweetbrier, or the vine,
> Or the twisted eglantine."

How it must have smitten the King's heart to re-member that the tender poet, whose melody none could appreciate better than he, was also the sturdy Puritan pamphleteer whose blows had thwacked so terribly upon the last props that held up his tottering throne!

Cromwell, as we have seen, gave Master Hartlib a pension; but whether on the score of his theological tracts, or his design for an agricultural college, would be hard to say. I suspect that the hop was the Pro-tector's favorite among flowering plants, and that his admiration of trees was measured by their capacity for timber. Yet that rare masculine energy, which he and his men carried with them in their tread all over

England, was a very wakeful stimulus to productive agriculture.

Charles II. loved tulips, and befriended Evelyn. In his long residence at Paris he had grown into a gieat fondness for the French gardens. He afterward sent for Le Notre — who had laid out Versailles at an expense of twenty millions of dollars — to superintend the planting of Greenwich and St. James. Fortunately, no strict imitation of Versailles was entered upon. The splendors of Chatsworth garden grew in this time out of the exaggerated taste, and must have delighted the French heart of Charles. Other artists have had the handling of this great domain since the days of Le Notre. A crazy wilderness of rock-work, amid which the artificial waters commit freak upon freak, has been strewed athwart the lawn ; a stately conservatory has risen, under which the Duke may drive, if he choose, in coach and four, amid palm-trees, and the monster vegetation of the Eastern archipelago ; the little glass temple is in the gardens, under which the Victoria lily was first coaxed into British bloom ; a model village has sprung up at the Park gates, in which each cottage is a gem, and seems transplanted from the last book on rural ornamentation. But the sight of the village oppresses one with a strange incongruity ; the charm of realism is wanting ; it needs a population out of one of Watteau's pictures, — clean

and deft as the painted figures; flesh and blood are
too gross, too prone to muddy shoes, and to — sneeze.
The rock-work, also, is incongruous; it belongs on no
such wavy roll of park-land; you see it a thousand
times grander, a half-hour's drive away, toward Matlock. And the stiff parterres, terraces, and alleys of
Le Notre are equally out of place in such a scene. If,
indeed, as at Versailles, they bounded and engrossed
the view, so that natural surfaces should have no claim
upon your eye, — if they were the mere setting to a
monster palace, whose colonnades and balusters of
marble edged away into colonnades and balusters of
box-wood, and these into a limitless extent of long
green lines, which are only lost to the eye where a distant fountain dashes its spray of golden dust into the
air, — as at Versailles, — there would be keeping. But
the Devonshire palace has quite other setting. Blue
Derbyshire hills are behind it; a grand, billowy slope
of the comeliest park-land in England rolls down from
its terrace-foot to where the Derwent, under hoary oaks,
washes its thousand acres of meadow-vale, with a flow
as charming and limpid as one of Virgil's eclogues. It
is such a setting that carries the great quadrangle of
Chatsworth Palace and its flanking artificialities of
rock and garden, like a black patch upon the face of a
fine woman of Queen Anne's court.

    This brings us upon our line of march again

Charles II. loved stiff gardens; James II. loved stiff
gardens; and William, with his Low-Country tastes,
outstiffened both, with his

"topiary box a-row."

Lord Bacon has commended the formal style to
public admiration by his advocacy and example. The
lesson was repeated at Cashiobury by the most noble
the Earl of Essex (of whom Evelyn writes, — " My
Lord is not illiterate beyond the rate of most noblemen
of his age "). So also that famous garden of Moor-
Park in Hertfordshire,* laid out by the witty Duchess
of Bedford, to whom Dr. Donne addresses some of his
piquant letters, was a model of old - fashioned and
stately graces. Sir William Temple praises it beyond
reason in his " Garden of Epicurus," and cautions
readers against undertaking any of those irregularities
of garden - figures which the Chinese so much affect.
He admires only stateliness and primness. " Among
us," he says, " the Beauty of Building and Planting is
placed chiefly in some certain Proportions, Symmetries,
or Uniformities; our Walks and our Trees ranged so as
to answer one another, and at exact Distances."

From all these it is clear what was the garden-drift
of the century. Even Waller, the poet, — who could
be more affluent with his moneys than most poets, —

---

* Not to be confounded with Temple's own home — of the same
same — in Surrey, where his heart was buried under an urn.

spent a large sum in levelling the hills about his rural home at Beaconsfields. (We shall find a different poet and treatment by-and-by in Shenstone.)

Only Milton, speaking from the very arcana of the Puritan rigidities, breaks in upon these geometric formalities with the rounded graces of the garden which he planted in Eden. There

> " the crisped brooks,
> Rolling on orient pearl and sands of gold
> With mazy error under pendent shades,
> Ran nectar, visiting each plant, and fed
> Flowers worthy of Paradise, which not nice Art
> In beds and curious knots, but Nature boon
> Poured forth profuse on hill and dale and plain."

Going far behind all conventionalities, he credited to Paradise — the ideal of man's happiest estate — variety, irregularity, profusion, luxuriance ; and to the fallen estate, precision, formality, and an inexorable Art, which, in place of concealing, glorified itself. In the next century, when Milton comes to be illustrated by Addison and the rest, we shall find gardens of a different style from those of Waller and of Hampton Court.

Old English Homes.

AND now from some lookout - point near to the close of the seventeenth century, when John Evelyn, in his age, is repairing the damages that Peter

12

the Great has wrought in his pretty Deptford home,
let us take a bird's-eye glance at rural England.

It is raining; and the clumsy Bedford coach, drawn
by stout Flemish mares, — for thorough-breds are as
yet unknown, — is covered with a sail-cloth to keep the
wet away from the six "insides." The grass, wherever
the land is stocked with grass, is as velvety as now.
The wheat in the near county of Herts is fair, and will
turn twenty bushels to the acre ; here and there an
enterprising landholder has a small field of dibbled
grain, which will yield a third more. John Worlidge's
drill is not in request, and is only talked of by a few
wiseacres who prophesy its ultimate adoption. The fat
bullocks of Bedford will not dress more than nine
hundred a head ; and the cows, if killed, would not
overrun five hundred weight. Horses "run at grass"
for eighteenpence per week; oxen and cows at sixpence
to a shilling, according to size.* There are occasional
fields of sainfoin and of turnips but these latter are
small, and no ridging or hurdling is yet practised.
From time to time appears a patch of barren moor-
land, which has been planted with forest-trees, in ac-
cordance with the suggestions of Mr. Evelyn, and under
the wet sky the trees are thriving. Wide reaches of
fen, measured by hundreds of miles, (which now bear

* *The Country Gentleman's Vade-Mecum*, by Giles Jacob, Gent,
1717.

great crops of barley,) are saturated with moisture, and tenanted only by ghost-like companies of cranes.

The gardens attached to noble houses, under the care of some pupil of John Rose or of Quintinie, have their espaliers, — their plums, their pears,* and their grapes. These last are rare, however, (Parkinson says sour, too,) and bear a great price in the London market. One or two horticulturists of extraordinary enterprise have built greenhouses, warmed, Evelyn says, " in a most ingenious way, by passing a brick flue underneath the beds."

But these were quite exceptional among the country-gentry, — fully as much so as the ruralist of our time who has his orchard-house, and who entertains his friends in May or June with a dwarf nectarine upon the table, in full bearing. I suspect that if we had wandered, in the days of which I speak, into the house of a Dorsetshire squire, we should have found in the great hall terriers, spaniels, and hounds lying about promiscuously, with, very likely, a litter of cats in a big armchair; there would have been an oaken table covered with cards and dice-boxes; in a cupboard of the wainscot I am sure we should have found a venison-pasty, and a black case-bottle of " something warming." Very

---

* Sir William Temple gives this list of his pears: — Blanquet, Robin, Rousselet, Pepin, Jargonel; and for autumn Buree, Vertlongue, and Bergamot.

likely upon some double-decked table which has the
air of an altar there would be a Bible and the "Book
of Martyrs"; but for all the flax-haired squire had to
do with them, they would be dusty; and ten to one a
hawk's-hood or a fox-skin might be lying on them.
Tobacco-pipes would not be out of sight, and a stale
scent of them would mingle with the smell of terriers
and half-dried otter-skins. Worlidge and Evelyn would
be as much sneered at (if ever heard of) by such a
squire as the progressive agriculturists are by our old-
fashioned men now; and like these last the old squire
would hold tenaciously upon life, — mounting a horse
at fourscore, and knowing nothing of spectacles.* I
can fancy such an old gentleman saying to his after-
dinner guest, with Shallow, (who lived so long before
him,) "Nay, you shall see mine orchard: where in an
arbor, we will eat a last year's pippin of my own graff-
ing, with a dish of carraways, and so forth."

Yet this flax-haired, rotund squire, so loud-mouthed
and tyrannic in his own household, would hardly venture up to London, for fear of the footpads on the
heath and the insolence of the blackguard Cockneys.
His wife should be some staid dame, lean, but rosy of
visage, learned at the brew-tub and in the buttery, who
could bandy words on occasions with the squire, yet
not speaking French, nor wearing hoops or patches.

* See Gilpin's *Forest Scenery*, Vol. II. pp. 23-26.

A daughter, it may be, illumines the place, (who knows?) —

" ycleped Dawsabel
  A maiden fair and free:
  And for she was her fathers heir
  Full well she was ycond the leir
    Of mickle courtesy.

" Her features all as fresh above,
  As is the grass that grows by Dove,
    And lythe as lass of Kent.
  Her skin as soft as Leinster wool,
  As white as snow on peakish Hull,
    Or swan that swims in Trent."

                              DRAYTON.

A great many of the older exotic plants would, I suppose, be domesticated at the door, and possibly wife or daughter would have plead successfully with the squire for the presence of a few rare bulbs from Holland; but whether these or not, we may be sure that there was a flaming parterre of peonies, of fleurs-de-lis, and of roses; yet all of these not half so much valued by the good-wife as her bed of marjoram and of thyme. She may read King James's Bible, or, if a Non - Conformist, Baxter's " Saint's Rest"; while the husband (if he ever reads at all) regales himself with a thumb-worn copy of " Sir Fopling Flutter," or, if he live well into the closing years of the century, with De Foe's " True-born Englishman."

A Brace of Pastorals.

POETIC feeling was more lacking in the country-life
than in the illustrative literature of the period.
To say nothing of Milton's brilliant little poems
" L' Allegro " and " Il Penseroso," which flash all over
with the dews, there are the charming " Characters " of
Sir Thomas Overbury, and the graceful discourse of
Sir William Temple. The poet Drummond wrought a
music out of the woods and waters which lingers allur-
ingly even now around the delightful cliffs and valleys
of Hawthornden. John Dryden, though a thorough
cit, and a man who would have preferred his arm-chair
at Will's Coffee-House to Chatsworth and the fee of all
its lands, has yet touched most tenderly the " daisies
white " and the spring, in his adaptation of " The Flower
and the Leaf."

But we skip a score of the poets, and bring our wet
day to a close with the naming of two honored pastorals. The first, in sober prose, is nothing more nor less
than Walton's " Angler." Its homeliness, its calm,
sweet pictures of fields and brooks, its dainty perfume of flowers, its delicate shadowing-forth of the
Christian sentiment which lived by old English firesides, its simple, artless songs, (not always of the
highest style, but of a hearty naturalness that is infi-
nitely better,) — these make the " Angler " a book that

stands among the thumb-worn. There is good mar-
rowy English in it; I know very few fine writers of
our times who could make a better book on such a subject to-day, — with all the added information, and all
the practice of the newspaper-columns. What Walton
wants to say he says. You can make no mistake about
his meaning; all is as lucid as the water of a spring.
He does not play upon your wonderment with tropes.
There is no chicane of the pen ; he has some pleasant
matters to tell of, and he tells of them — straight.

Another great charm about Walton is his childlike
truthfulness. I think he is almost the only earnest
trout-fisher I ever knew (unless Sir Humphry Davy
be excepted) whose report could be relied upon for the
weight of a trout. I have many excellent friends —
capital fishermen — whose word is good upon most
concerns of life, but in this one thing they cannot be
confided in. I excuse it; I take off twenty per cent.
from their estimates without either hesitation, anger, or
reluctance.

I do not think I should have trusted in such a matter Charles Cotton, although he was agricultural as
well as piscatory, — having published a " Pianter's
Manual." I think he could, and did, draw a long bow.
I suspect innocent milkmaids were not in the habit of
singing Kit Marlowe's songs to the worshipful Mr.
Cotton.

One pastoral remains to mention, published at the very opening of the year 1600, and spending its fine forest-aroma thenceforward all down the century. I mean Shakspeare's play of " As You Like It."

From beginning to end the grand old forest of Arden is astir overhead; from beginning to end the brooks brawl in your ear; from beginning to end you smell the bruised ferns and the delicate-scented wood-flowers. It is Theocritus again, with the civilization of the added centuries contributing its spangles of reason, philosophy, and grace. Who among all the short-kirtled damsels of all the eclogues will match us this fair, lithe, witty, capricious, mirthful, buxom Rosalind ? Nowhere in books have we met with her like, — but only at some long-gone picnic in the woods, where we worshipped " blushing sixteen " in dainty boots and white muslin. There, too, we met a match for sighing Orlando, — mirrored in the water; there, too, some diluted Jaques may have "moralized " the excursion for next day's " Courier," and some lout of a Touchstone (there are always such in picnics) passed the ices, made poor puns, and won more than his share of the smiles.

Walton is English all over; but " As You Like It is as broad as the sky, or love, or folly, or hope.

SIXTH DAY.

A British Tavern.

I'T is a pelting November rain. No leaves are left upon the branches save a few yellow flutterers on the tips of the willows and poplars, and the bleached company that will be clinging to the beeches and the white-oaks for a month to come. All others are whipped away by the night-winds into the angles of old walls, or are packed under low-limbed shrubberies, there to swelter and keep warm the rootlets of the newly planted weigelias and spruces, until the snows and February suns and April mists and May heats shall have transmuted them into fat and unctuous mould. A close, pelting, unceasing rain, trying all the leaks of the mossy roof, testing all the newly laid drains, pressing the fountain at my door to an exuberant gush, — a rain that makes outside work an impossibility; and as I sit turning over the leaves of an old book of engravings, wondering what drift my rainy·

day's task shall take, I come upon a pleasant view of
Dovedale in Derbyshire, a little exaggerated, perhaps,
in the luxuriance of its trees and the depth of its
shadows, but recalling vividly the cloudy April morning on which, fifteen years agone, I left the inn of the
" Green Man and Black's Head," in the pretty town of
Ashbourne, and strolled away by the same road or
which Mr. Charles Cotton opens his discourse of fish-
ing with Master " Viator," and plunged down the steep
valley-side near to Thorpe, and wandered for three
miles and more, under towering crags, and on soft,
spongy bits of meadow, beside the blithe river where
Walton had cast, in other days, a gray palmer-fly, —
past the hospitable hall of the worshipful Mr. Cotton,
and the wreck of the old fishing-house, over whose
lintel was graven in the stone the interlaced initials of
" Piscator, Junior," and his great master of the rod. As
the rain began to patter on the sedges and the pools, I
climbed out of the valley, on the northward or Derbyshire side, and striding away through the heather,
which belongs to the rolling heights of this region, I
presently found myself upon the great London and
Manchester highway. A broad and stately thoroughfare it had been in the old days of coaching ; but now a
close, fine turf invested it all, save one narrow strip of
Macadam in the middle. The mile-stones, which had
been showy, painted affairs of iron, were now deeply

bitten and blotched with rust. Two of them I had
passed, without sight of house or of other traveller,
save one belated drover, who was hurrying to the fair
at Ashbourne; as I neared the third, a great hulk of
building appeared upon my left, with a crowd of aspir-
ing chimneys, from which only one timid little pennant
of smoke coiled into the harsh sky.

The gray, inhospitable-looking pile proved to be one
of the old coach-inns, which, with its score of vacant
chambers and huge stable-court, was left stranded upon
the deserted highway of travel. It stood a little space
back from the road, so that a coach and four, or, indeed, a half-dozen together, might have come up to
the door-way in dashing style. But it must have been
many years since such a demand had been made upon
the resources of bustling landlord and of attendant
grooms and waiters. The doors were tightly closed;
even the sign-board creaked uneasily in the wind, and
a rampant growth of ivy that clambered over the porch
so covered it with leaves and berries that I could not
at all make out its burden. I gave a sharp ring to the
bell, and heard the echo repeated from the deserted
stable-court; there was the yelp of a hound somewhere
within, and presently a slatternly-dressed woman received me, and, conducting me down a bare hall,
showed me into a great dingy parlor, where a murky
fire was struggling in the grate. A score of roistering

travellers might have made the stately parlor gay; and
I dare say they did, in years gone; but now I had only
for company — their heavy old arm-chairs, a few prints
of " fast coaches " upon the wall, and a superannuated
greyhound, who seemed to scent the little meal I had
ordered, and presently stalked in and laid his thin nose,
with an appealing look, in my hands. His days of
coursing — if he ever had them — were fairly over;
and I took a charitable pride in bestowing upon him
certain tough morsels of the rump-steak, garnished with
horse-radish, with which I was favored for dinner.

I had intended to push on to Buxton the same after
noon; but the deliberate sprinkling of the morning
had quickened by two o'clock into a swift, pelting
rain, the very counterpart of that which is beating on
my windows to-day.   There was nothing to be done
but to make my home of the old coach-inn for the
night; and for my amusement — besides the slumber-
ous hound, who, after dinner, had taken up position
upon the faded rug lying before the grate — there was
a " Bell's Messenger " of the month past, and, as good
luck would have it, a much-bethumbed copy of a work
on horticulture and kindred subjects, first printed somewhere about the beginning of the eighteenth century,
and entitled " The Clergyman's Recreation, showing
the Pleasure and Profit of the Art of Gardening,' by
the Reverend John Laurence.

It was a queer book to be found in this preten tious old coach-inn, with its silken bell-pulls and stately parlors; and I thought how the roisterers who came thundering over the road years ago, and chucked the barmaids under the chin, must have turned up their noses, after their pint of crusted Port, at the " Clergyman's Recreation." Yet, for all that, the book had a rare interest for me, detailing, as it did, the methods of fruitculture in England a hundred and forty years ago, and showing with nice particularity how the espaliers could be best trained, and how a strong infusion of walnut-leaf tea will destroy all noxious worms.

And now, when, upon this other wet day, and in the quietude of my own library, I come to measure the claims of this ancient horticulturist to consideration, I find that he was the author of some six or seven distinct works on kindred subjects, showing good knowledge of the best current practice ; and although he incurred the sneers of Mr. Tull, who hoped " he preached better than he ploughed," there is abundant evidence that his books were held in esteem.

Early English Gardeners.

CONTEMPORARY with the Rev. Mr. Laurence were London and Wise, the famous horticulturists of Brompton, (whose nursery, says Evelyn, " was the greatest work of the kind ever seen or heard of, eithei in books or travels,") also Switzer, a pupil of the .atter and Professor Richard Bradley.

Mr. London was the director of the royal gardens under William and Mary, and at one time had in his charge some three or four hundred of the most considerable landed estates in England. He was in the habit of riding some fifty miles a day to confer with his subordinate gardeners, and at least two or three times in a season traversed the whole length and breadth of England, — and this at a period, it must be remembered, when travelling was no holiday-affair, as is evident from the mishaps which befell those well-known contemporaneous travellers of Fielding, — Joseph Andrews and Parson Adams. Traces of the work of Mr. London are to be seen even now in the older parts of the grounds of Blenheim and of Castle Howard in Yorkshire.

Stephen Switzer was an accomplished gardener, well known by a great many horticultural and agricultural works, which in his day were " on sale at his seed-shop in Westminster Hall." Chiefest among these was the "Ichnographia Rustica," which gave general directions for the management of country-estates, while it indulged in some prefatory magniloquence upon the dignity and antiquity of the art of gardening. It is the first of all arts, he claims; for " tho' Chirurgery

may plead high, inasmuch as in the second chapter of
Genesis that *operation* is recorded of taking the rib
from Adam, wherewith woman was made, yet the very
current of the Scriptures determines in favor of Gardening." It surprises us to find that so radical an in-
vestigator should entertain the belief, as he clearly did,
that certain plants were produced without seed by the
vegetative power of the sun acting upon the earth.
He is particularly severe upon those Scotch gardeners,
" Northern lads," who, with " a little learning and a
great deal of impudence, know, or pretend to know,
more in one twelvemonth than a laborious, honest
South-country man does in seven years."

His agricultural observations are of no special value,
nor do they indicate any advance from the practice of
Worlidge. He deprecates paring and burning as exhaustive of the vegetable juices, advises winter fallow-
ing and marling, and affirms that " there is no super-
ficies of earth, how poor soever it may be, but has in
its own bowels something or other for its own improve-
ment."

In gardening, he expresses great contempt for the
clipped trees and other excesses of the Dutch school,
yet advises the construction of terraces, lays out his
ponds by geometric formulæ, and is so far devoted to
out-of-door sculpture as to urge the establishment of a
royal institution for the instruction of ingenious young

men, who, on being taken into the service of noblemen
and gentlemen, would straightway people their grounds
with statues.   And this notwithstanding Addison had
published his famous papers on the " Pleasures of the
Imagination " three years before.*

Richard Bradley was the Dr. Lardner of his day, — a
man of general scientific acquirement, an indefatigable
worker, venturing hazardous predictions, writing some
fifteen or twenty volumes upon subjects connected with
agriculture, foisting himself into the chair of Botany
at Cambridge by noisy reclamation, selling his name to
the booksellers for attachment to other men's wares,†
and, finally, only escaping the indignity of a removal
from his professor's chair by sudden death, in 1732.
Yet this gentleman's botanical dictionary ("Historia
Plantarum," etc.) was quoted respectfully by Linnæus,
and his account of British cattle, their races, proper
treatment, etc., was, by all odds, the best which had
appeared up to his time.   The same gentleman, in his
" New Improvements of Planting and Gardening," lays
great stress upon a novel " invention for the more
speedy designing of garden-plats," which is nothing
more than an adaptation of the principle of the kalei ·

* The *Spectators* 414 and 477, which urge particularly a better
taste in gardening, are dated 1712; and the first volume of the *Ichnographia* (under a different name, indeed) appeared in 1715.

† This is averred of the translation of the *Œconomics* of Xenophon, before cited in these papers, and published under Professor
Bradley's name.

ioscope. The latter book is the sole representative of this author's voluminous agricultural works in the Astor collection; and, strange to say, there are only two (if we may believe Mr. Donaldson) in the library of the British Museum.

I take, on this dreary November day, (with my Ca-tawbas blighted,) a rather ill-natured pleasure in reading how the Duke of Rutland, in the beginning of the last century, was compelled to "keep up fires from Lady-day to Michaelmas behind his sloped walls," in order to insure the ripening of his grapes; yet winter grapes he had, and it was a great boast in that time. The quiet country - squires — such as Sir Roger de Coverley — had to content themselves with those old-fashioned fruits which would struggle successfully with out-of-door fogs. Fielding tells us that the garden of Mr. Wilson, where Parson Adams and the divine Fanny were guests, showed nothing more rare than an alley bordered with filbert-bushes.*

In London and its neighborhood the gourmands fared better. Cucumbers, which in Charles's time never came in till the close of May, were ready in the shops of Westminster (in the time of George I.) in early March. Melons were on sale, for those who could pay roundly, at the end of April; and the season of cauliflowers,

---

* *Joseph Andrews*, Bk. III. cn. 4, where Fielding, thief that he was, appropriates the story that Xenophon tells of Cyrus.

which used to be limited to a single month, now reached over a term of six months.

Mr. Pope, writing to Dr. Swift, somewhere about 1730, says, — "I have more fruit - trees and kitchen - garden than you have any thought of; nay, I have good melons and pine-apples of my own growth." Nor was this a small boast; for Lady Wortley Montague, describing her entertainment at the table of the Elector of Hanover, in 1716, speaks of "pines" as a fruit she had never seen before.

Ornamental gardening, too, was now changing its complexion Dutch William was dead and buried. Addison had written in praise of the natural disposition of the gardens of Fontainebleau, and, at his place near Rugby, was carrying out, so far as a citizen might, the suggestions of those papers to which I have already alluded. Milton was in better odor than he had been, and people had begun to realize that an arch-Puritan might have exquisite taste. Possibly, too, cultivated landholders had seen that charming garden - picture where the luxurious Tasso makes the pretty sorceress Armida spread her nets.

Pope affected a respect for the views of Addison; but his Twickenham garden was a very stiff affair. Bridgman was the first practical landscape-gardener who ventured to ignore old rules; and he was followed closely by William Kent, a broken-down and unsucces-

ful landscape-painter, who came into such vogue as a
man of taste that he was employed to fashion the furniture of scores of country-villas ; and Walpole * tells us
that he was even beset by certain fine ladies to design
Birthday gowns for them : — " The one he dressed in
a petticoat decorated with columns of the five orders ;
the other, like a bronze, in a copper-colored satin, with
ornaments of gold."

Clermont, the charming home of the exiled Orléans
family, shows vestiges of the taste of Kent, who always
accredited very much of his love for the picturesque to
the reading of Spenser. It is not often that the poet
of the " Faerie Queene " is mentioned as an educator.

Jethro Tull.

AND now let us leave gardens for a while, to discuss Mr. Jethro Tull, the great English cultivator
of the early half of the eighteenth century. I suspect
that most of the gentry of his time, and cultivated people, ignored Mr. Tull, — he was so rash and so headstrong and so noisy. It is certain, too, that the educated farmers, or, more strictly, the writing farmers,
opened battle upon him, and used all their art to ward
off his radical tilts upon their old methods of culture.
And he fought back bravely ; I really do not think that

* *Works of Earl of Orford* Vol. III. p. 490.

an editor of a partisan paper to-day could improve upon him, — in vigor, in personality, or in coarseness.

Unfortunately, the biographers and encyclopædists who followed upon his period have treated his name with a neglect that leaves but scanty gleanings for his personal history. His father owned landed property in Oxfordshire, and Jethro was a University-man ; he studied for the law, (which will account for his address in a wordy quarrel,) made the tour of Europe, returned to Oxfordshire, married, took the paternal homestead, and proceeded to carry out the new notions which he had gained in his Southern travels. Ill health drove him to France a second time, whence he returned once more, to occupy the famous " Prosperous Farm " in Berkshire ; and here he opened his batteries afresh upon the existing methods of farming. The gist of his proposed reform is expressed in the title of his book, " The Horse-hoeing Husbandry." He believed in the thorough tillage, at frequent intervals, of all field-crops, from wheat to turnips. To make this feasible, drilling was, of course, essential ; and to make it economical, horse-labor was requisite : the drill and the horse-hoe were only subsidiary to the main end of THOROUGH TILLAGE.

Sir Hugh Platt, as we have seen, had before sug-gested dibbling, and Worlidge had contrived a drill; but Tull gave force and point and practical efficacy to their suggestions. He gives no credit, indeed, to these old gentlemen ; and it is quite possible that his theory may have been worked out from his own observations. He certainly gives a clear account of the growth of his belief, and sustains it by a great many droll notions about the physiology of plants, which would hardly be admissible in the botanies of to-day.

Shall I give a sample ?

" Leaves," he says, " are the parts, or bowels of a plant, which perform the same office to sap as the lungs of an animal do to blood ; that is, they purify or cleanse it of the recrements, or fuliginous steams, received in the circulation, being the unfit parts of the food, and per-haps some decayed particles which fly off the vessels through which blood and sap do pass respectively."

It does not appear that the success of Tull upon " Prosperous Farm " was such as to give a large war-rant for its name. His enemies, indeed, alleged that he came near to sinking two estates on his system ; this, however, he stoutly denies, and says, " I propose no more than to keep out of debt, and leave my estate be-hind me better than I found it. Yet, owned it must be, that, had I, when I first began to make trials, known as much of the system as I do now, the practice of it would have been more profitable to me." Farmers in other parts of England, with lands better adapted to the new husbandry, certainly availed themselves of it, very much to their advantage. Tull, like a great many earnest reformers, was almost always in difficulty with those immediately dependent on him ; over and over he insists upon the " inconveniency and slavery attending the exorbitant power of husbandry servants and laborers over their masters." He quarrels with their wages, and with the short period of their labor. Pray, what would Mr. Tull have thought, if he had dealt with the Drogheda gentlemen in black satin waistcoats, who are to be conciliated by the farmers of to-day?

I think I can fancy such an encounter for the querulous old reformer. "Mike! blast you, you booby, you've broken my drill!" And Mike, (putting his thumb deliberately in the armlet of his waistcoat,) " Meester Tull, it's not the loikes o' me'll be leestening to insoolting worrds. I'll take me money, if ye plase." And with what a fury "Meester" Tull would have slashed away, after this, at "Equivocus," and all his newspaper-antagonists !

I wish I could believe that Tull always told the exact truth ; but he gives some accounts of the perfection to which he had brought his drill * to which I can lend only a most meagre trust ; and it is unquestionable that his theory so fevered his brain at last as to make him utterly contemptuous of all old-fashioned methods of procedure. In this respect he was not alone among

* See Chap. VII. p. 104, Cobbett's edition.

reformers. He stoutly affirmed that tillage would supply
the lack of manure, and his neighbors currently reported
that he was in the habit of dumping his manure-carts
in the river. This charge Mr. Tull firmly denied, and
I dare say justly. But I can readily believe that the
rumors were current ; country-neighborhoods offer good
starting-points for such lively scandal. The writer of
this book has heard, on the best possible authority, that
he is in the habit of planting shrubs with their roots in
the air.

In his loose, disputative way, and to magnify the importance of his own special doctrine, Tull affirms that
the ancients, and Virgil particularly, urged tillage for the
simple purpose of destroying weeds.* In this it seems
to me that he does great injustice to our old friend
Maro. Will the reader excuse a moment's dalliance
with the Georgics again ?

> " Multum adeo, rastris *glebas* qui *frangit inertes,*
> Vimineasque trahit crates, juvat arva ; . . . .
> Et qui proscisso quæ suscitat æquore terga
> Rursus in obliquum verso perrumpit aratro,
> Exercetque frequens tellurem, atque *imperat* arvis." †

That "*imperat*" looks like something more than

* Chap. IX. p. 136, Cobbett's edition.
† "He does his land great service who breaks the sluggish clods with
barrows, and drags over them the willow hurdles ; . . . . who tears
up the ridges of his furrowed plain, and ploughs crosswise, and over
and over again stirs his field, and with masterly hand subdues it."

weed-killing ; it looks like subjugation ; it looks like
pulverization at the hands of an imperious master.

But behind all of Tull's exaggerated pretension, and
unaffected by the noisy exacerbation of his speech
there lay a sterling good sense, and a clear comprehen-
sion of the existing shortcomings in agriculture, which
gave to his teachings prodigious force, and an influence
measured only by half a century of years. There were
few, indeed, who adopted literally and fully his plans, or
who had the hardihood to acknowledge the irate Jethro
as a safe and practical teacher ; yet his hints and his
example gave a stimulus to root-culture, and an attention to the benefits arising from thorough and repeated
tillage, that added vastly to the annual harvests of England. Bating the exaggerations I have alluded to, his
views are still reckoned sound ; and though a hoed crop
of wheat is somewhat exceptional, the drill is now almost universal in the best cultivated districts of Great
Britain and the Continent ; and a large share of the
forage-crops owe their extraordinary burden to horse-
hoeing husbandry.

Even the exaggerated claims of Tull have had their
advocates in these last days ; and the energetic farmer
of Lois-Weedon, in Northamptonshire, is reported to
be growing heavy crops of wheat for a succession of
years, without any supply of outside fertilizers, and rely-
ing wholly upon repeated and perfect pulverization of

the soil.* And Mr. Way, the distinguished chemist of the Royal Society in a paper on " The Power of Soils to absorb Manure," † propounds the question as follows : — " Is it likely, on theoretical considerations, that the air and the soil together can by any means be made to yield, without the application of manure, and year after year continuously, a crop of wheat of from thirty to thirty-five bushels per acre ? " And his reply is this : — " I confess I do not see why they should not do so.' A practical farmer, however, (who spends only his wet days in-doors,) would be very apt to suggest here, that the validity of this *dictum* must depend very much on the original constituents of the soil.

Under the lee of the Coombe Hills, on the extreme southern edge of Berkshire, and not far removed from the great highway leading from Bath to London, lies the farmery where this restless, petulant, suffering, earnest, clear-sighted Tull put down the burden of life, a hundred and twenty years ago. The house is unfortunately largely modernized, but many of the out-buildings remain unchanged ; and not a man thereabout, or in any other quarter, could tell me where the former occupant, who fought so bravely his fierce battle of the drill, lies buried.

* It is to be remarked, however, that the Rev. Mr. Smith, (farmer of Lois-Weedon,) by the distribution of his crop, avails himself virtually of a clean fallow, every alternate year.
† *Transactions*, V ℒ. XXX. p. 140.

Hanbury and Lancelot Brown.

ABOUT the middle of the last century, there li˟ ed in the south of Leicestershire, in the parish of Church-Langton, an eccentric and benevolent clergy‑ man by the name of William Hanbury, who conceived the idea of establishing a great charity which was to be supported by a vast plantation of trees. To this end he imported a great variety of seeds and plants from the Continent and America, established a nursery of fifty acres in extent, and published " An Essay on Planting, and a Scheme to make it Conducive to the Glory of God and the Advantage of Society."

But the Reverend Hanbury was beset by aggressive and cold-hearted neighbors, — among them two strange old "gentlewomen," Mistress Pickering and Mistress Byrd, who malevolently ordered their cattle to be turned loose into his first plantation of twenty thousand young and thrifty trees. And not content with this, they served twenty-seven different copies of writs upon him in .one day, for trespass. Of all this he gives de‑ tailed account in his curious history of the " Charitable Foundations at Church-Langton." He tells us that the ' venomous rage " of these old ladies (who died shortly after, worth a million of dollars) did not even spare his dogs ; but that his pet spaniel and greyhound were cruelly killed by a table-fork thrust into their entrails.

Nay, their game-keeper even buried two dogs alive, which belonged to his neighbor, Mr. Wade, a substantial grazier. His story of it is very Defoe-like and pitiful : — " I myself heard them," he says, " *ten days* after they had been buried, and, seeing some people at a distance, inquired what dogs they were. *'They are some dogs that are lost, Sir,'* said they ; *'they have been lost some time.'* I concluded only some poachers had been there early in the morning, and by a precipitate flight had left their dogs behind them. In short, the howling and barking of these dogs was heard for near three weeks, when it ceased. Mr. Wade's dogs were missing, but he could not suspect those dogs to be his ; and the noise ceasing, the thoughts, wonder, and talking about them soon also ceased. Some time after, a person, being amongst the bushes where the howling was heard, discovered some disturbed earth, and the print of men's heels ramming it down again very close, and, seeing Mr. Wade's servant, told him he thought something had been buried there. ' *Then,*' said the man, '*it is our dogs, and they have been buried alive. I will go and fetch a spade, and will find them, if I dig all Caudle over.*' He soon brought a spade, and upon removing the top earth, came to the blackthorns, and then to the dogs, the biggest of which had eat the loins, and greatest share of the hind parts, of the little one."

The strange ladies who were guilty of this slaughter

of innocents showed "a dying blaze of goodness" by bequeathing twelve thousand pounds to charitable societies ; and "thus ended," says Hanbury, "these two poor, unhappy, uncharitable, charitable old gentlewomen."

The good old man describes the beauty of plants and trees with the same delightful particularity which he spent on his neighbors and the buried dogs.

I cannot anywhere learn whether or not the charity-plantation of Church-Langton is still thriving.

About this very time, Lancelot Brown, who was for a long period the kitchen-gardener at Stowe, came into sudden notoriety by his disposition of the waters in Blenheim Park, where, in the short period of one week, he created perhaps the finest artificial lake in the world. Its indentations of shore, its bordering declivities of wood, and the graceful swells of land dipping to its margin, remain now in very nearly the same condition in which Brown left them more than a hundred years ago. All over England the new man was sent for; all over England he rooted out the mossy avenues, and the sharp rectangularities, and laid down his flowing lines of walks, and of trees. He (wisely) never contracted to execute his own designs, and — from lack of facility, perhaps — he always employed assistants to draw his plans. But the quick eye which at first sight recognized the "capabilities" of a place, and which leaped to the recognition of its matured graces, was all his own. He was accused of sameness ; but the man who at one time held a thousand lovely landscapes unfolding in his thought could hardly give a series of contrasts without startling affectations.

I mention the name of Lancelot Brown, however, not to discuss his merits, but as the principal and largest illustrator of that taste in landscape-gardening which just now grew up in England, out of a new reading of Milton, out of the admirable essays of Addison, out of the hints of Pope, out of the designs of Kent, and which was stimulated by Gilpin, by Horace Walpole, and, still more, by the delightful little landscapes of Gainsborough.

William Shenstone.

ENOUGH will be found of Mr. Brown, and of his style, in the professional treatises, upon whose province I do not now infringe. I choose rather, for the entertainment of my readers, if they will kindly find it, to speak of that sad, exceptional man, William Shenstone, who, by the beauties which he made to appear on his paternal farm of Leasowes, fairly rivalled the best of the landscape-gardeners, — and who, by the graces and the tenderness which he lavished on his verse, made no mean rank for himself at a

time when people were reading the "Elegy" of Gray
the Homer of Pope, and the "Cato" of Addison.

I think there can hardly be any doubt, however, that
poor Shenstone was a wretched farmer ; yet the Leasowes was a capital grazing farm, when he took it in
charge, within fair marketable distance of both Wor-
cester and Birmingham. I suspect that he never put
his fine hands to the plough-tail ; and his plaintive
elegy, that dates from an April day of 1743, tells, I am
sure, only the unmitigated truth : —

> "Again the laboring hind inverts the soil;
> Again the merchant ploughs the tumid wave;
> Another spring renews the soldier's toil,
> *And finds me vacant in the rural cave.*"

Shenstone, like many another of the lesser poets,
was unfortunate in having Dr. Johnson for his biogra-
pher.* It is hard to conceive of a man who would show
less of tenderness for an elaborate parterre of flowers,
or for a poet who affectedly parted his gray locks on one

---

* Mrs. Piozzi says, " He [Dr. Johnson] hated to hear about pros-
pects and views, and laying out ground, and taste in gardening; —
' That was the best garden,' he said, ' which produced most roots and
fruits; and that water was most to be prized which contained most
fish. Walking in a wood when it rained was, I think, the only rural
image which pleased his fancy. He loved the sight of fine forest-
trees, however, and detested Brighthelmstone Downs, ' because it was
a country so truly desolate,' he said, ' that if one had a mind to hang
one's self for desperation at being obliged to live there, it would be
difficult to find a tree on which to fasten the rope.' " — Croker's *Boswell,* Vol. II p. 209.

side of his head, wore a crimson waistcoat, and warbled in anapæstics about kids and shepherds' crooks. Only fancy the great, snuffy, wheezing Doctor, with his hair-powder whitening half his shoulders, led up before some charming little extravaganza of Boucher, wherein all the nymphs are simpering marchionesses, with rosettes on their high-heeled slippers that out-color the sky! With what a " Faugh ! " the great gerund-grinder would thump his cane upon the floor, and go lumbering away! And Shenstone, or rather his memory, caught the besom of just such a sneer.

But other critics were more kindly and appreciative; among them, Dodsley the bookselling author, who wrote " The Economy of Human Life," * (the " Proverbial Philosophy " of its day,) and Whately, who gave to the public the most elegant and tasteful discussion of artificial scenery that was perhaps ever written.

Shenstone studied, as much as so indolent a man ever could, at Pembroke College, Oxford. His parents died when he was young, leaving to him a very considerable estate, which fortunately some relative administered for him, until, owing to this supervisor's death, it lapsed into the poet's improvident hands. Even then a sensible tenant of his own name, and a

* Dodsley was also the author of a still and unreadable poem on Agriculture "

distant relative, managed very snugly the farm of
Leasowes; but when Shenstone came to live with him,
neither house nor grounds were large enough for the
joint occupancy of the poet, who was trailing his
walks through the middle of the mowing, and of the
tenant, who had his beeves to fatten and his rental to
pay.

So Shenstone became a farmer on his own account;
and, according to all reports, a very sorry account he
made of it. The good soul had none of Mr. Tull's
petulance and audacity with his servants; if the
ploughman broke his gear, I suspect the kind bal
lad-master allowed him a holiday for the mending.
The herdsman stared in astonishment to find the
"beasts" ordered away from their accustomed graz-
ing-fields. A new thicket had been planted, which
must not be disturbed; the orchard was uprooted to
give place to some parterre; a fine bit of meadow was
flowed with a miniature lake; hedges were shorn away
without mercy; arbors, grottos, rustic seats, Arcadian
temples, sprang up in all outlying nooks; so that the
annual product of the land came presently to be limited, almost entirely, to the beauty of its disposition.*

---

* Repton is somewhat severe in his condemnation of Leasowes and
of Shenstone's taste, not, that I can perceive, because he objects to
errors of detail, but because he ignores *in toto* the practicability of
uniting farm-culture with any tasteful management of landscape. I
have no doubt that Leasowes was a wretchedly managed farm eco-

I think that the poet, unlike most, was never very
thoroughly satisfied with his poems, and that, therefore,
the vanity possessed him to vest the sense of beauty
which he felt tingling in his blood in something more
palpable than language.   Hence came the charming
walks and woods and waters of Leasowes.   With this
ambition holding him and mastering him, what mat-
tered a mouldy grain-crop, or a debt?   If he had only
an ardent admirer of his walks, his wilderness, his
grottos, — this was his customer.   He longed for such,
in troops, — as a poet longs for readers, and as a farmer longs for sun and rain.

And he had them.   I fancy there was hardly a cultivated person in England, but, before the death of
Shenstone, had heard of the rare beauty of his home
of Leasowes.   Lord Lyttelton, who lived near by, at
the elegant seat of Hagley, brought over his guests
to see what miracles the hare-brained, sensitive poet
had wrought upon his farm.   And I can fancy the
proud, shy creature watching from his lattice the company of distinguished guests, — maddened, if they look
at his alcove from the wrong direction, — wondering
if that shout that comes booming to his sensitive ear
means admiration, or only an unappreciative surprise,

nomically speaking; yet I see no reason to forbid the conjurction,
under proper hands, of a great deal of landscape-beauty with a profit-
ably conducted grazing-farm.

14

— dwelling on the memory of the visit, as a poet dwells on the first public mention of his poem. In his " Egotisms," (well named,) he writes, — " Why repine ? I have seen mansions on the verge of Wales that convert my farm-house into a Hampton Court, and where they speak of a glazed window as a great piece of magnificence. All things figure by comparison."

And this reflection, with its flavor of philosophy, was, I dare say, a sweet morsel to him. He saw very little of the world in his later years, save that part of it which at odd intervals found its way to the delights of Leasowes ; indeed, he was not of a temper to meet the world upon fair terms. " The generality of mankind," he cynically says, "are seldom in good humor but whilst they are imposing upon you in some shape or other." *

Our farmer of Leasowes published a pastoral that was no way equal to the pastoral he wrote with trees, walks, and water upon his land ; yet there are few cultivated readers who have not some day met with it, and been beguiled by its mellifluous seesaw. How its jingling resonance comes back to me to-day from the " Reader " book of the High School !

> " I have found out a gift for my fair ;
> I have found where the wood-pigeons breed :
> But let me that plunder forbear ;

---

* *Detached Thoughts on Men and Manners :* Wm. Shenstone.

She will say 't was a baroarous deed.
For he ne'er could be true, she averred,
Who could rob a poor bird of its young:
And I loved her the more, when I heard
Such tenderness fall from her tongue."

And what a killing look over at the girl in the corner, in check gingham, with blue bows in her hair, as I read (always on the old school-benches), —

" I have heard her with sweetness unfold
How tha⁺ pity was due to—a dove:
That it ever attended the bold;
And she called it *the sister of love*.
But her words such a pleasure convey,
So much I her accents adore
Let her speak, and whatever she say,
Methinks I should love her the more."

There is a rhythmic prettiness in this ; but it is the prettiness of a lover in his teens, and not the kind we look for from a man who stood five feet eleven in his stockings, and wore his own gray hair. Strangely enough, Shenstone had the *physique* of a ploughman or a prize-fighter, and with it the fine, sensitive brain of a woman; a Greek in his refinements, and a Greek in indolence. I hope he gets on better in the other world than he ever did in this.

SEVENTH DAY.

John Abercrombie.

I BEGIN my day with a canny Scot, who was born in Edinburgh in 1726, near which city his father conducted a large market-garden. As a youth, aged nineteen, John Abercrombie (for it is of him I make companion this wet morning) saw the Battle of Preston Pans, at which the Highlanders pushed the King's-men in defeat to the very foot of his father's garden-wall. Whether he shouldered a matchlock for the Castle-people and Sir John Cope, or merely looked over from the kale-beds at the victorious fighters for Prince Charley I cannot learn ; it is certain only that before Culloden, and the final discomfiture of the Pretender, he avowed himself a good King's-man, and in many an after-year, over his pipe and his ale, told the story of the battle which surged wrathfully around his father's kale-garden by Preston Pans.

But he did not stay long in Scotland ; he became gardener for Sir James Douglas, into whose family (below-stairs) he eventually married; afterwards he had experience in the royal gardens at Kew, and in Leicester Fields. Finally he became proprietor of a patch of ground in the neighborhood of London; and his success here, added to his success in other service, gave him such reputation that he was one day waited upon (about the year 1770) by Mr. Davies, a London bookseller, who invited him to dine at an inn in Hackney; and at the dinner he was introduced to a certain Oliver Goldsmith, an awkward man, who had published four years before a book called "The Vicar of Wakefield." Mr. Davies thought John Abercrombie was competent to write a good practical work on gardening, and the Hackney dinner was intended to warm the way toward such a book. Dinners are sometimes given with such ends even now. The shrewd Mr. Davies was a little doubtful of Abercrombie's style, but not at all doubtful of the style of the author of " The Traveller." Dr. Goldsmith was not a man averse to a good meal, where he was to meet a straightforward, out-spoken Scotch gardener; and Mr. Davies, at a mellow stage of the dinner, brought forward his little plan, — which was that Abercrombie should prepare a treatise upon gardening, to be revised and put in shape by the author of " The Deserted Village." The dinner at Hackney was, I dare say, a good one : the scheme looked promising to a man whose vegetable-

carts streamed every morning into London, and to the
Doctor, mindful of his farm-retirement at the six-mile
stone on the Edgeware Road; so it was all arranged
between them.

But, like many a publisher's scheme, it miscarried.
The Doctor perhaps saw a better bargain in the Lives
of Bolingbroke and Parnell;* or perhaps his appoint-
ment as Professor of History to the Royal Academy put
him too much upon his dignity. At any rate, the world
has to regret a gardening-book in which the shrewd
practical knowledge of Abercrombie would have been
refined by the grace and the always alluring limpidity
of the style of Goldsmith.

I know that the cultivators pretend to spurn graces
of manner, and affect only a clumsy burden of language,
under which, I am sorry to say, the best agriculturists
have most commonly labored; but if the transparen*
simplicity of Goldsmith had once been thoroughly infused with the practical knowledge of Abercrombie,
what a book on gardening we should have had! What
a lush verdure of vegetables would have tempted us!
What a wealth of perfume would have exuded from the
flowers!

But the scheme proved abortive. Goldsmith said, " I
think our friend Abercrombie can write better about
plants than I can." And so doubtless he could, so far as

* Published 1770–'71.

knowledge of their habits went. Eight years after,
Abercrombie prepared a book called " Every Man his
own Gardener "; but so doubtful was he of his own
reputation, that he paid twenty pounds to Mr. Thomas
Mawe, the fashionable gardener of the Duke of Leeds,
for the privilege of placing Mr. Mawe's name upon the
title-page. I am sorry to record such a scurvy bit of
hypocrisy in so competent a man. The book sold, however, and sold so well, that, a few years after, the elegant
Mr. Mawe begged a visit from the nursery-man of Tottenham Court, whom he had never seen ; so Abercrombie goes down to the seat of the Duke of Leeds, and
finds his gardener so bedizened with powder, and wearing such a grand air, that he mistakes him for his Lordship ; but it is a mistake, we may readily believe, which
the elegant Mr. Mawe forgives, and the two gardeners
become capital friends.

Abercrombie afterward published many works under
his own name ; * among these was " The Gardener's
Pocket Journal," which maintained an unflagging popularity as a standard book for a period of half a century.
This hardy Scotchman lived to be eighty ; and when he
could work no longer, he was constantly afoot among
the botanical gardens about London. At the last it was
a fall " down-stairs in the dark " that was the cause of
death ; and fifteen days after, as his quaint biographers

* Johnson enumerates fifteen.

tell us, "he expired, just as the clock upon St. Paul's struck twelve, — between April and May": as if the ripe old gardener could not tell which of these twin gar- den - months he loved the best; and so, with a foot planted in each, he made the leap into the realm of eter- nal spring.

A noticeable fact in regard to this out-of-door old gentleman is, that he never took "doctors'-stuff" in his life, until the time of that fatal fall in the dark. He was, however, an inveterate tea-drinker; and there was another aromatic herb (I write this with my pipe in my mouth) of which he was, up to the very last, a most ardent consumer.

A Philosopher and Two Poets.

IN the year 1766 was published for the first time a posthumous work by John Locke, the great philos- opher and the good Christian, entitled, "Observations upon the Growth and Culture of Vines and Olives," * — written, very likely, after his return from France, down in his pleasant Essex home, at the seat of Sir Francis Masham. Were the book by me, I should love to give the reader a sample of the manner in which

---

* Most of the bibliographers have omitted mention of this treatise. It may be found in the collected edition of Locke's works, London 1823, Vol. X.

the author of " An Essay concerning Human Under-
standing " wrote regarding horticultural matters. No
one can doubt but there is wisdom in it. " I believe
you think me," he writes in a private letter to a friend,
" too proud to undertake anything wherein I should
acquit myself but unworthily." This is a sort of pride
— not very common in our day — which does *not* go
before a fall.

I name a poet next, — not because a great poet, for
he was not, nor yet because he wrote "The English
Garden," * for there is sweeter garden-perfume in many
another poem of the day that does not pique our curiosity by its title. But the Reverend William Mason, if
not among the foremost of poets, was a man of most
kindly and liberal sympathies. He was a devoted Whig,
at a time when Whiggism meant friendship for the
American Colonists ; and the open expression of this
friendship cost him his place as a Royal Chaplain. I
will remember this longer than I remember his " English
Garden," — longer than I remember his best couplet
of verse : —

" While through the west, where sinks the crimson day,
Meek twilight slowly sails, and waves her banners gray."

It was alleged, indeed, by those who loved to say ill-

* Of which the first book was published in 1772. This author is to
be distinguished from George Mason, who in 1768 published *An Essay
on Design in Gardening*

natured things, (Horace Walpole among them,) that is
the later years of his life he forgot his first love of Lib-
eralism and became politically conservative. But it
must be remembered that the good poet lived into the
time when the glut and gore of the French Revolution
made people hold their breath, and when every man
who lifted a humane plaint against the incessant creak
and crash of the guillotine was reckoned by all mad reformers a conservative. I think, if I had lived in that
day, I should have been a conservative, too, — however
much the pretty and bloody Desmoulins might have
made faces at me in the newspapers.

I can find nothing in Mason's didactic poem to quote.
There are tasteful suggestions scattered through it, better every way than his poetry. The grounds of his vic-
arage at Aston must have offered charming loitering-
places. I will leave him idling there, — perhaps con-
ning over some letter of his friend the poet Gray ; perhaps lounging in the very alcove where he had inscribed
this omitted verse of the " Elegy," —

> " Here scattered oft, the loveliest of the year,
>   By hands unseen, are showers of violets found;
> The redbreast loves to build and warble here,
>   And little footsteps lightly print the ground."

If, indeed, he had known how to strew such gems
through his " English Garden," we should have had a
poem that would have outshone " The Seasons."

And this mention reminds me, that, although I have slipped past his period, I have said no word as yet of the Roxburgh poet; but he shall be neglected no longer. (The big book, my boy, upon the third shelf, with a worn back, labelled THOMSON.)

This poet is not upon the gardeners' or the agricultural lists. One can find no farm-method in him, — indeed, little method of any sort; there is no description of a garden carrying half the details that belong to Tasso's garden of Armida, or Rousseau's in the letter of St. Preux.* And yet, as we read, how the country, with its woods, its valleys, its hill-sides, its swains, its toil-ing cattle, comes swooping to our vision! The leaves rustle, the birds warble, the rivers roar a song. The sun beats on the plains; the winds carry waves into the grain; the clouds plant shadows on the mountains. The minuteness and the accuracy of his observation are something wonderful; if farmers should not study him, our young poets may. *He* never puts a song in the throat of a jay or a wood-dove; he never makes a mother-bird break out in bravuras; he never puts a sickle into green grain, or a trout in a slimy brook; he could picture no orchis growing on a hill-side, or colum-bine nodding in a meadow. If the leaves shimmer, you may be sure the sun is shining; if a primrose light-ens on the view, you may be sure there is some covert

* Lettre XI. Liv. IV. *Nouvelle Héloise.*

which the primroses love ; and never by any license
does a white flower come blushing into his poem.

I will not quote, where so much depends upon the atmosphere which the poet himself creates as he waves
his enchanter's wand. Over all the type his sweet
power compels a rural heaven to lie reflected; I go
from budding spring to blazing summer at the turning
of a page; on all the meadows below me (though it is
March) I see ripe autumn brooding with golden wings;
and winter howls and screams in gusts, and tosses tem-
pests of snow into my eyes — out of the book my boy
has just now brought me.

One verse, at least, I will cite, — so full it is of all
pastoral feeling, so brimming over with the poet's passion for the country : it is from " The Castle of Indolence " : —

> " I care not, Fortune, what you me deny:
>   You cannot rob me of free Nature's grace;
>   You cannot shut the windows of the sky,
>   Through which Aurora shows her brightening face·
>   You cannot bar my constant feet to trace
>   The woods and lawns, by living stream at eve:
>   Let health my nerves and finer fibres brace,
>   And I their toys to the great children leave;
>   Of fancy, reason, virtue, nought can me bereave."

Lord Kames.

A NOTHER Scotchman, Lord Kames (Henry Home by name,) who was Senior Lord of Sessions in Scotland about the year 1760, was best known in his own day for his discussion of " The Principles of Equity "; he is known to the literary world as the author of an elegant treatise upon the " Elements of Criticism "; I beg leave to introduce him to my readers to-day as a sturdy, practical farmer. The book, indeed, which serves for his card of introduction, is called " The Gentleman Farmer ";* but we must not judge it by our experience of the class who wear that title nowadays. Lord Kames recommends no waste of money, no extravagant architecture, no mere prettinesses. He talks of the plough in a way that assures us he has held it some day with his own hands. People are taught, he says, more by the eye than the ear; *show* them good culture, and they will follow it.

As for what were called the principles of agriculture, he found them involved in obscurity; he went to the book of Nature for instruction, and commenced, like Descartes, with doubting everything. He condemns the Roman husbandry as fettered by superstitions, and gives a piquant sneer at the absurd rhetoric and verbos-

* First published in 1766.

ity of Varro.*　Nor is he any more tolerant of Scotch superstitions.　He declares against wasteful and care‑less farming in a way that reminds us of our good friend Judge ———, at the last county-show.

He urges good ploughing as a primal necessity, and insists upon the use of the roller for rendering the sur‑face of wheat-lands compact, and so retaining the moist‑ure; nor does he attempt to reconcile this declaration with the Tull theory of constant trituration.　A great many excellent Scotch farmers still hold to the views of his Lordship, and believe in "keeping the sap" in fresh-tilled land by heavy rolling; and so far as regards a wheat or rye crop upon *light* lands, I think the weight of opinion, as well as of the rollers, is with them.

Lord Kames, writing before the time of draining‑tile, dislikes open ditches, by reason of their interfer‑ence with tillage, and does not trust the durability of brush or stone underdrains.　He relies upon ridging, and the proper disposition of open furrows, in the old Greek way.　Turnips he commends without stint, and the Tull system of their culture.　Of clover he thinks as highly as the great English farmer, but does not be‑lieve in his notion of economizing seed: "Idealists," he says, "talk of four pounds to the acre; but when sown for cutting green, I would advise twenty-four

---

* Citing, in confirmation, that passage commencing, — "*Nunc dicam agri quibus rebus colantur,*" etc.

pounds." This amount will seem a little startling, I fancy, even to farmers of our day.

He advises strongly the use of oxen in place of horses for all farm-labor ; they cost less, keep for less, and sell for more ; and he enters into arithmetical calculations to establish his propositions. He instances Mr. Burke, who ploughs with four oxen at Beaconsfield. How drolly it sounds to hear the author of " Letters on a Regicide Peace " cited as an authority in practical farming ! He still further urges his ox-working scheme, on grounds of public economy : it will cheapen food, forbid importation of oats, and reduce wages. Again, he recommends soiling,* by all the arguments which are used, and vainly used, with us. He shows the worthlessness of manure dropped upon a parched field, compared with the same duly cared for in court or stable ; he proposes movable sheds for feeding, and enters into a computation of the weight of green clover which will be consumed in a day by horses, cows, or oxen : "a horse, ten Dutch stone daily ; an ox or cow, eight stone ; ten horses, ten oxen, and six cows, two hundred and wenty-eight stone per day," — involving constant cart-age : still he is convinced of the profit of the method.

His views on feeding ordinary store-cattle, or accustoming them to change of food, are eminently practical. After speaking of the desirableness of provid-

* Pp. 177-179, edition of 1802, Edinburgh.

ing a good stock of vegetables, he continues, — "And
yet, after all, how many indolent farmers remain, who
for want of spring food are forced to turn their cattle
out to grass before it is ready for pasture! which not
only starves the cattle, but lays the grass-roots open to
be parched by sun and wind."

Does not this sound as if I had clipped it from the
" Country Gentleman" of last week? And yet it was
written nearly ninety years ago, by one of the most
accomplished Scotch judges, and in his eightieth year,
— another Varro, packing his luggage for his last voy-
age.

One great value of Lord Kames's talk lies in the
particularity of his directions : he does not despise
mention of those minutiæ a neglect of which makes so
many books of agricultural instruction utterly useless.
Thus, in so small a matter as the sowing of clover-
seed, he tells how the thumb and finger should be
held, for its proper distribution; in stacking, he directs
how to bind the thatch; he tells how mown grass
should be raked, and how many hours spread;* and
his directions for the making of clover-hay could not
be improved upon this very summer. " Stir it not the
day it is cut. Turn it in the swath the forenoon of the
next day ; and in the afternoon put it up in small
cocks. The third day put two cocks into one, enlarg

* Pp. 166, 167.

ing eveiy day the cocks till they are ready for the
tramp rick [temporary field-stack]." The reader wil!
not fail to remark how nearly this method agrees with
the one cited in my First Day, from the treatise of
Heresbach.

A small portion of his book is given up to the discussion of the theory of agriculture; but he fairly
warns his readers that he is wandering in the dark
If all theorists were as honest! He deplores the ig
norance of Tull in asserting that plants feed on earth;
air and water alone, in his opinion, furnish the supply
of plant-food. All plants feed alike, and on the same
material ; degeneracy appearing only in those which
are not native : white clover never deteriorates in England, nor bull-dogs.

But I will not linger on his theories. He is repre-
sented to have been a kind and humane man ; but this
did not forbid a hearty relish (appearing often in his
book) for any scheme which promised to cheapen labor.
" The people on landed estates," he says, " are trusted
by Providence to the owner's care, and the proprietor
is accountable for the management of them to the
Great God, who is the Creator of both." It does not
seem to have occurred to the old gentleman that some
day people might decline to be " managed."

He gave the best proof of his practical tact, in the
conduct of his estate of Blair-Drummond, — uniting

15

there all the graces of the best landscape-gardening with profitable returns.

I take leave of him with a single excerpt from his admirable chapter on Gardening in the "Elements of Criticism" : — "Other fine arts may be perverted to excite irregular, and even vicious emotions; but gardening, which inspires the purest and most refined pleasures, cannot fail to promote every good affection. The gayety and harmony of mind it produceth inclineth the spectator to communicate his satisfaction to others, and to make them happy as he is himself, and tends naturally to establish in him a habit of humanity and benevolence."

It is humiliating to reflect that a thievish orator at one of our Agricultural Fairs might appropriate page after page out of the " Gentleman Farmer" of Lord Kames, written in the middle of the last century, and the county-paper, and the aged directors, in clean shirt-collars and dress-coats, would be full of praises " of the enlightened views of our esteemed fellow-citizen." And yet at the very time when the critical Scotch judge was meditating his book, there was erected a land light-house, called Dunston Column, upon Lincoln Heath, to guide night travellers over a great waste of land that lay a half-day's ride south of Lincoln. And when Lady Robert Manners, who had a seat at Bloxholme, wished to visit Lincoln, a groom or two were

sent out the morning before to explore a good path
and families were not unfrequently lost for days * together in crossing the heath. This same heath —
made up of a light fawn-colored sand, lying on "dry,
thirsty stone" — was, twenty years since at least, bloom-
ing all over with rank, dark lines of turnips ; trim, low
hedges skirted the level highways; neat farm-cottages
were flanked with great saddle-backed ricks ; thousands upon thousands of long-woolled sheep cropped
the luxuriant pasturage, and the Dunston column was
but an idle monument of a waste that existed no
longer.

Claridge, Mills, and Miller.

ABOUT the time of Lord Kames's establishment
at Blair-Drummond, or perhaps a little earlier,
a certain Master Claridge published "The Country
Calendar ; or, The Shepherd of Banbury's Rules to
know of the Change of the Weather." It professed
to be based upon forty years' experience, and is said
to have met with great favor. I name it only because it embodies these old couplets, which still lead a
vagabond life up and down the pages of country-
almanacs : —

* See Article of Philip Pusey, M. P., in *Transactions of the Royal
Society*, Vol. XIV.

"If the grass grows in Janiveer,
It grows the worst for 't all the year."

" The Welshman had rather see his dam on the bier
Than to see a fair Februeer."

" When April blows his horn,
It 's good both for hay and corn."

" A cold May and a windy
Makes a full barn and a findy."

" A swarm of bees in May
Is worth a load of hay;
But a swarm in July
Is not worth a fly."

Will any couplets of Tennyson reap as large a fame?

About the same period, John Mills, a Fellow of the Royal Society, published a work of a totally different character, — being very methodic, very full, very clear. It was distributed through five volumes. He enforces the teachings of Evelyn and Duhamel, and is commendatory of the views of Tull.   The Rotherham plough is figured in his work, as well as thirteen of the natural grasses. He speaks of potatoes and turnips as established crops, and enlarges upon their importance. He clings to the Virgilian theory of small farms, and to the better theory of thorough tillage.

In 1759 was issued the seventh edition of Miller's

" Gardener's Dictionary," * in which was for the first
time adopted (in English) the classical system of Linnæus. If I have not before alluded to Philip Miller,
it is not because he is undeserving. He was a correspondent of the chiefs in science over the Continent
of Europe, and united to his knowledge a rare practical
skill. He was superintendent of the famous Chelsea
Gardens of the Apothecaries Company. He lies
buried in the Chelsea Church-yard, where the Fellows
of the Linnæan and Horticultural Societies of London
have erected a monument to his memory. Has the
reader ever sailed up the Thames, beyond Westminster? And does he remember a little spot of garden-
ground, walled in by dingy houses, that lies upon the
right bank of the river near to Chelsea Hospital?
If he can recall two gaunt, flat-topped cedars which
sentinel the walk leading to the river-gate, he will
have the spot in his mind, where, nearly two hundred
years ago, and a full century before the Kew parterres
were laid down, the Chelsea Garden of the Apothecaries Company was established. It was in the open
country then; and even Philip Miller, in 1722, walked
to his work between hedge-rows, where sparrows
chirped in spring, and in winter the fieldfare chat-
tered: but the town has swallowed it; the city-smoke
has starved it; even the marble image of Sir Hans

---

* First published in 1724.

Sloane in its centre is but the mummy of a statue.
Yet in the Physic Garden there are trees struggling
still which Philip Miller planted; and I can readily
believe, that, when the old man, at seventy - eight,
(through some quarrel with the Apothecaries,) took
his last walk to the river-bank, he did it with a sinking at the heart which kept by him till he died.

Thomas Whately.

I COME now to speak of Thomas Whately, to whom
I have already alluded, and of whom, from the
scantiness of all record of his life, it is possible to say
only very little. He lived at Nonsuch Park, in Surrey,
not many miles from London, on the road to Epsom.
He was engaged in public affairs, being at one time
secretary to the Earl of Suffolk, and also a member of
Parliament. But I enroll him in my wet-day service
simply as the author of the most appreciative and most
tasteful ˙ treatise upon landscape-gardening which has
ever been written, — not excepting either Price or
Repton. It is entitled, "Observations on Modern
Gardening," and was first published in 1770. It was
the same year translated into French by Latapie, and
was to the Continental gardeners the first revelation
of the graces which belonged to English cultivated
landscape. In the course of the book he gives vivid

descriptions of Blenheim, Hagley, Leasowes, Clare-
mont, and several other well-known British places.
He treats separately of Parks, Water, Farms, Gardens, Ridings, etc., illustrating each with delicate and
tender transcripts of natural scenes. Now he takes
us to the cliffs of Matlock, and again to the farm-flats
of Woburn. His criticisms upon the places reviewed
are piquant, full of rare apprehension of the most
delicate natural beauties, and based on principles
which every man of taste must accept at sight. As
you read him, he does not seem so much a theorizer
or expounder as he does the simple interpreter of
graces which had escaped your notice. His suggestions come upon you with such a momentum of truthfulness, that you cannot stay to challenge them.

There is no argumentation, and no occasion for it.
On such a bluff he tells us wood should be planted,
and we wonder that a hundred people had not said
the same thing before; on such a river-meadow the
grassy level should lie open to the sun, and we wonder
who could ever have doubted it. Nor is it in matters
of taste alone, I think, that the best things we hear
seem always to have a smack of oldness in them, —
as if we remembered their virtue. " Capital!" we say ;
" but has n't it been said before?" or, " Precisely !
I wonder I did n't do or say the same thing myself."
Whenever you hear such criticisms upon any perform

ance, you may be sure that it has been directed by a
sound instinct. It is not a sort of criticism any one
is apt to make upon flashy rhetoric, or upon flash gardening.

Whately alludes to the analogy between landscape-
painting and landscape-gardening : the true artists in
either pursuit aim at the production of rich pictorial
effects, but their means are different. Does the
painter seek to give steepness to a declivity ? — then
he may add to his shading a figure or two toiling up.
The gardener, indeed, cannot plant a man there ; but
a copse upon the summit will add to the apparent
height, and he may indicate the difficulty of ascent
by a hand-rail running along the path. The painter
will extend his distance by the *diminuendo* of his
mountains. or of trees stretching toward the horizon :
the gardener has, indeed, no handling of successive
mountains. but he may increase apparent distance by
leafy avenues leading toward the limit of vision ; he
may even exaggerate the effect still further by so grad-
uating the size of his trees as to make a counterfeit
perspective.

When I read such a book as this of Whately's, —
so informed and leavened as it is by an elegant taste,
— I am most painfully impressed by the shortcomings
of very much which is called good landscape-gardening with us. As if serpentine walks, and glimpses of

elaborated turf-ground, and dots of exotic evergreens
in little circlets of spaded earth, compassed at all those
broad effects which a good designer should keep in
mind! We are gorged with *petit-maître*-ism, and pretty
littlenesses of all kinds. We have the daintiest of
walks, and the rarest of shrubs, and the best of drainage; but of those grand, bold effects which at once
seize upon the imagination, and inspire it with new wor-
ship of Nature, we have great lack. In private grounds
we cannot of course command the opportunity which
the long tenure under British privilege gives; but the
conservators of public parks have scope and verge;
let them look to it, that their resources be not wasted
in the niceties of mere gardening, or in elaborate ar-
chitectural devices. Banks of blossoming shrubs and
tangled wild vines and labyrinthine walks will count
for nothing in park-effect, when, fifty years hence,
the scheme shall have ripened, and hoary pines pile
along the ridges, and gaunt single trees spot here
and there the glades, to invite the noontide wayfarer.
A true artist should keep these ultimate effects always
in his eye, — effects that may be greatly impaired, if
not utterly sacrificed, by an injudicious multiplication
of small and meretricious beauties, which in no way
conspire to the grand and final poise of the scene.

But I must not dwell upon so enticing a topic, or
my wet day will run over into sunshine. One word

more, however, I have to say of the personality of the author who has suggested it. The reader of Sparks's Works and Life of Franklin may remember, that, in the fourth volume, under the head of " Hutch- inson's Letters," the Doctor details difficulties which he fell into in connection with "certain papers" he obtained indirectly from one of His Majesty's officials, and communicated to Thomas Cushing, Speaker of the House of Representatives of Massachusetts Bay. The difficulty involved others besides the Doctor, and a duel came of it between William Whately and Mr. Temple. This William Whately was the brother of Thomas Whately, — the author in question, and the secretary to Lord Grenville,* in which capacity he died in 1772.† The " papers " alluded to were letters from Governor Hutchinson and others, expressing sympathy with the British Ministry in their efforts to enforce a grievous Colonial taxation. It was cur- rently supposed that Mr. Thomas Whately was the recipient of these letters; and upon their being made public after his death, Wm. Whately, his brother and executor, conceived that Mr. Temple was the instru- ment of their transfer. Hence the duel. Dr. Frank- lin, however, by public letter, declared that this alle- gation was ill - founded, but would never reveal the

---

* I find him named, in Dodsley's *Annual Register* for 1771, " Keeper of His Majesty's Private Roads."

† Loudon makes an error in giving 1780 as the year of his death.

name of the party to whom he was indebted. The
Doctor lost his place of Postmaster General for the
Colonies, and was egregiously insulted by Wedder-
burn in open Council; but he could console himself
with the friendship of such men as Lawyer Dunning,
(one of the suspected authors of " Junius,") and with
the eulogium of Lord Chatham.

Horace Walpole.

THERE are three more names belonging to this
period, which I shall bring under review, to finish
up my day. These are Horace Walpole, (Lord Orford,) Edmund Burke, and Oliver Goldsmith. Walpole was the proprietor of Strawberry Hill, and wrote
upon gardening: Burke was the owner of a noble farm
at Beaconsfield, which he managed with rare sagacity:
Goldsmith could never claim land enough to dig a
grave upon, until the day he was buried ; but he wrote
the story of " The Vicar of Wakefield," and the sweet
poem of " The Deserted Village."

I take a huge pleasure in dipping from time to time
into the books of Horace Walpole, and an almost equal
pleasure in cherishing a hearty contempt for the man.
With a certain native cleverness, and the tact of a
showman, he paraded his resources, whether of garden,
or villa, or memory, or ingenuity, so as to carry a larger

reputation for ability than he ever has deserved. His
money, and the distinction of his father, gave him an
association with cultivated people, — artists, politicians,
poets, — which the metal of his own mind would never
have found by reason of its own gravitating power.
He courted notoriety in a way that would have made
him, if a poorer man, the toadying Boswell of some
other Johnson giant, and, if very poor, the welcome
buffoon of some gossiping journal, who would never
weary of contortions, and who would brutify himself
at the death, to kindle an admiring smile.

He writes pleasantly about painters, and condescend-
ingly of gardeners and gardening. Of the special
beauties of Strawberry Hill he is himself historiog-
rapher; elaborate copper plates, elegant paper, and
a particularity that is ludicrous, set forth the charms
of a villa which never supplied a single incentive to
correct taste, or a single scene that has the embalm-
ment of genius. He tells us grandly how this room
was hung with crimson, and that other with gold; how
"the tea-room was adorned with green paper and
prints, ... on the hearth, a large green vase of
German ware, with a spread eagle, and lizards for
handles," — which vase (if the observation be not
counted disloyal by sensitive gentlemen) must have
been a very absurd bit of pottery. "On a shelf and
brackets are two *pot-pourris* of Nankin china; two

pierced blue and white basons of old Delft; and two sceaus [sic] of coloured Seve; a biue and white vase and cover; and two old Fayence bottles."

When a man writes about his own furniture in this style for large type and quarto, we pity him more than if he had kept to such fantastic nightmares as the "Castle of Otranto." The Earl of Orford speaks in high terms of the literary abilities of the Earl of Bath: have any of my readers ever chanced to see any literary work of the Earl of Bath? If not, I will supply the omission, in the shape of a ballad, "to the tune of a former song by George Bubb Doddington." It is entitled, "Strawberry Hill."

> "Some cry up Gunnersbury,
>   For Sion some declare;
> And some say that with Chiswick House
>   No villa can compare.
> But ask the beaux of Middlesex,
>   Who know the country well,
> If Strawb'ry Hill, if Strawb'ry Hill
>   Don't bear away the bell?
>
> Since Denham sung of Cooper's,
>   There's scarce a hill around
> But what in song or ditty
>   Is turned to fairy ground.
> Ah, peace be with their memories!
>   1 wish them wondrous well;
> But Strawb'ry Hill, but Strawb'ry Hill
>   Must bear away the bell."

It is no way surprising that a noble poet capable of writing such a ballad should have admired the villa of Horace Walpole: it is no way surprising that a proprietor capable of admiring such a ballad should have printed his own glorification of Strawberry Hill.

I am not insensible to the easy grace and the piquancy of his letters; no man could ever pour more delightful twaddle into the ear of a great friend; no man could more delight in doing it, if only the friend were really great. I am aware that he was highly cultivated, — that he had observed widely at home and abroad, — that he was a welcome guest in distinguished circles; but he never made or had a sterling friend; and the news of the old man's death caused no severer shock than if one of his Fayence pipkins had broken.

But what most irks me is the absurd dilettanteism and presumption of the man. He writes a tale as if he were giving dignity to romance; he applauds an artist as Dives might have thrown crumbs to Lazarus; vain to the last degree of all that he wrote or said, he was yet too fine a gentleman to be called author; if there had been a way of printing books, without recourse to the vulgar *media* of type and paper, — a way of which titled gentlemen could command the monopoly, — I think he would have written more. As I turn over the velvety pages of his works, and look at his catalogues, his *bon-mots*, his drawings, his affectations of magnifi-

cence, I seem to see the fastidious old man shuffling
with gouty step up and down, from drawing-room to li
brary, — stopping here and there to admire some newly
arrived bit of pottery, — pulling out his golden snuff-
box, and whisking a delicate pinch into his old nostrils,
— then dusting his affluent shirt-frill with the tips of his
dainty fingers, with an air of gratitude to Providence
for having created so fine a gentleman as Horace Walpole, and of gratitude to Horace Walpole for having
created so fine a place as Strawberry Hill.

Edmund Burke.

I TURN from this ancient specimen of titled elegance
to a consideration of Mr. Burke, with much the
same relief with which I would go out from a perfumed
drawing-room into the breezy air of a June morning.
Lord Kames has told us that Mr. Burke preferred oxen
to horses for field-labor; and we have Burke's letters
to his bailiff, showing a nice attention to the economies
of farming, and a complete mastery of its working details. But more than anywhere else does his agricultural sagacity declare itself in his " Thoughts and Details on Scarcity." *

Will the reader pardon me the transcript of a passage or two? " It is a perilous thing to try experiments

* Presented to William Pitt, 1795.

on the farmer. The farmer's capital (except in a few persons, and in a very few places) is far more feeble than is commonly imagined. The trade is a very poor trade; it is subject to great risks and losses. The capital, such as it is, is turned but once in the year; in some branches it requires three years before the money is paid; I believe never less than three in the turnip and grass-land course. . . . . It is very rare that the most prosperous farmer, counting the value of his quick and dead stock, the interest of the money he turns, together with his own wages as a bailiff or overseer, ever does make twelve or fifteen *per centum* by the year on his capital. In most parts of England which have fallen within my observation, I have rarely known a farmer who to his own trade has not added some other employment or traffic, that, after a course of the most unremitting parsimony and labor, and persevering in his business for a long course of years, died worth more than paid his debts, leaving his posterity to continue in nearly the same equal conflict between industry and want in which the last predecessor, and a long line of predecessors before him, lived and died."

In confirmation of this last statement, I may mention that Samuel Ireland, writing in 1792, (" Picturesque Views on the River Thames,") speaks of a farmer named Wapshote, near Chertsey, whose ancestors had resided on the place ever since the time of Alfred the Great;

and amid all the chances and changes of centuries, not one of the descendants had either bettered or marred his fortunes. The truthfulness of the story is confirmed in a number of the " Monthly Review " for the same year.

Mr. Burke commends the excellent and most useful works of his " friend Arthur Young," (of whom I shall have somewhat to say another time,) but regrets that he should intimate the largeness of a farmer's profits. He discusses the drill-culture, (for wheat,) which, he says, is well, provided " the soil is not excessively heavy, or encumbered with large, loose stones,* and provided the most vigilant superintendence, the most prompt activity, *which has no such day as to-morrow in its calendar*, combine to speed the plough ; in this case I admit," he says, " its superiority over the old and general methods." And again he says, — " It requires ten times more of labor, of vigilance, of attention, of skill, and, let me add, of good fortune also, to carry on the business of a farmer with success, than what belongs to any other trade."

May not a farmer take a little pride in such testimony as this ?

One of his biographers tells us, that, in his later years, the neighbors saw him on one occasion, at his home

---

* At that day, horse-hoeing, at regular intervals, was understood to form part of what was counted drill-culture.

16

of Beaconsfield, leaning upon the shoulder of a favorite
old horse, (which had the privilege of the lawn,) and
sobbing. Whereupon the gossiping villagers reported
the great man crazed. Ay, crazed, — broken by the
memory of his only and lost son Richard, with whom
this aged saddle-horse had been a special favorite, —
crazed, no doubt, at thought of the strong young hand
whose touch the old beast waited for in vain, — crazed
and broken, — an oak, ruined and blasted by storms.
The great mind in this man was married to a great
heart.

Goldsmith.

DO I not name a fitting companion for a wet day
in the country, when I name Oliver Goldsmith?
Yet he can tell me nothing about farming, or about
crops. He knew nothing of them and cared nothing
for them. He would have made the worst farmer in
the world. A farmer should be prudent and fore-
sighted, whereas poor Goldsmith was always as improvident as a boy. A farmer should be industrious and
methodical: Goldsmith had no conception of either
industry or method. A farmer should be willing to be
taught every day of his life, and Goldsmith was willing
to be taught nothing.

He had no more knowledge of gardening and of its
proper appliances, than he had of economy   I have

no doubt that the grafting of a cherry-tree would have
been as abstruse a problem for him as the balancing
of his account-book. Nay, if we may believe his own
story, he had very little eye for the picturesque. He
was delighted with the flat land and canals of Holland
and reckoned them far prettier than the hills and rocks
of Scotland. Writing to an early friend of the country about Leyden, he says, "Nothing can equal its
beauty. Wherever I turn my eyes, fine houses, elegant gardens, statues, grottos, vistas, present themselves; but when you enter their towns, you are
charmed beyond description. . . . . In Scotland hills
and rocks intercept every prospect; here, 'tis all a
continued plain. The Scotch may be compared to
a tulip planted in dung; but I never see a Dutch-
man in his own house, but I think of a magnificent Egyptian temple dedicated to an ox." I have
no doubt that this indifference to the picturesque aspects of Nature was as honest as his debts. And yet,
for all this, and though circled about by rural scenes,
I do still keep his "Essays" or his "Vicar" in my
hand, or in my thought most lovingly. He carried
with him out of Kilkenny West the heart of an Irish
country-lad, and the odor of the meadows of West-
meath never wholly left his thought.

The world is accustomed to regard his little novel,
which Dr. Johnson bargained away for sixty guineas.

as a rural tale: it is so quiet; it is so simple; its at
mosphere is altogether so redolent of the country
And yet all, save some few critical readers, will be
surprised to learn that there is not a picture of natural
scenery in the book of any length; and wherever an
allusion of the kind appears, it does not bear the im-
press of a mind familiar with the country, and practically at home there. The Doctor used to go out
upon the Edgeware road, — not for his love of trees,
but to escape noise and duns. Yet we overlook liter-
alness, charmed as we are by the development of his
characters and by the sweet burden of his story. The
statement may seem extraordinary, but I could tran-
scribe every rural, out-of-door scene in the " Vicar of
Wakefield " upon a single half-page of foolscap. Of
the first home of the Vicar we have only this account:
— " We had an elegant house, situated in a fine country and a good neighborhood." Of his second home
there is this more full description : — " Our little habitation was situated at the foot of a sloping hill, sheltered
with a beautiful underwood behind, and a prattling river
before : on one side a meadow, on the other a green.
My farm consisted of about twenty acres of excellent
land, having given a hundred pounds for my predecessor's good-will. Nothing could exceed the neatness of
my little enclosures : the elms and hedge-rows appear
ing with inexpressible beauty. My house consisted of

but one story, and was covered with thatch, which gave it an air of great snugness." It is quite certain that an author familiar with the country, and with a memory stocked with a multitude of kindred scenes, would have given a more determinate outline to this picture. But whether he would have given to his definite outline the fascination that belongs to the vagueness of Goldsmith, is wholly another question.

Again, in the sixth chapter, Mr. Burchell is called upon to assist the Vicar and his family in " saving an after-growth of hay." " Our labors," he says, " went on lightly ; we turned the swath to the wind." It is plain that Goldsmith never saved much hay ; turning the swath to the wind may be a good way of making it, but it is a slow way of gathering it. In the eighth chapter of this charming story, the Doctor says, — " Our family dined in the field, and we sat, or rather reclined, round a temperate repast, *our cloth spread upon the hay.* To heighten our satisfaction, the blackbirds answered each other from opposite hedges, the familiar redbreast came and pecked the crumbs from our hands, and every sound seemed but the echo of tranquillity." This is very fascinating ; but it is the veriest romanticism of country-life. Such sensible girls as Olivia and Sophia would, I am quite sure, never have spread the dinner cloth upon hay, which would most certainly have set all the gravy aflow, if the platters had not been fairly over turned; and as for the redbreasts, (with that rollicking boy Moses in my mind,) I think they must have been terribly tame birds.

But this is only a farmer's criticism, — a Crispin feeling the bunions on some Phidian statue. And do I think the less of Goldsmith, because he wantoned with the literalism of the country, and laid on his prismatic colors of romance where only white light lay? Not one whit. It only shows how Genius may discard utter faithfulness to detail, if only its song is charged with a general simplicity and truthfulness that fill our ears and our hearts.

As for Goldsmith's verse, who does not love it? Who does not find tender reminders of the country in it?

> " Sweet was the sound, when oft, at evening's close,
> Up yonder hill the village murmur rose:
> There, as I passed with careless steps and slow,
> The mingled notes came softened from below;
> The swain responsive as the milkmaid sung,
> The sober herd that lowed to meet their young;
> The noisy geese that gabbled o'er the pool,
> The playful children just let loose from school;
> The watch-dog's voice that bayed the whispering wind,
> And the loud laugh that spoke the vacant mind; —
> These all in sweet confusion sought the shade,
> And filled each pause the nightingale had made."

And yet the nightingale is a myth to us; the milkmaid's song comes all the way from a century back in Ireland

neither one nor the other charms our ear, listen faith
fully as we may; but there is a subtile rural aroma per-
vading the lines I have quoted, which calls at every
couplet a responsive memory, — which girls welcome as
they welcome fresh flowers, — which boys welcome as
they welcome childish romp, — which charms middle
age away from its fierce wrestle with anxieties, and laps
it in some sweet Elysium of the past. Not all the arts
of all the modernists, — not " Maud," with its garden-
song, — not the caged birds of Killingworth, singing up
and down the village-street, — not the heather-bells out
of which the springy step of Jean Ingelow crushes
perfume, —shall make me forget the old, sweet, even
flow of the " Deserted Village."

Down with it, my boy! — (from the third shelf).
G-O-L-D-S-M-I-T-H — a worker in gold — is on the back.

And I sit reading it to myself, as a fog comes welter-
ing in from the sea, covering all the landscape, save
some half-dozen of the city-spires, which peer above
the drift like beacons.

EIGHTH DAY.

Arthur Young.

IN these notes upon the Farm-Writers and the Pastorals, I have endeavored to keep a certain chronologic order; and upon this wet morning I find myself embayed among those old gentlemen who lived in the latter part of the eighteenth century. George III. is tottering under his load of royalty; the French Revolution is all asmoke. Fox and Sheridan and Burke and the younger Pitt are launching speeches at this Gallic tempest of blood, — each in his own way. Our American struggle for liberty has been fought bravely out; and the master of it has retired to his estates upon the Potomac. There, in his house at Mount Vernon, he receives one day a copy of the early volumes of Young's "Annals of Agriculture," with the author's compliments, and the proffer of his services to execute orders for seeds, implements, cattle, or "anything else that might contribute to the General's rural amusements."

The General, in his good old-fashioned way, returns the compliments with interest, and says, " I will give you the trouble, Sir, of providing and sending to the care of Wakelin Welch, of London, merchant, the fol-lowing articles: —

" Two of the simplest and best-constructed ploughs for land which is neither very heavy nor sandy; to be drawn by two horses; to have spare shares and coulters ; and a mould, on which to form new irons, when the old ones are worn out, or will require repair-ing. I will take the liberty to observe, that, some years ago, from a description or a recommendation thereof which I had somewhere met with, I sent to England for what was then called the Rotherham or patent plough ; and, till it began to wear and was ruined by a bungling country-smith, that no plough could have done better work, or appeared to have gone easier with two horses ; but, for want of a mould, which I neglected to order with the plough, it became useless after the irons which came with it were much worn.

" A little of the best kind of cabbage seed for field-culture.

" Twenty pounds of the best turnip seed.

" Ten bushels of sainfoin seed.

" Eight bushels of the winter vetches.

" Two bushels of rye-grass seed.

" Fifty pounds of hop-clover seed."

The curious reader may be interested to know tha this shipment of goods, somewhat injured by stowage in the hold of the vessel, reached Mount Vernon just one week after Washington had left it to preside over the sittings of the Constitutional Convention. And amidst all the eagerness of those debates under which the ark of our nationality was being hammered into shape, this great man of system did not omit to send to his farm-manager the most minute directions in respect to the disposition of the newly arrived seeds.

Of those directions, and of the farm-method at the home of Washington, I may possibly have something to say at another time: I have named the circumstance only to show that Arthur Young had a world-wide reputation as an agriculturist at this day, (1786–7,) although he lived for more than thirty years beyond it.

Arthur Young was born at a little village near to Bury St. Edmund's, (evermore famous as the scene of Pickwickian adventure,) in the year 1741. He had his schooling like other boys, and was for a time in a counting-room at Lynn, where he plunged into literature at the unfledged age of seventeen, by writing a tract on the American-French war; and this he followed up with several novels, among which was one entitled "The Fair American." *   I greatly fear that the book

---

* By an odd coincidence, I observe that Washington made one of his first shipments of tobacco (after his marriage with Mrs. Curtis)

was not even with the title: it has certainly slipped
away from the knowledge of all the bibliographers.

At twenty-two he undertook the management of the
farm upon which his mother was living, and of which the
lease was about expiring : here, by his own account, he
spent a great deal more than he ever reaped. A little
later, having come to the dignity of a married man, he
leased a farm in Essex, (Samford Hall,) consisting of
some three hundred acres. This, however, he abandoned in despair very shortly, — giving a brother-farmer
a hundred pounds to take it off his hands. Thereupon
he advertises for another venture, gallops through all
the South of England to examine those offered to his
notice, and ends with renting a hundred-acre farm in
Hertfordshire, which proved of "a hungry vitriolic
gravel," where, he says, "for nine years, I occupied
the jaws of a wolf."

Meantime, however, his pen has not been idle ; for,
previous to 1773, he had written and published no less
than sixteen octavo volumes relating mostly to agricultural subjects, besides two ponderous quartos filled with
tabular details of "Experiments on the Cultivation of
all Sorts of Grain and Pulse, both in the Old and New
Methods."

This last was the most pretentious of his books, the

upon a vessel called " The Fair American." Did the ship p:ssibly
give a name to the novel, or the novel a name to the ship?

result of most painstaking labor, and by far the most useless and uninteresting; it passed long ago into the waste-paper shops of London. A very full synopsis of it, however, may be found in four or five consecutive numbers of the old "Monthly Review" for 1771.

The great fault of the book is, (and it is the fault of a good many books,) it does not prove what the author wants to prove. He had hoped by a long - continued course of minute experiments (and those detailed in his book count a thousand, and extend over a period of five years) to lay down an exact law of procedure for the guidance of his brother-farmers. But the brother-farmers did not weary themselves over his tables; or if they did, they found themselves as much muddled as the experimenter himself. A good rule for dry weather was a bad one for wet; and what might be advisable for Suffolk would be wrong in Herts. Upon one occasion, where he shows a loss of nearly three pounds to the acre on drilled wheat, against a loss of two shillings fourpence on broadcast-sowing, he observes, — "Reason is so often mistaken in matters of husbandry, that it is *never fully* to be trusted, even in deducing consequences evident from experiment itself." By which we may safely conclude that the experiment disappointed his expectations. It must be remembered, however, that Mr. Young was quite youthful and inexperienced at the time of conducting these trials, and that he pos-

sessed none of that scientific accuracy which character-
izes the analysis of farm-experiments at Rothamstead or
at Bechelbron. He says, with a diverting sincerity
that he was never " absent more than a single week at
a time from the field of his observations without leaving
affairs in charge of a trusty bailiff." He was too full of
a constitutional unrest, and too much wedded to a habit
of wide and rapid generalization, to acquit himself well
in the task of laborious and minute observation.

His " Tours " through the English counties, and his
" Letters to Farmers," were of great service, and were
widely read. His " Farmer's Calendar " became a
standard work. He entertained at one time the project
of emigrating to America; but, abandoning this, he
enlisted as Parliamentary reporter for the " Morning
Post," — walking seventeen miles to his country-home
every Saturday evening, and returning afoot every
Monday morning. His energy and industry were immense ; his information upon all subjects connected with
agriculture, whether British or Continental, entirely
unmatched. The Empress of Russia sent three lads to
him to be taught the arts of husbandry, — at which, I
venture, his plodding neighbors who " made the ends
meet " laughed incontinently. He had also pupils from
France, America, Italy, Poland, Sicily, and Portugal.

In 1784 he commenced the publication of his famous
" Arnals of Agriculture," which grew to the enorm ous

mass of forty-five volumes, and in the course of which dukes and princes and kings and republican generals were his correspondents. At the formation of the Board of Agriculture, he was named Secretary, with a salary and duties that kept him mostly in London' where he died at an advanced age in 1820.

It is a somewhat remarkable fact, that a man so dis-tinguished in agriculture, so full of information, so ear-nest in advocacy of improved methods of culture, so doggedly industrious, should yet never have undertaken farming on his own account save at a loss. I attribute this very much to his zeal for experiments. If he could establish, or controvert, some popular theory by the loss of his crop, he counted it no loss, but a gain to hus-bandry. Such men are benefactors; such men need salaries; and if any such are afloat with us, unprovided for, I beg to recommend them for clerkships in the Agricultural Bureau at Washington; and if the Com-missioner shall hit upon one Arthur Young among the score of his *protégés*, the country will be better repaid than it usually is.

Ellis and Bakewell.

THE " Practical Farmer," and other books of Wil-liam Ellis, Hertfordshire, were in considerable vogue in the days of Young, and received a little faint

praise from him, while he says that through half his
works he is "a mere old woman."

I notice that Ellis recommends strongly the plough·
ing in of buckwheat,* — a practice which Washington
followed extensively at Mount Vernon. He tells us
that a cow is reckoned in his day to pay a clear profit
of four pounds a year (for butter and cheese) ; but he
adds, " Certain it is that no one knows what a cow wil.
pay, unless she has her constant bellyful of requisite
meat." And his talk about cider has such a relishy
smack of a " mere old woman " that I venture to quote
it.

" I have drank," he says, " such Pippin Cyder, as I
never met with anywhere, but at Ivinghoe, just under
our *Chiltern* Hills, where their Soil is partly a chalky
Loam : It was made by its Owner, a Farmer, and on
my Recommendation our Minister went with me to
prove it, and gave it his Approbation. This was made
from the Holland Pippin: And of such a wholesome
Nature is the Pippin of any Sort above all others, that
I remember there is a Relation of its wonderful influences, I think it was in Germany : A Mother and two
or three of her Sons having a Trial at Law, were asked
what they eat and drank to obtain such an Age, which
was four or five hundred years that they all made up
amongst them ; they answered, chiefly by eating the

* *Practical Farmer*, by William Ellis. London, 1759.

Apple, and drinking its Juice. And I knew an emi
nent, rich Lawyer, almost eighty Years old, who was
very much debilitated through a tedious Sickness, on
the telling him this Story, got Pippins directly, sliced
them to the number of a dozen at a Time, and infused
them in Spring-Water, and made it his common Drink,
till Cyder - Time came on ; also he fell on planting a
number of Pippin-Trees in order to his enjoying their
salubrious Quality, and a fine Plantation there is at this
Day in his Gardens a few miles from me. This Practice
of his drinking the Pippin Liquor and Cyder, answered
extraordinary well, for he lived several Years after, in a
pretty good State of Health."

The next name I come upon, in this rainy-day service, starts a pleasant picture to my mind, — not offset
by a British landscape, but by one of our own New
England hills. A group of heavy, overgrown chestnuts
stand stragglingly upon a steep ascent of pasture ; they
are flanked by a wide reach of velvety turf covering
the same swift slope of hill ; gray boulders of granite,
scattered here and there, show gleaming spangles of
mica ; clumps of pokeweed lift sturdily a massive luxuriance of stems and a great growth of purple berries ;
occasional stumps are cushioned over with mosses,
green and gray ; and, winding among stumps and rocks,
there comes trending down the green hill-side a comely
flock of great, long-woolled sheep : they nibble at stray

clover-blossoms; they lift their heads and look, — it is
only the old dog who is by me, — they know him; they
straggle on. I strew the salt here and there upon a
stone; " Dandie " pretends to sleep; and presently the
woolly company is all around me, — the " Bakewell "
flock.

Robert Bakewell,* who gave the name to this race
of sheep, (afterward known as New-Leicesters,) lived at
Dishley, upon the highway from Leicester to Derby,
and not very far from that Ashby de la Zouche where
Scott plants the immortal scene of the tournament in
" Ivanhoe." He was a farmer's son, with limited education, and with limited means; yet, by due attention
to crosses, he succeeded in establishing a flock which
gained a world-wide reputation. His first letting of
bucks at some fifteen shillings the season was succeeded in the year 1774 by lettings at a hundred guineas
a head; and there were single animals in his flock from
which he is reported to have received, in the height of
his fame, the sum of twelve hundred pounds.

Nor was Bakewell less known for his stock of neat
cattle, for his judicious crosses, and for a gentleness of
management by which he secured the utmost docility.
A writer in the " Gentleman's Magazine " of his date

---

* The geologist, Robert Bakewell, who lived many years later,
wrote of the " Influence of the Soil on Wool," and for that reason,
perhaps, is frequently confounded by agricultural writers with the
great breeder.

says, — " This docility seemed to run through the herd
At an age when most of his brethren are either foam·
ing or bellowing with rage and madness, old ' Comely'
had all the gentleness of a lamb, both in his look and
action.   He would lick the hand of his feeder; and if
any one patted or scratched him, he would bow himself
down almost on his knees."

The same writer, describing Mr. Bakewell's kitchen,
(which served as hall,) says, — " The separate joints
and points of each of the more celebrated of his cattle
were preserved in pickle, or hung up there side by side,
— showing the thickness of the flesh and external fat
on each, and the smallness of the offal.   There were also
skeletons of the different breeds, that they might be
compared with each other, and the comparative difference marked."

Arthur Young, in his " Eastern Tour," says, " All his
bulls stand still in the field to be examined; the way
of driving them from one field to another, or home, is
by a little switch ; he or his men walk by their side, and
guide them with the stick wherever they please ; and
they are accustomed to this method from being calves."

He was a tall, stout, broad - shouldered man of a
swarthy complexion, clad usually in a brown loose coat,
with scarlet waistcoat, leather breeches, and top-boots
In this dress, and in the kitchen I have above described
he entertained Russian princes, French and German

royal dukes, British peers and farmers, and sight-seers of every degree. All his guests, whether high or low, were obliged to conform to the farmer's rules: "Breakfast at eight o'clock, dinner at one, supper at nine, bed at eleven o'clock"; at half-past ten — let who would be there — he knocked out his last pipe.

He left no book for future farmers to maltreat, — not even so much as a pamphlet; and the sheep that bore his name are now refined by other crosses, or are supplanted by the long-woolled troop of "New-Oxfordshire."

William Cowper.

ON the way from Leicestershire to London, one passed, in the old coach-days, through Northampton; and from Northampton it is one of the most charming of drives for an agriculturist over to the town of Newport-Pagnell. I lodged there, at the Swan tavern, upon a July night some twenty years gone; and next morning I rambled over between the hedge-rows and across meadows to the little village of Weston, where I lunched at the inn of "Cowper's Oak." The house where the poet had lived with good Mrs. Unwin was only next door, and its front was quite covered over with a clambering rose-tree. The pretty waitress of the inn showed me the way, and a wheezing old man — half gardener and half butler — introduced me to the

rooms where Cowper had passed so many a dreary hour
and where he had been cheered by the blithe company
of Cousin Lady Hesketh.

My usher remembered the crazy recluse, and, when
we had descended to the garden, told me how much he,
with other village-boys, stood in awe of him,—and
how the poet used to walk up and down the garden-
alleys in dressing-gown and white-tasselled cotton cap,
muttering to himself; but what mutterings some of
them were!

> " Thy silver locks, once auburn bright,
> Are still more lovely in my sight
> Than golden beams of orient light,
>   My Mary!

> " For could I view nor them nor thee,
> What sight worth seeing could I see?
> The sun would rise in vain for me,
>   My Mary!

> " Partakers of thy sad decline,
> Thy hands their little force resign,
> Yet, gently pressed, press gently mine,
>   My Mary!"

Afterward the shuffling old usher turns a key in
a green gate, and shows me into the " Wilderness."
Here I come presently upon the Temple,—sadly shat-
tered,—and upon the urns with their mouldy inscrip-
tions; I wander through the stately avenue of lindens

to the Alcove, and, so true are the poet's descriptions, I recognize at once the seat of the Throckmortons, the " Peasant's Nest," the " Rustic Bridge," and far away a glimpse of the spire of Olney.

Plainly as I see to-day the farm-flat of Edgewood smoking under the spring rains below me, I see again the fat meadows that lie along the sluggish Ouse reeking with the heats of July. And I bethink me of the bewildered, sensitive poet, shrinking from the world, loving Nature so dearly, loving friends like a child, loving God with reverence, and yet with a great fear that is quickened by the harsh hammering of John Newton's iron Calvinism into a wild turbulence of terror. From this he seeks escape in the walks of the " Wilderness," and paces moodily up and down from temple to alcove, — in every shady recess still haunted by " a fearful looking-for of judgment," and from every sunny bit of turf clutching fancies by eager handful, to strew over his sweet poem of the " Task."

A sweet poem, I repeat, though not a finished or a grand one; but there is in it such zealous, earnest overflow of country-love that we farmers must needs welcome it with open hearts.

I should not like such a man as Cowper for a tenant, where any bargains were to be made, or any lambs to be killed; nor do I think that the mere memory of his verse would have put me upon that July walk from

Newport to Weston; but his letters and his sad life, throughout which trees and flowers were made almost his only confidants, led me to the scene where that strange marriage with Nature was solemnized. And though the day was balmy, and the sun fairly golden, the garden and the alley and the trees and the wilderness were like a widow in her weeds.

Gilbert White.

GILBERT WHITE, of Selborne, belongs to this epoch; and no lover of the country or of country-things can pass him by without cordial recognition and genial praise. There is not so much of incident or of adventure in his little book as would suffice to pepper the romances of one issue of a weekly paper in our day. The literary mechanicians would find in him no artful contrivance of parts and no rhetorical jangle of language. It is only good Parson White, who, wandering about the fields and the brook-sides of Selborne, scrutinizes with rare clearness and patience a thousand miracles of God's providence, in trees, in flowers, in stones, in birds, — and jots down the story of his scrutiny with such simplicity, such reverent trust in His power and goodness, such loving fondness for almost every created thing, that the reading of it charms like Walton's story of the fishes.

We Americans, indeed, do not altogether recognize his chaffinches and his titlarks; his daws and his fern-owl are strange to us ; and his robin-redbreast, though undoubtedly the same which in our nursery-days flitted around the dead " Children in the Wood," (while tears stood in our eyes,) and

> " painfully
> Did cover them with leaves,"

is by no means our American redbreast. For one, I wish it were otherwise; I wish with all my heart that I could identify the old, pitying, feathered mourners in the British wood with the joyous, rollicking singer who perches every sunrise, through all the spring, upon the thatch of the bee - house, within stone's - throw of my window, and stirs the dewy air with his loud *bravura*.

Notwithstanding, however, the dissimilarity of species, the studies of this old naturalist are directed with a nice particularity, and are colored with an unaffected home-liness, which are very charming ; and I never hear the first whisk of a swallow's wing in summer but I feel an inclination to take down the booklet of the good old Parson, drop into my library-chair, and follow up at my leisure all the gyrations and flutterings and incuba-tions of all the *hirundines* of Selborne. Every country-liver should own the book, and be taught from it — nicety of observation.

Trusler and Farm-Profits.

THERE was another clergyman of a different stamp — the Reverend John Trusler of Cobham, Surrey, — who wrote about this time a book on chronology, a few romances, a book on law, and another upon farming. He commenced public life as an apothecary; from his drug-shop he went to the pulpit, thence to book-selling, and finally to book-making. I am inclined to think that he found the first of these two trades the more profitable one : it generally is.

Mr. Trusler introduces his agricultural work by declaring that it " contains all the knowledge necessary in the plain business of farming, unincumbered with theory, speculation, or experimental inquiry "; — by which it will be seen that the modesty of the author was largely overborne by the enterprise of the book-seller. The sole value of his treatise lies in certain statistical details with regard to the cost and profits of different crops, prices of food, rates of wages, etc. By his showing, the profit of an acre of wheat in 1780 was £2 10s. ; of barley, £3 3s. 6d. ; of buckwheat, £2 19s. ; and a farm of one hundred and fifty acres, judiciously managed, would leave a profit of £379.

These estimates of farm-profits, however, at all times, are very deceptive. A man can write up his own balance - sheet, but he cannot make up his neighbor's

There will be too many screws — or pigs — loose, which he cannot take into the reckoning. The agricultural journals give us from time to time the most alluring "cash-accounts" of farm-revenue, which make me re-gard, for a month or two thereafter, every sober-sided farmer I meet as a Rasselas, — "choring" and "team-ing it" in a Happy Valley; but shortly I come upon some retired citizen, turned farmer, and active member of a Horticultural Society, slipping about the doors of some "Produce and Commission Store" for his winter's stock of vegetables, butter, and fruits, — and the fact impresses me doubtfully and painfully. It is not often, unfortunately, that printed farm-accounts — most of all, model-farm-accounts — will bear close scrutiny. Some-times there is delicate reservation of any charge for personal labor or superintendence; sometimes an equally cheerful reticence in respect to any interest upon capi-tal; and in nearly all of them such miniature expression of the cost of labor as gives a very shaky consistency to the exhibit.

Farmers, I am aware, are not much given to figures; but outside "averagers" are; and agricultural writers, if they indulge in figures, ought to show some decent respect for the proprieties of arithmetic. I have before me now the " Bi-Monthly Report of the United States Agricultural Department for January and February, 1864," in the course of which it is gravely asserted, that, in the event of a certain suggested tax on **tobacco**, " the tobacco-grower would find at the end of the year two hundred and ten per cent. of his crops unsold." Now I am not familiar with the tobacco-crop, and still less familiar with the Washington schemes of taxation; but whatever may be the exigencies of the former, and whatever may be the enormities of the latter, I find myself utterly unable to measure, even proximately, the misfortune of a tobacco-grower who should find himself stranded with two hundred and ten per cent. of his crop, after his sales were closed ! It is plainly a case involving a pretty large *quid pro quo*, if it be not a clear one of *nisi quid.*

Sinclair and Others.

SIR JOHN SINCLAIR, so honorably known in connection with British agriculture, dealt with an estate in Scotland of a hundred thousand acres. He parcelled this out in manageable farms, advanced money to needy tenants, and by his liberality and enterprise gave enormous increase to his rental. He also organized the first valid system for obtaining agricultural statistics through the clergymen of the different parishes in Scotland, thus bringing together a vast amount of valuable information, which was given to the public at intervals between 1790 and 1798. And

I notice with interest that the poet Burns was a contributor to one of these volumes,* over the signature
of " A Peasant," in which he gives account of a farmers' library established in his neighborhood, and adds,
in closing, — " A peasant who can read and enjoy such
books is certainly a much superior being to his neighbor, who, perhaps, stalks beside his team, very little removed, except in shape, from the brutes he drives."

There is reason to believe that Sir John Sinclair, at
one time, — in the heat of the French Revolution, —
projected emigration to America; and I find in one of
Washington's letters † to him the following allusion to
the scheme: — " To have such a tenant as Sir John
Sinclair (however desirable it might be) is an honor I
dare not hope for; and to alienate any part of the fee-
simple estate of Mount Vernon is a measure I am not
inclined to."

Another British cultivator of this period, whose name
is associated with the Mount Vernon estate, was Richard Parkinson of Doncaster, who wrote " The Experienced Farmer," and who not only proposed at
one time to manage one of the Washington farms, but
did actually sail for America, occupied a place called
Orange-Hill, near Baltimore, for a year or more, travelled through the country, making what sale he could

* Third volume *Statistics*, p. 598.
† Dated December, 1796. Sparks's *Life and Letters*, Vol. XII. p
323.

of his " Experienced Farmer," and, on his return to
England, published " A Tour in America," which is to
be met with here and there upon the top-shelves of
old libraries, and which is not calculated to encourage
immigration.

He sets out by saying, — " The great advantages
held out by different authors, and men travelling from
America with commission to sell land, have deluded
persons of all denominations with an idea of becoming
land-owners and independent. They have, however,
been most lamentably disappointed, — particularly the
farmers, and all those that have purchased land ; for,
notwithstanding the low price at which the American
lands are sold, *the property of the soil is such* as to make
it not to pay for labor ; therefore the greater part have
brought themselves and their families to total ruin."

He is distressed, too, by the independence of the laborers, — being " often forced to rise in the morning
to milk the cows, when the servants were in bed."

Among other animals which he took with him, he
mentions " two race-horses, ten blood mares, a bull and
cow of the North Devon, a bull and cow of the no-
horned York, a cow (with two calves and in calf again)
of the Holderness, five boar- and seven sow-pigs of four
different kinds."

On arriving at Norfolk, Virginia, in November, he
inquired for hay, and " was informed that American

cattle subsisted on blades and slops, and that no hay
was to be had." He found, also, that "American cows
eat horse-dung as naturally as an English cow eats hay;
and as America grows no grass, the street is the cheap-
est place to keep them in." This would make an admirable item for the scientific column of the London
"Athenæum." Again he says, with a delightful pointedness of manner, — "No transaction in America re-
flects any discredit on a man, unless he loses money by
it. . . . . I remember an Englishman, after repeating
all the things that could fill a stranger's mind with
trouble and horror, said, with a very heavy sigh, as
he was going out of the house, 'It is the Devil's own
country, to be sure!'"

The "Times" newspaper never said a prettier word
than that!

Mr. Robert Brown was a worthier man, and, I suspect, a better farmer; he was one of the earlier types
of those East-Lothian men who made their neighborhood the garden of Scotland. He was also the author
of a book on "Rural Affairs," the editor for fifteen
years of the well-known "Edinburgh Farmers' Magazine," and (if I am not mistaken) communicated the
very valuable article on "Agriculture" to the old "Encyclopædia Britannica."

At this period, too, I find an Earl of Dundonald
(Archibald Cochrane) writing upon the relations of

chemistry to agriculture, — and a little later Richard
Kirwan, F. R. S., indulging in vagaries upon the same
broad, and still unsettled, subject.

Joseph Cradock, a quiet, cultivated gentleman, who
had been on terms of familiarity with Johnson, Gar-
rick, and Goldsmith, published in 1775 his "Village
Memoirs," in which Lancelot Brown has a little fun
pointed at him, under the name of "Layout," the general "undertaker" for gardens.   Sir Uvedale Price,
too, a man of somewhat stronger calibre, and of great
taste, (fully demonstrated on his own place of Foxley,)
made poor Brown the target for some well-turned witticisms, and, what was far better, demonstrated the near
relationship which should always exist between the
aims of the landscape-painter and those of the landscape-gardener.   I am inclined to think that Brown
was a little unfairly used by these new writers, and that
he had won a success which provoked a great deal of
jealousy.   A popularity too great is always dangerous.
Sir Uvedale was a man of strong conservative tenden-
cies, and believed no more in the levelling of men than
in the levelling of hills.   He found his love for the
picturesque sated in many of those hoary old avenues
which, under Brown, had been given to the axe.   I suspect he would have forgiven the presence of a clipped
yew in a landscape where it had thriven for centuries,
the moss of age could give picturesqueness even to

formality. He speaks somewhere of the kindly work of his uncle, who had disposed his walks so as to be a convenience to the poor people of an adjoining parish, and adds, with curious *naïveté*, — " Such attentive kindnesses are amply repaid by affectionate regard and reverence ; and were they general throughout the kingdom, they would do much more towards guarding us against democratical opinions than ' twenty thousand soldiers armed in proof.' "

Richard Knight (a brother of the distinguished horticulturist) illustrated the picturesque theory of Price in a passably clever poem, called " The Landscape," which had not, however, enough of outside merit to keep it alive. Humphrey Repton, a professional designer of gardens, whose work is to be found in almost every county of England, took issue with Price in respect to his picturesque theory, — as became an independent gardener who would not recognize allegiance to the painters. But the antagonism was only one of those petty wars about non-essentials, and significance of terms, into which eager book-makers are so apt to run.

Old Age of Farmers.

IN the course of one of my earlier Wet Days I took occasion to allude to the brave old age that was reached by the classic veterans, — Xerophon, Cato, and Varro; and now I find among the most eminent British agriculturists and gardeners of the close of the last century a firm grip on life that would have matched the hardihood of Cato. Old Abercrombie of Preston Pans, as we have already seen, reached the age of eighty. Walpole, though I lay no claim to him as farmer or gardener, yet, thanks to the walks and garden-work of Strawberry Hill, lived to the same age. Philip Miller was an octogenarian. Lord Kames was aged eighty-seven at his death (1782). Arthur Young, though struggling with blindness in his later years, had accumulated such stock of vitality by his out-door life as to bridge him well over into the present century: he died in 1820, aged seventy-nine. Parson Trusler notwithstanding his apothecary-schooling, lived to be eighty. In 1826 died Joseph Cradock of the "Village Memoirs," and a devoted horticulturist, aged eighty-five. Three years after, (1829,) Sir Uvedale Price bade final adieu to his delightful seat of Foxley, at the age of eighty-three. Sir John Sinclair lived fairly into our own time, (1835,) and was eighty-one at his death.

William Speechley, whom Johnson calls the best gardener of his time, and who established the first effective system of hot-house culture for pines in England, died in 1819, aged eighty-six; and in the same year, William Marshal, a voluminous agricultural writer and

active farmer, died at the age of eighty. And I must
mention one more, Dr. Andrew Duncan, a Scotch physician, who cultivated his garden with his own hands,
— inscribing over the entrance-gate, " *Hinc salus,* —
and who was the founder of the Hoiticultural Society
of Edinburgh. This hale old doctor died in 1828, at
the extreme age of eighty-four ; and to the very last
year of his life he never omitted going up to the top
of Arthur's Seat every May-Day morning, to bathe
his forehead in the summer's dew.

As a country-liver, I like to contemplate and to boast
of the hoary age of these veterans. The inscription
of good old Dr. Duncan was not exaggerated. Every
man who digs his own garden, and keeps the weeds
down thoroughly, may truthfully place the same writing
over the gate, — " *Hinc salus* " (wherever he may place
his " *Hinc pecunia* "). Nor is the comparative safety
of active gardening or farming pursuits due entirely
to the vigorous bodily exercise involved, but quite as
much, it seems to me, to that enlivening and freshening
influence which must belong to an intimate and loving
and intelligent companionship with Nature. It may be
an animal view of the matter, — but, in estimating the
comparative advantages and disadvantages of a country-life, I think we take too little account of that glow
and exhilaration of the blood which come of every-
day dealings with the ground and flowers and trees,

18

and which, as age approaches, subside into a calm
equanimity that looks Death in the face no more fear-
ingly than if it were a frost.   I have gray-haired neighbors around me who have come to a hardy old age upon
their little farms, — buffeting all storms, — petting the
cattle which have come down to them from ten gen-
erations of short-lived kine, gone by, — trailing ancient
vines, that have seen a quarter of a century of life,
over their door-steps, — turning over soil, every cheery
season of May, from which they have already gathered
fifty harvests ; and I cannot but regard their serene
philosophy, and their quiet, thankful, and Christian enjoyment of the bounties of Nature, as something quite
as much to be envied as the distinctions of town-craft.
I ask myself, — If these old gentlemen had plunged
into the whirlpool of a city five-and-fifty years ago,
would they have been still adrift upon this tide of time,
where we are all serving our apprenticeships ? — and
if so, would they have worn the same calm and cheerful equanimity amid the harvests of traffic or the blight
of a panic ? — and if not adrift, would they have carried a clearer and more justifying record to the hearing
of the Great Court than they will carry hence when
our village-bell doles out the funeral march for them ?

The rain is beating on my windows ; the rain is
beating on the plain ; a mist is driving in from the
Sound, over which I see only the spires, — those Chris

tian beacons. And (by these hints, that always fret the
horizon) calling to mind that bit of the best of all pray-
ers, " *Lead us not into temptation*," it seems to me that
many a country-liver might transmute it without offence,
and in all faith, into words like these, — " Lead us not
into cities." To think for a moment of poor farmer
Burns, with the suppers of Edinburgh, and the orgies
of the gentlemen of the Caledonian hunt, inflaming his
imagination there in the wretched chamber of his low
farm-house of Ellisland !

But all this, down my last two pages, relates to the
physical and the moral aspects of the matter, — aspects
which are, surely, richly worthy of consideration. The
question whether country-life and country-pursuits will
bring the intellectual faculties to their strongest bent
is quite a distinct one. There may be opportunity for
culture ; but opportunity counts for nothing, except it
occur under conditions that prompt to its employment.
The incitement to the largest efforts of which the mind
is capable comes ordinarily from mental attrition, — an
attrition for which the retirement demanded by rural
pursuits gives little occasion. Milton would never have
come to his stature among pear-trees, — nor Newton, nor
Burke. They may have made first-rate farmers or horticulturists ; they may have surpassed all about them ;
but their level of action would have been a far lower
one than that which they actually occupied. There is a

great deal of balderdash written and talked upon this
subject, which ought to have an end ; it does not help
farming, it does not help the world, — simply because
it is untrue.   Rural life offers charming objects of
study ; but to most minds it does not offer the prompt-
ings for large intellectual exertion.   It ripens health-
fully all the receptive faculties ; it disposes to that judicial calmness of mind which is essential to clearness
and directness of vision ; but it does not kindle the
heat of large and ambitious endeavor.   Hence we often
find that a man who has passed the first half of his life
in comparative isolation, cultivating his resources quietly, unmoved by the disturbances and the broils of
civic life, will, on transfer to public scenes, and stirred
by that emulation which comes of contact with the
world, feel all his faculties lighted with a new glow,
and accomplish results which are as much a wonder to
himself as to others.

Burns and Bloomfield.

I HAVE alluded to the poet-farmer Burns, — a capital ploughman, a poor manager, an intemperate
lover, a sad reveller, a stilted letter-writer, a rare good-
fellow, and a poet whose poems will live forever   It is
no wonder he did not succeed as farmer ; Moss-giel had
an ugly wet subsoil, and draining-tiles were as yet not

in vogue ; but from all the accoun's I can gather, there
was never a truer furrow laid than was laid by Robert
Burns in his days of vigor, upon that same damp upland
of Moss-giel ; his "fearings" were all true, and his head-
lands as clear of draggled sod as if he had used the best
" Ruggles, Nourse, and Mason " of our time. Alas for
the daisies! he must have turned over perches of them
in his day ; and yet only one has caught the glory of
his lamentation !

Ellisland, where he went later, and where he hoped
to redeem his farm-promise, was not over-fertile ; it had
been hardly used by scurvy tenants before him, and
was so stony that a rain-storm made a fresh-rolled field
of sown barley look like a paved street. He tells us
this ; and we farmers know what it means. But it lay
in Nithsdale ; and the beauty of Nithsdale shed a regal
splendor on his home. It was the poet that had chosen
the farm, and not the grain-grower.

Then there were the "callants" coming from Edinburgh, from Dumfries, from London, from all the world,
to have their " crack " with the peasant-poet, who had
sung the " Lass of Ballochmyle." Can this man, whose
tears drip (in verse) for a homeless field-mouse, keep by
the plough, when a half-score of good-fellows are up
from Dumfries to see him, and when Joh n Barleycorn
stands frothing in the cupboard ?

Consider, again, that his means, notwithstanding the

showy and short-lived generosity of his Edinburgh friends, enabled him only to avail himself of the old Scotch plough; his harrow, very likely, had wooden teeth; he could venture nothing for the clearing of gorse and broom; he could enter upon no system of drainage, even of the simple kind recommended by Lord Kames; he had hardly funds to buy the best quality of seed, and none at all for "liming," or for "wrack" from the shore. Even the gift of a pretty heifer he repays with a song.

Besides all this, he was exciseman; and he loved galloping over the hills in search of recreants, and cosy sittings in the tap of the "Jolly Beggars" of Mauchline, better than he loved a sight of the stunted barley of Ellisland.

No wonder that he left his farm; no wonder that he went to Dumfries, — shabby as the street might be where he was to live; no wonder, that, with his mad pride and his impulsive generosity, he died there, leaving wife and children almost beggars. But, in all charity, let us remember that it is not alone the poor exciseman who is dead, but the rare poet, who has intoned a prayer for ten thousand lips, —

"That He, who stills the raven's clamorous nest,
    And decks the lily fair in flowery pride,
Would, in the way His wisdom sees the best,
    For them and for their little ones provide,
But chiefly in their hearts with grace divine preside."

Let no one fancy that Burns was a poor farmer because he was a poet: he was a poor farmer simply because he gave only his hand to the business, and none of his brain. He had enough of good sense and of clear-sightedness to sweep away every agricultural obstacle in his path, and to make Ellisland "pay well"; but good-fellowship, and the "Jolly Beggars," and his excise-galloping among the hills by Nithsdale made an end of the farmer, — and, in due time, made an end of the man.

Robert Bloomfield was another poet-farmer of these times, but of a much humbler calibre. I could never give any very large portion of a wet day to his reading. There is truthfulness of description in him, and a certain grace of rhythm, but nothing to kindle any glow. The story of Giles, and of the milking, and of the spot-ted heifers, may be true enough ; but every day, in my barn-yard, I find as true and as lively a story. The fact is, that the details of farm-life — the muddy boots, the sweaty workers, the amber-colored pools, the wallowing pigs — are not of a kind to warrant or to call out any burning imprint of verse. Theme for this lies in the breezes, the birds, the waving-wooded mo: ntains (Νήριτον εἰνοσίφυλλον), the glorious mornings

"Gilding pale streams with heavenly alchemy,"

— and for these the poet must soar above the barn-yard and the house-tops. There is more of the spirit of true poesy in that little fragment of Jean Ingelow's, beginning,—

> " What change has made the pastures sweet,
> And reached the daisies at my feet,
> And cloud that wears a golden hem? "

than in all the verse of Bloomfield, if all of Bloomfield were compressed into a single song. And yet, if we had lived in those days, we should all have subscribed for the book of the peasant-bard, perhaps have read it,—but, most infallibly, have given it away to some country-cousin.

Country Story-Tellers.

I WILL not leave the close of the last century without paying my respects to good Mrs. Barbauld,— not so much for her pleasant " Ode to Spring," about which there is a sweet odor of the fields, as for her partnership in those " Evenings at Home " which are associated — I scarce can remember how — with roaring fires and winter nights in the country; and not less strongly with the first noisy chorus of the frogs in the pools, and the first coy uplift of the crocuses and the sweet violets. There are pots of flowers, and glowing fruit-trees, and country hill-sides scattered up and down those little stories, which, though my eye has not lighted on them these twenty odd years past, are still fresh in my mind, and full of a sweet pastoral fragrance. The sketches may be very poor, with few artist-like touches in them ; it may be only a boyish caprice by which I cling to them ; but what pleasanter or more grateful whim to cherish than one which brings back all the aroma of childhood in the country, — floating upon the remnant-patches of a story that is only half recalled ? The cowslips are there ; the pansies are there ; the overhanging chestnuts are there ; the dusty high-road is there ; the toiling wagons are there ; and, betimes, the rain is dripping from the cottage-eaves — as the rain is dripping to-day.

And from Mrs. Barbauld I am led away to speak of Miss Austen, — belonging, it is true, to a little later date, and the tender memory of her books to an age that had outgrown " Evenings at Home." Still, the association of her tales is strongest with the country, and with country - firesides. I sometimes take up one of her works upon an odd hour even now ; and how like finding old-garret clothes — big bonnets and scant skirts — is the reading of such old-time story ! How the " proprieties " our grandmothers taught us come drifting back upon the tide of those buckram conventionalities of the " Dashwoods " ! * Ah, Marianne, how we once loved you ! Ah, Sir John, how we once thought you a profane swearer ! — as you really were.

* *Sense and Sensibility.*

There are people we know between the covers of Miss Austen : Mrs. Jennings has a splutter of tease, and crude incivility, and shapeless tenderness, that you and I see every day; — not so patent and demonstrative in our friend Mrs. Jones ; but the difference is only in fashion : Mrs. Jennings was in scant petticoats, and Mrs. Jones wears hoops, thirty springs strong.

How funny, too, the old love - talk ! " My beloved Amanda, the charm of your angelic features enraptures my regard." It is earnest ; but it 's not the way those things are done.

And what visions such books recall of the days when they were read, — the girls in pinafores, — the boys in roundabouts, — the elders looking languishingly on, when the reader comes to tender passages ! And was not a certain Mary Jane another Ellinor ? And was not Louisa (who lived in the two - story white house on the corner) another Marianne, — gushing, tender ? Yes, by George, she was ! (that was the form our boyish oaths took). And was not the tall fellow who offered his arm to the girls so gravely, and saw them home from our evening visits so cavalierly, — was he not another gay deceiver, — a Lothario, a Willoughby ? He could kiss a girl on the least provocation ; he took pay out, for his escort, that way. It was wonderful, — the fellow's effrontery. It never forsook him I do not know about the romance in his family; but he went into the grocery - line, and has become a contractor now, enormously rich. He offers his arm to Columbia, who wishes to get home before dark; and takes pay in rifling her of golden kisses. Yes, by George, he does!

NINTH DAY.

British Progress in Agriculture.

AS I sit in my library-chair listening to the welcome drip from the eaves, I bethink me of the great host of English farm-teachers who in the last century wrote and wrought so well, and wonder why their precepts and their example should not have made a garden of that little British island. To say nothing of the inherited knowledge of such men as Sir Anthony Fitz-herbert, Hugh Platt, Markham, Lord Bacon, Hartlib, and the rest, there was Tull, who had blazed a new path between the turnip and the wheat-drills — to fortune; there was Lord Kames, who illustrated with rare good sense, and the daintiness of a man of letters, all the economies of a thrifty husbandry; Sir John Sinclair proved the wisdom of thorough culture upon tracts that almost covered counties; Bakewell (of Dishley) — that fine old farmer in breeches and top-boots, who received Russian princes and French marquises at his kitchen-fireside — demonstrated how fat might be laid on sheep or cattle for the handling of a butcher ; in fact, he succeeded so far, that Dr. Parkinson once told Paley that the great breeder had " the power of fattening his sheep in whatever part of the body he chose, directing it to shoulder, leg, or neck, as he thought proper, — and this," continued Parkinson, is the great *problem* of his art."

" It 's a lie, Sir," said Paley, — " and that 's the *solution* of it."

Besides Bakewell, there was Arthur Young, as we have seen, giving all England the benefit of agricultural comparisons by his admirable "Tours"; Lord Dundonald had brought his chemical knowledge to the aid of good husbandry; Abercrombie and Speechley and Marshal had written treatises on all that regarded good gardening. The nurseries of Tottenham Court Road, the parterres of Chelsea, and the stoves of the Kew Gardens were luxuriant witnesses of what the enterprising gardener might do.

Agriculture, too, had a certain dignity given to it by the fact that " Farmer George " (the King) had written his experiences for a journal of Arthur Young, the Duke of Bedford was one of the foremost advocates of improved farming, and Lord Townshend took a pride in his *sobriquet* of " Turnip Townshend."

Yet, for all this, at the opening of the present century England was by no means a garden. Over more than half the kingdom, turnips, where sown at all, were sown broadcast. In four counties out of five, a bare fallow was deemed essential for the recuperation of cropped lands. Barley and oats were more often grown than wheat. Dibbling or drilling of grain, notwithstanding Platt and Jethro Tull, were still rare. The wet clay-lands had, for the most part, no drainage, save the open furrows which were as old as the teachings of Xeno-phon; indeed, it will hardly be credited, when I state that it is only so late as 1843 that a certain gardener, John Reade by name, at the Derby Show of the Royal Agricultural Society, exhibited certain cylindrical pipes, which he had formed by wrapping damp clay around a smooth billet of wood, and with which he "had been in the habit of draining the hot-beds of his master." A sagacious engineer who was present, and saw these, examined them closely, and, calling the attention of Earl Spencer (the eminent agriculturist) to them, said, "My Lord, with these I can drain all England."

It was not until about 1830 that the subsoil-plough of Mr. Smith of Deanston was first contrived for special work upon the lands of Perthshire. Notwith-standing all the brilliant successes of Bakewell, long-legged, raw-boned cattle were admired by the majority of British farmers at the opening of this century, and elephantine monsters of this description were dragged about England in vans for exhibition. It was only in

1798 that the "Smithfield Club" was inaugurated for the show of fat cattle, by the Duke of Bedford, Lord Somerville, Arthur Young, and others; and it was about the same period that young Jonas Webb used to ride upon the Norfolk bucks bred by his grandfather, and, with a quick sense of discomfort from their sharp backs, vowed, that, when he "grew a man, he'd make better saddles for them"; and he did, — as every one knows who has ever seen a good type of the Brabaham flock.

The Royal Agricultural Society dates from 1838. In 1835 Sir Robert Peel presented a farmers' club at Tamworth with " two iron ploughs of the best construction," and when he inquired after them and their work the following year, the report was that the wooden mould-board was better: " We tried 'em, but we be all of one mind, that the iron made the weeds grow." And I can recall a bright morning in January of 1845, when I made two bouts around a field in the middle of the best dairy-district of Devonshire, at the stilts of a plough so cumbrous and ineffective that a thrifty New-England farmer would have discarded it at sight. Nor can I omit, in this connection, to revive, so far as I may, the image of a small Devon farmer, who had lived, and I dare say will die, utterly ignorant of the instructions of Tull, or of the agricultural labors of Arthur Young: a short, wheezy, rotund figure of a man, with

ruddy face, — fastening the *h*s in his talk most blunder.
ingly, — driving over to the market-town every fair.
day, with pretty samples of wheat or barley in his dog.
cart, — believing in the royal family like a gospel, —
limiting his reading to glances at the " Times " in the
tap-room, — looking with an evil eye upon railways,
(which, in that day, had not intruded farther than Exeter into his shire,) — distrusting terribly the spread
of " eddication ": it " doan't help the work-folk any ;
for, d' ye see, they 've to keep a mind on their pleughing
and craps ; and as for the b'ys, the big uns must mind
the beasts, and the little uns 's got enough to do a-scar-
ing the demed rooks. Gads ! what hodds to them,
please your Honor, what Darby is a-dooin' up in Lun-
nun, or what Lewis-Philup is a-dooin' with the French-
ers ? " And the ruddy farmer-gentleman stirs his toddy
afresh, lays his right leg caressingly over his left leg,
admires his white-topped boots, and is the picture of
British complacency. I hope he is living ; I hope he
stirs his toddy still in the tap-room of the inn by the
pretty Erme River ; but I hope that he has grown wiser
as he has grown older, and that he has given over his
wheezy curses at the engine as it hurtles past on the
iron way to Plymouth and to Penzance

Thus we find that the work was not all done for the
agriculture and the agriculturist of England in the last
century ; it is hardly all done yet ; it is doubtful if it

will be done so as to close investigation and ripen method in our time. There was room for a corps of fresh workers at the opening of the present century nor was such a corps lacking.

Opening of the Century.

ABOUT the year 1808, John Christian Curwen, Member of Parliament, and dating from Cumberland, wrote " Hints on Agricultural Subjects," a big octavo volume, in which he suggests the steaming of potatoes for horses, as a substitute for hay ; but it does not appear that the suggestion was well received. To his credit, however, it may be said, that, in the same book, he urged the system of " soiling " cattle, — a system which even now needs its earnest expounders, and which would give full warrant for their loudest exhortation.

I notice, too, that, at about the same period, Dr. Beddoes, the friend and early patron of Sir Humphry Davy at the Pneumatic Institution of Bristol, wrote a book with the quaint title, " Good Advice to Husbandmen in Harvest, and for all those who labor in Hot Berths, and for others who will take it — in Warm Weather." And with the recollection of Davy's description of the Doctor in my mind, — " uncommonly short and fat," *

* *Life of Sir Humphry Davy,* London, 1839, p. 46.

19

— I have felt a great interest in seeing what such a man should have to say upon harvest-heats; but his book, so far as I know, is not to be found in An.erica.

John Harding, of St. James Street, London, published, in 1809, a tract upon " The Use of Sugar in Feeding Cattle," in which were set forth sundry experiments which went to show how bullocks had been fattened on molasses, and had been rewarded with a premium. I am indebted for all knowledge of this anomalous trac-tate to the " Agricultural Biography " of Mr. Donaldson, who seems disposed to give a sheltering wing to the curious theory broached, and discourses upon it with a lucidity and coherence worthy of a state-paper. I must be permitted to quote Mr. Donaldson's language : — " The author's ideas are no romance or chimera, but a very feasible entertainment of the undertaking, when a social revolution permits the fruits of all climes to be used in freedom of the burden of value that is imposed by monopoly, and restricts the legitimate appropriation."

George Adams, in 1810, proposed " A New System of Agriculture and Feeding Stock," of which the nov-elty lay in movable sheds, (upon iron tram-ways,) for the purpose of soiling cattle. The method was cer-tainly original; nor can it be regarded as wholly vis-ionary in our time, when the iron conduits of Mr. Mechi, under the steam-thrust of the Tip-Tree en-gines, are showing a percentage of profit.

Charles Drury, in the same year, recommended, in an elaborate treatise, the steaming of straw, roots, and hay, for cattle-food, — a recommendation which, in our time, has been put into most successful practice.*

Mowbray, who was for a long time the great authority upon Domestic Fowls and their Treatment, published his book in 1803, which he represents as having been compiled from the memoranda of forty years' experience.

Sir Humphry Davy.

NEXT, as illustrative of the rural literature of the early part of this century, I must introduce the august name of Sir Humphry Davy. This I am warranted in doing on two several counts: first, because he was an accomplished fisherman and the author of " Salmonia," and next, because he was the first scientific man of any repute who was formally invited by a Board of Agriculture to discuss the relations of Chemistry to the practice of farming.

Unfortunately, he was himself ignorant of practical agriculture,† when called upon to illustrate its relations

---

* The success of the method has been most abundantly proved, so far as relates to the feeding of milch-cows; for beef- or store-cattle steamed food is of more doubtful policy, while for horses the best breeders condemn it without reserve.

† See letter of Thomas Poole, p. 322, *Fragmentary Remains of Sir Humphry Davy.*

to chemistry; but, like an earnest man, he set about informing himself by communication with the best farmers of the kingdom. He delivered a very admirable series of lectures, and it was without doubt most agreeable to the country-gentlemen to find the great waste from their fermenting manures made clear by Sir Humphry's retorts; but Davy was too profound and too honest a man to lay down for farmers any chemical high-road to success. He directed and stimulated inquiry; he developed many of the principles which underlay their best practice; but he offered them no safety-lamp. I think he brought more zeal to his investigations in the domain of pure science; he loved well-defined and brilliant results; and I do not think that he pushed his inquiries in regard to the way in which the forage-plants availed themselves of sulphate of lime with one-half the earnestness or delight with which he conducted his discovery of the integral character of chlorine, or with which he saw for the first time the metallic globules bubbling out from the electrified crust of potash.

Yet he loved the country with a rare and thorough love, as his descriptions throughout his letters prove; and he delighted in straying away, in the leafy month of June, to the charming place of his friend Knight, upon the Teme in Herefordshire. His " Salmonia " is, in its way, a pastoral; not, certainly, to be compared

with the original of Walton, lacking its simple homeliness, for which its superior scientific accuracy can make
but poor amends. I cannot altogether forget, in reading it, that its author is a fine gentleman from London.
Neither fish, nor alders, nor eddies, nor purling shal-
lows, can drive out of memory the fact that Sir Humphry must be back at "The Hall" by half-past six, in
season to dress for dinner. Walton, in slouch-hat,
bound about with "leaders," sat upon the green turf
to listen to a milkmaid's song. Sir Humphry (I think
he must have carried a camp-stool) recited some verses
written by "a noble lady long distinguished at court." *

In fact, there was always a great deal of the fine gentleman about the great chemist, — almost too fine for
the quiet tenor of a working-life. Those first brilliant
successes of his professional career at the Royal Institution of London, before he was turned of thirty, and in
which his youth, his splendid elocution, his happy discoveries, his attractive manner, all made him the mark
for distinguished attentions, went very far, I fancy, to
carry him to that stage of social intoxication under
which he was deluded into marrying a wealthy lady of
fashion, and a confirmed blue-stocking, — the brilliant
Mrs. Apreece.

Little domestic comfort ever came of the marriage.
Yet he was a chivalrous man, and took the issue calmly

* *Salmonia*, p. 5, London, Murray, 1851.

It is always in his letters, — "My dear Jane," and " God
bless you! Yours affectionately." But these expres-
sions bound the tender passages. It was altogether a
gentlemanly and a lady-like affair. Only once, as I can
find, he forgets himself in an honest repining; it is in
a letter to his brother, under date of October 30,
1823 :* — "To add to my annoyances, I find my house,
as usual, after the arrangements made by the mistress of
it, without female servants; but in this world we have
to suffer and bear, and from Socrates down to humble
mortals, domestic discomfort seems a sort of philosoph-
ical fate."

If only Lady Davy could have seen this Xantippe
touch, I think Sir Humphry would have taken to
angling in some quiet country-place for a month thereafter !

And even when affairs grow serious with the Baro-
net, and when, stricken by the palsy, he is loitering
among the mountains of Styria, he writes, — "I am
glad to hear of your perfect restoration, and with health
and the society of London, *which you are so fitted to
ornament and enjoy*, your ' *viva la felicità* ' is much more
secure than any hope belonging to me."

And again, " You once *talked* of passing *this* winter in
Italy ; but I hope your plans will be entirely guided by
the state of your health and feelings. Your society

* *Fragmentary Remains*, p. 242.

would undoubtedly be a very great resource to me, but I am so well aware of my own present unfitness for society that I would not have you risk the chance of an uncomfortable moment on my account."

The dear Lady Jane must have had a *penchant* for society to leave a poor palsied man to tumble into his tomb alone.

Yet once again, in the last letter he ever writes, dated Rome, March, 1829, he gallantly asks her to join him ; it begins, — "I am still alive, though expecting every hour to be released."

And the Lady Jane, who is washing off her fashionable humors in the fashionable waters of Bath, writes, — "I have received, my beloved Sir Humphry, the letter signed by your hand, with its precious wish of tenderness. I start to-morrow, *having been detained here* by Doctors Babington and Clarke till to-day. . . . . I cannot add more " (it is a letter of half a page) " than that your fame is a deposit, and your memory a glory, your life still a hope."

Sweet Lady Jane ! Yet they say she mourned him duly, and set a proper headstone at his grave. But, for my own part, I have no faith in that affection which will splinter a loving heart every day of its life, and yet, when it has ceased to beat, will make atonement with an idle swash of tears.

Birkbeck, Beatson, and Finlayson.

THERE was a British farmer by the name of Morris Birkbeck, who about the year 1814 wrote an account of an agricultural tour in France; and who subsequently established himself somewhere upon our Western prairies, of which he gave account in " Letters from Illinois," and in " Notes on a Journey in America, from the Coast of Virginia to the Territory of Illinois," with maps, etc.   Cobbett once or twice names him as " poor Birkbeck," — but whether in allusion to his having been drowned in one of our Western rivers, or to the poverty of his agricultural successes, it is hard to determine.

In 1820 Major-General Beatson, who had been Aid to the Marquis of Wellesley in India, published an account of a new system of farming, which he claimed to have in successful operation at his place in the County of Sussex.   The novelty of the system lay in the fact that he abandoned both manures and the plough, and scarified the surface to the depth of two or three inches, after which he burned it over.   The Major-General was called to the governorship of St. Helena before his system had made much progress.   I am led to allude to the plan as one of the premonitory hints of that rotary method which is just now enlisting a large degree of attention in the agricultural world, and which promises to supplant the plough on all wide stretchts of land, within the present century.

Finlayson, a brawny Scot, born in the parish of Mauchline, who was known from " Glentuck to the Rutton-Ley " as the best man for " putting the stone," or for a " hop, step, and leap," contrived the self-cleaning ploughs (with circular beam) and harrows which bore his name. He was also — besides being the athlete of Ayrshire — the author of sundry creditable and practical works on agriculture.

William Cobbett.

BUT the most notable man in connection with rural literature, of this day, was, by all odds, William Cobbett. His early history has so large a flavor of romance in it that I am sure my readers will excuse me for detailing it.

His grandfather was a day-laborer; he died before Cobbett was born ; but the author says that he used to visit the grandmother at Christmas and Whitsuntide. Her home was " a little thatched cottage, with a garden before the door. She used to give us milk and bread for breakfast, an apple-pudding for dinner, and a piece of bread and cheese for our supper. Her fire was made of turf cut from the neighboring heath ; and her evening light was a rush dipped in grease." His father was a

small farmer, and one who did not al.ow his boys to
grow up in idleness. "My first occupation," he tells us,
"was driving the small birds from the turnip-seed, and
the rook from the pease; when I first trudged a-field,
with my wooden bottle and my satchel swung over my
shoulders, I was hardly able to climb the gates and
stiles; and at the close of the day, to reach home was a
task of infinite difficulty." *

At the age of eleven he speaks of himself as occupied
in clipping box-edgings and weeding flower-beds in the
garden of the Bishop of Winchester; and while here
he encounters, one day, a workman who has just come
from the famous Kew Gardens of the King. Young
Cobbett is fired by the glowing description, and resolves
that he must see them, and work upon them too. So he
sets off, one summer's morning, with only the clothes he
has upon his back, and with thirteen halfpence in his
pocket, for Richmond. And as he trudges through the
streets of the town, after a hard day's walk, in his blue
smock-frock, and with his red garters tied under his
knees, staring about him, he sees in the window of a
bookseller's shop the "Tale of a Tub," price threepence;
it piques his curiosity, and, though his money is nearly
all spent, he closes a bargain for the book, and throwing
himself down upon the shady side of a hay-rick, makes
his first acquaintance with Dean Swift. He reads till

---

* *Life and Adventures of Peter Porcupine.*

It is dark, without thought of supper or of bed, — then tumbles down upon the grass under the shadow of the stack, and sleeps till the birds of the Kew Gardens wake him.

He finds work, as he had determined to do; but it was not fated that he should pass his life amid the pleasant parterres of Kew. At sixteen, or thereabout, on a visit to a relative, he catches his first sight of the Channel waters, and of the royal fleet riding at anchor at Spithead. And at that sight, the " old Armada,' and the " brave Rodney," and the " wooden walls," of which he had read, come drifting like a poem into his thought, and he vows that he will become a sailor, — maybe, in time, the Admiral Cobbett. But here, too, the fates are against him: a kind captain to whom he makes application suspects him for a runaway, and advises him to find his way home.

He returns once more to the plough; " but " he says, " I was now spoiled for a farmer." He sighs for the world; the little horizon of Farnham (his native town) is too narrow for him ; and the very next year he makes his final escapade.

" It was on the 6th of May, 1783, that I, like Don Quixote, sallied forth to seek adventures. I was dressed in my holiday clothes, in order to accompany two or three lasses to Guildford fair. They were to assemble at a house about three miles from my home, where I was to attend them ; but, unfortunately for me, I had to cross the London turnpike-road. The stage-coach had just turned the summit of a hill, and was rattling down towards me at a merry rate. The notion of going to London never entered my mind till this very moment; yet the step was completely determined on before the coach had reached the spot where I stood. Up I got, and was in London about nine o'clock in the evening."

His immediate adventure in the metropolis proves to be his instalment as scrivener in an attorney's office. No wonder he chafes at this; no wonder, that, in his wanderings about town, he is charmed by an advertisement which invited all loyal and public-spirited young men to repair to a certain "rendezvous"; he goes to the rendezvous, and presently finds himself a recruit in one of His Majesty's regiments which is filling up for service in British America.

He must have been an apt soldier, so far as drill went; for I find that he rose rapidly to the grade of corporal, and thence to the position of sergeant-major. He tells us that his early habits, his strict attention to duty, and his native talent were the occasion of his swift promotion. In New Brunswick, upon a certain winter's morning, he falls in with the rosy-faced daughter of a sergeant of artillery, who was scrubbing her pans at sunrise, upon the snow. " I made up my mind," he says, "that she was the very girl for me. . . . . This matter was at once settled as firmly as if written in the book of fate."

To this end he determines to leave the army as soon as possible. But before he can effect this, the artillery-man is ordered back to England, and his pretty daughter goes with him. But Cobbett has closed the compact with her, and placed in her hands a hundred and fifty pounds of his earnings, — a free gift, and an earnest of his troth.

The very next season, however, he meets, in a sweet rural solitude of the Province, another charmer, with whom he dallies in a lovelorn way for two years or more. He cannot quite forget the old; he cannot cease befondling the new. If only the " remotest rumor had come," says he, " of the faithlessness of the brunette in England, I should have been fastened for life in the New-Brunswick valley." But no such rumor comes; and in due time he bids a heart-rending adieu, and recrosses the ocean to find his first love maid-of-all-work in a gentleman's family at five pounds a year ; and she puts in his hand, upon their first interview, the whole of the b ndred and fifty pounds, untouched. This rekindles his admiration and respect for her judgment, and she becomes his wife, — a wife he never ceases thereafter to love and honor.

He goes to France, and thence to America. Establishing himself in Philadelphia, he enters upon the career of authorship, with a zeal for the King, and a hatred of Dr. Franklin and all Democrats, which give him a world of trouble. His foul bitterness of speech finds its climax at length in a brutal onslaught upon Dr. Rush, for which he is prosecuted, convicted, and mulcted in a sum that breaks down his bookselling and interrupts the profits of his authorship.

He retires to England, opens shop in Pall-Mall, and edits the " Porcupine," which bristles with envenomed arrows discharged against all Liberals and Democrats. Again he is prosecuted, convicted, imprisoned. His boys, well taught in all manner of farm-work, send him, from his home in the country, hampers of fresh fruits, to relieve the tedium of Newgate. Discharged at length, and continuing his ribaldry in the columns of the " Register," he flies before an Act of Parliament, and takes new refuge in America. He is now upon Long Island, earnest as in his youth in agricultural pursuits. His political opinions had undergone modification ; there was not so much declamation against democracy, — not so much angry zeal for royalty and the state-church. Nay, he committed the stupendous absurdity of carry-ing back with him to England the bones of Tom Paine, as the grandest gift he could bestow upon his mother-land. No great ovations greeted this strange luggage of his ; I think he was ashamed of it afterwards, — if Cobbett was ever ashamed of anything. He became

candidate for Parliament in the Liberal interest; he undertook those famous " Rural Rides " which are a rare
jumble of sweet rural scenes and crazy political objur-
gation. Now he hammers the " parsons," — now he
tears the paper-money to rags, — and anon he is bitter
upon Malthus, Ricardo, and the Scotch " Feelosofers,"
— and closes his anathema with the charming picture of
a wooded " hanger," up which he toils (with curses on
the road) only to rejoice in the view of a sweet Hamp-
shire valley, over which sleek flocks are feeding, and
down which some white stream goes winding, and cheat-
ing him into a rare memory of his innocent boyhood.
He gains at length his election to Parliament; but he
is not a man to figure well there, with his impetuosity
and lack of self-control. He can talk by the hour to
those who feel with him; but to be challenged, to have
his fierce invective submitted to the severe test of an
inexorable logic, — this limits his audacity; and his audacity once limited, his power is gone.

His energy, his promptitude, his habits of thrift, would
have made him one of the best of farmers. His book
on gardening is even now one of the most instructive
that can be placed in the hands of a beginner. He
ignores physiology and botany, indeed; he makes
crude errors on this score; but he had an intuitive
sense of the right method of teaching. He is plain and
clear, to a comma   He knows what needs to be told;

and he tells it straightforwardly. There is no better model for agricultural writers than "Cobbett on Gardening."

His "Cottage Economy," too, is a book which every small landholder in America should own; there is a sterling merit in it which will not be outlived. He made a great mistake, it is true, in insisting that Indian-corn could be grown successfully in England. But being a man who did not yield to influences of climate himself, he did not mean that his crops should; and if he had been rich enough, I believe that he would have covered his farm with a glass roof, rather than yield his conclusion that Indian-corn could be grown successfully under a British sky.

A great, impracticable, earnest, headstrong man, the like of whom does not appear a half-dozen times in a century. Being self-educated, he was possessed, like nearly all self-educated men, of a complacency and a self-sufficiency which stood always in his way. Affecting to teach grammar, he was ignorant of all the etymology of the language; knowing no word of botany, he classified plants by the "fearings" of his turnip-field. He was vain to the last degree; he thought his books were the best books in the world, and that everybody should read them.* He was industrious, restless, cap-

* On the fly-leaf to his *Woodlands* he wrote, — " When I am asked what books a young man or young woman should read, I always answer, ' Let him or her read all the books that I have written ' "

tious, and, although humane at heart, was the most malignant slanderer of his time. He called a political antagonist a "pimp," and thought a crushing argument lay in the word; he called parsons scoundrels, and bade his boys be regular at church.

In June, 1835, while the Parliament was in session, he grew ill, — talked feebly about politics and farming, (to his household,) "wished for 'four days' rain' for the Cobbett corn," and on Wednesday, (16th June,) desired to be carried around the farm, and criticised the work that had been done, — grew feeble as evening drew on, and an hour after midnight leaned back heavily in his chair, and died.

Grahame and Crabbe.

I MUST give a paragraph, at least, to the Rev. James Grahame, the good Scotch parson, were it only because he wrote a poem called "British Georgics." They are not so good as Virgil's; nor did he ever think it himself. In fact, he published his best poem anonymously, and so furtively that even his wife took up an early copy, which she found one day upon her table, and, charmed with its pleasant description of Scottish braes and burn-sides, said, "Ah! Jemmy, if ye could only mak' a book like this!" And I will venture to say that "Jemmy" never had rarer or pleasanter praise.

I suspect good Mistress Grahame was not a very strong-minded woman.

Crabbe, who was as keen an observer of rural scenes as the Scotchman, had a much better faculty of verse; indeed, he had a faculty of language so large that it carried him beyond the real drift of his stories. I do not *know* the fact, indeed; but I think, that, notwithstanding the Duke of Rutland's patronage, Mr. Crabbe must have written inordinately long sermons. It is strange how many good men do, — losing point and force and efficiency in a welter of words! If there is one rhetorical lesson which it behooves all theologic or academic professors to lay down and enforce, (if need be with the ferule,) it is this, — Be short.

George Crabbe wrote charming rural tales; but he wrote long ones. There is minute observation, dramatic force, tender pathos, but there is much of tedious and coarse description. If by some subtile alchemy the better qualities could be thrown down from the turbid and watery flux of his verse, we should have an admirable pocket-volume for the country; as it is, his books rest mostly on the shelves, and it requires a strong breath to puff away the dust that has gathered on the topmost edges.

I think of the Reverend Mr. Crabbe as an amiable, absent-minded old gentleman, driving about on weekdays in a heavy, square-topped gig, (his wife holding

the reins,) in search of way-side gypsies, and on Sunday pushing a discourse — which was good up to the
" fourthly" — into the " seventhly."

Charles Lamb.

CHARLES LAMB, if he had been clerically disposed, would, I am sure, have written short sermons ; and I think that his hearers would have carried
away the gist of them clean and clear.

He never wrote anything that could be called strictly
pastoral ; he was a creature of streets and crowding
houses ; no man could have been more ignorant of the
every-day offices of rural life ; I doubt if he ever knew
from which side a horse was to be mounted or a cow to
be milked, and a sprouting bean was a source of the
greatest wonderment to him. Yet, in spite of all this,
what a book those Essays of his make, to lie down with
under trees ! It is the honest, lovable simplicity of his
nature that makes the keeping good. He is the Izaak
Walton of London streets, — of print-shops, of pastry-
shops, of mouldy book-stalls ; the chime of Bow-bells
strikes upon his ear like the chorus of a milkmaid's
song at Ware.

There is not a bit of rodomontade in him about the
charms of the country, from beginning to end ; if there
were, we should despise him. He can find nothing to

say of Skiddaw but that he is "a great creature"; and
he writes to Wordsworth, (whose sight is failing,, on
Ambleside, "I return you condolence for your decaying
sight, — not for anything there is to see in the country,
but for the miss of the pleasure of reading a London
newspaper."

And again to his friend Manning, (about the date of
1800,) — "I am not romance-bit about *Nature*. The
earth and sea and sky (when all is said) is but as a
house to dwell in. If the inmates be courteous, and
good liquors flow like the conduits at an old coronation,
— if they can talk sensibly, and feel properly, I have
no need to stand staring upon the gilded looking-glass,
(that strained my friend's purse-strings in the purchase,)
nor his five-shilling print, over the mantel-piece, of old
Nabbs, the carrier. Just as important to me (in a sense)
is all the furniture of my world, — eye-pampering, but
satisfies no heart. Streets, streets, streets, markets,
theatres, churches, Covent Gardens, shops sparkling
with pretty faces of industrious milliners, neat seam-
stresses, ladies cheapening, gentlemen behind counters
ying, authors in the street with spectacles, lamps lit at
night, pastry-cooks' and silver-smiths' shops, beautiful
Quakers of Pentonville, noise of coaches, drowsy cry
of mechanic watchmen at night, with bucks reeling
home drunk, — if you happen to wake at midnight, cries
of 'Fire!' and 'Stop thief!' — inns c⁽court with their

learned air, and halls, and butteries, just like Cambr.dge
colleges, — old book-stalls, 'Jeremy Taylors,' 'Burtons
on Melancholy,' and 'Religio Medicis,' on every stall.
These are thy pleasures, O London-with-the-many-sins!
— for these may Keswick and her giant brood go
hang!"

Does any weak-limbed country-liver resent this hon-
esty of speech? Surely not, if he be earnest in his
loves and faith; but, the rather, by such token of un-
bounded naturalness, he recognizes under the waistcoat
of this dear, old, charming cockney the traces of close
cousinship to the Waltons, and binds him, and all the
simplicity of his talk, to his heart, for aye. There is
never a hill-side under whose oaks or chestnuts I lounge
upon a smoky afternoon of August, but a pocket Elia is
as coveted and as cousinly a companion as a pocket
Walton, or a White of Selborne. And upon wet days in
my library, I conjure up the image of the thin, bent old
gentleman — Charles Lamb — to sit over against me,
and I watch his kindly, beaming eye, as he recites with
poor stuttering voice, — between the whiffs of his pipe,
— over and over, those always new stories of " Christ's
Hospital," and the cherished " Blakesmoor," and Mack-
ery End."

(No, you need not put back the book, my boy; 't is
always in place.)

The Ettrick Shepherd.

I NEVER admired greatly James Hogg, the Ettrick
Shepherd ; yet he belongs of double right in the
coterie of my wet-day preachers.   Bred a shepherd, he
tried farming, and he wrote pastorals.   His farming (if
we may believe contemporary evidence) was by no
means so good as his verse.   The Ettrick Shepherd of
the " Noctes Ambrosianæ " is, I fancy, as much becol-
ored by the wit of Professor Wilson as any daughter
of a duchess whom Sir Joshua changed into a nymph.
I think of Hogg as a sturdy sheep-tender, growing re-
bellious among the Cheviot flocks, crazed by a reading
of the Border minstrelsy, drunken on books, (as his
fellows were with " mountain-dew,") and wreaking his
vitality on Scottish rhymes, — which, it is true, have a
certain blush and aroma of the heather-hills, but which
never reached the excellence that he fondly imagined
belonged to them.   I fancy, that, when he sat at the
laird's table, (Sir Walter's,) and called the laird's lady
by her baptismal name, and — not abashed in any presence — uttered his Scotch gibes for the wonderment of
London guests, — that he thought far more of himself
than the world has ever been inclined to think of him.

It may not be commonly known that the Ettrick
Shepherd was an agricultural author, and wrote " Hogg
on Sheep," for which, as he tells us, he received the sum

of eighty-six pounds. It is an octavo book, and relates
to the care, management, and diseases of the black-faced
mountain-breed, of which alone he was cognizant. It
had never a great reputation ; and I think the sheep-
farmers of the Cheviots were disposed to look with dis-
trust upon the teachings of a shepherd who supped with
" lords " at Abbotsford, and whose best venture in verse
was in " The Queen's Wake." A British agricultural
author, speaking of him in a pitiful way, says, — " He
passed years of busy authorship, and encountered *the
usual difficulties of that penurious mode of life.*" *

This is good ; it is as good as anything of Hogg's.

Loudon.

I APPROACH the name of Mr. Loudon, the author
of the Encyclopædias of Gardening and Agriculture,
with far more of respect. If nothing else in him laid
claim to regard, his industry, his earnestness, his indefatigable labor in aid of all that belonged to the progress of British gardening or farming, would demand it.
I take a pride, too, in saying, that, notwithstanding his
literary labors, he was successful as a farmer, during
the short period of his farm-holding.

Mr. Loudon was a Scotchman by birth, was educated

* *Agricultural Biography*, etc. London, 1854. *Printed for the
Author.*

in Edinburgh, and was for a time under the tutelage
of Mr. Dickson, the famous nurseryman of Leith-Walk.
Early in the present century he made his first appear-
ance in London, — contributed to the journals certain
papers on the laying-out of the public squares of the
metropolis, and shortly after was employed by the Earl
of Mansfield in the arrangement of the palace-gar-
dens at Scone.   In 1806 he published a work upon the
management of country-residences, and at about the
same period entered upon the business of farming,
which he followed with great success until 1813.   In
this and the succeeding year he travelled on the Continent very widely, making the gardens of most repute
the special objects of his study; and in 1822 he gave
to the world his "Encyclopædia of Gardening"; that
on Agriculture followed shortly after, and his book of
Rural Architecture in 1833.   But these labors, enormous as they were, had interludes of other periodical
work, and were crowned at last by his *magnum opus*,
the "Arboretum."

"For months," says Mrs. Loudon, speaking of the
preparation of the Encyclopædias, "he and I used to
sit up the greater part of every night, never having
more than four hours' sleep, and drinking strong coffee
to keep ourselves awake."   And this persistency of
labor was the more extraordinary from the fact that he
was a man of naturally feeble constitution, and as early

as the date of his first considerable work was broke:. by disease. In the year 1806 a night's exposure upon a coach-box in travelling brought upon him a rheumatic fever which resulted in a permanent anchylosis of the left knee. Subsequently his right arm became affected, and he submitted to shampooing. In this process it was broken so near to the shoulder that it could not be set in the usual manner; somewhat later it was again broken, and finally amputated in 1826. Meantime his left hand became so affected (rheumatically) that he could use only the third and little finger. But though after this time always obliged to employ an amanuensis and draughtsman, he wrought on bravely and constantly until the year 1843, when he was attacked with infla-mation of the lungs. To this, however, he did not yield himself a willing prey; but with his right arm gone, his left side paralyzed, his sight miserably defec-tive, and his lungs one mass of disease, he kept by his desk and his work, up to the very day of his death.

This veteran author massed together an amount of information upon the subjects of which he treated that is quite unmatched in the whole annals of agricultural literature. Columella, Heresbach, Worlidge, and even the writers of the " Geoponica," dwindle into insignifi-cance in the comparison. He is not, indeed, always absolutely accurate on historical points; * but in all

* I ought, perhaps, to make definite exception in the case of a writer

essentials his books are so complete as to have made them standard works up to a time long subsequent to their issue.

No notice of the agricultural literature of the early part of this century would be at all complete without mention of the Magazines and Society "Transactions," in which alone some of the best and most scientific cultivators communicated their experience or suggestions to the public. Loudon was himself the editor of the "Gardener's Magazine"; and the earlier Transactions of the Horticultural Society are enriched by the papers of such men as Knight, Van Mons, Sir Joseph Banks, Rev. William Herbert, Messrs. Dickson, Haworth, Wedgwood, and others. The works of individual authors lost ground in comparison with such an array of reports from scientific observers, and from that time forth periodical literature has become the standard teacher in what relates to good culture. I do not know what extent of good the newly instituted Agri-

so universally accredited. In his *Encyclopædia of Gardening*, he speaks of the *Geoponica* as the work of "modern Greeks," written after the transfer of the seat of empire to Constantinople; whereas the bulk of those treatises were written long before that date. He speaks of Varro as first in order of time of Roman authors on agriculture; yet Varro was born 116 B. C., and Cato died as early as 149 B. C. Crescenzi he names as an author of the fifteenth century; he should be credited to the fourteenth. He also commits the very common error in writers on gardening, of confounding the Tuscan villa of Pliny with that at Tusculum. These two places of the Roman Consul were entirely distinct. In his Epist. 6 (*Apollinari*) Pliny says, "*Habes causas cur ego Tuscos meos Tusculanis, Tyburtinis, Prænestinisque meis præponam.*"

cultural Colleges of this country may effect ; but I feel
quite safe in saying that our agricultural journals will
prove always the most effective teachers of the great
mass of the farming-population. The London Horticultural Society at an early day established the Chiswick
Gardens, and these, managed under the advice of the
Society's Directors, have not only afforded an accurate
gauge of British progress in horticulture, but they have
furnished to the humblest cultivator who has strolled
through their enclosures practical lessons in the craft of
gardening. It is to be hoped that the American Agricultural Colleges will adopt some similar plan, and
illustrate the methods they teach upon lands which
shall be open to public inspection, and upon whose
culture and its successes systematic reports shall be
annually made.

A Bevy of Poets.

WRITING thus, during these in-door hours, of
country-pursuits, and of those who have illustrated them, or who have in any way quickened the
edge with which we farmers rasp away the weeds or
carve out our pastoral entertainment, I come upon the
names of a great bevy of poets, belonging to the earlier
quarter of this century, that I find it hard to pass by.
Much as 1 love to bring to mind, over and over again,

"Ivanhoe" and "Waverley," I love quite as much to summon to my view Walter Scott, the woodsman of Abbotsford, with hatchet at his girdle, and the hound Maida in attendance. I see him thinning out the saplings that he has planted upon the Tweed banks. I can fancy how the master would have lopped away the boughs for a little looplet through which a burst of the blue Eildon Hills should come. His favorite seat, overshadowed by an arbor-vitæ, (of which a leaf lies pressed in the "Scotch Tourist" yonder,) was so near to the Tweed banks that the ripple of the stream over its pebbly bottom must have made a delightful lullaby for the toil-worn old man. But beyond wood-craft, I could never discover that Sir Walter had any strong agricultural inclination; indeed, in one of his letters, dated about the time of his commercial involvement, (1826,) he says, — after enumerating other prospective retrenchments, — "then I give up an expensive farm, *which I always hated,* and turn all my odds and ends into cash." * Again, (and I count this a surer indication,) he puts in the mouth of Cromwell (" Woodstock ") a mixed metaphor of which no apt farmer could have been guilty. The Puritan general is speaking of the arch-loyalist Dr. Rochecliffe, and says, "I know his stiffneckedness of old, though I have made him plough in my *furrow*, when he thought he was turning up his

* Lockhart's *Life*, Vol. IV. ch. i.

own *swathe.*" Nor do I think that the old gentleman
had much eye for the picturesque; no landscape-gardener of any reputation would have decided upon such
a site for such a pile as that of Abbotsford : * the spot
is low; the views are not extended or varied ; the very
trees are all of Scott's planting ; but the master loved
the murmur of the Tweed, — loved the nearness of
Melrose, and in every old bit of sculpture that he
walled into his home he found pictures of far-away
scenes that printed in vague shape of tower or abbey
all his limited horizon.

Christopher North carried his Scotch love of mountains to his home among the English lakes. I think
he counted Skiddaw something more than "a great
creature." In all respects — saving the pipes and the
ale — he was the very opposite of Charles Lamb. And
yet do we love him more? A stalwart, hearty man,
with a great redundance of flesh and blood, who could
" put the stone " with Finlayson, or climb with the
hardiest of the Ben-Nevis guides, or cast a fly with the
daintiest of the Low-Country fishers, — redundant of
imagination, redundant of speech, and with such exu-

---

* This is the more remarkable as Scott wrote most appreciatively
on the subject of landscape-gardening. I allude particularly to that
charming essay of his in the *Quarterly Review* for March, 1828, based
upon Sir Henry Steuart's scheme for the safe removal of large forest-
trees, — a scheme which unfortunately promised more than it has per
formed.

berance in him that we feel surfeit from the overflow
as at the reading of Spenser's " Faëry Queene," and
lay him down with a wearisome sense of mental indigestion.

Nor yet is it so much an indigestion as a feeling of
plethora, due less to the frothiness of the condiments
than to a certain fulness of blood and brawn. The
broad-shouldered Christopher, in his shooting-jacket, (a
dingy green velveteen, with pocket-pouches all stuffed,)
strides away along the skirts of Cruachan or Loch
Lochy with such a tearing pace, and greets every lassie
with such a clamorous outbreak of song, and throws
such a wonderful stretch of line upon every pool, and
amazes us with such stupendous " strikes " and such a
whizzing of his reel, that we fairly lose our breath.

Not so of the " White Doe of Rylstone"; nay, we
more incline to doze over it than to lose our breath.
Wilson differs from Wordsworth as Loch Awe, with
its shaggy savagery of shore, from the Sunday quietude and beauty of Rydal-Water. The Strid of Wordsworth was bounded by the slaty banks of the " Crystal
Wharf," and the Strid of Wilson, in his best moments,
was as large as the valley of Glencoe. Yet Wordsworth loved intensely all the more beautiful aspects of
the country, and of country-life. No angler and no
gardener, indeed, — too severely and proudly meditative for any such sleight-of-hand. The only great weight

which he ever lifted, I suspect, was one which he carried with him always, — the immense dignity of his poetic priesthood. His home and its surroundings were fairly typical of his tastes : a cottage, (so called,) of homely material indeed, but with an ambitious elevation of gables and of chimney-stacks ; a velvety sheen of turf, as dapper as that of a suburban haberdasher ; a mossy urn or two, patches of flowers, but rather fragrant than showy ones ; behind him the loveliest of wooded hills, all toned down by graceful culture, and before him the silvery mirrors of Windermere and Rydal-Water.

We have to credit him with some rare and tender description, and fragments of great poems ; but I cannot help thinking that he fancied a profounder meaning lay in them than the world has yet detected.

John Clare was a contemporary of Wordsworth's, and was most essentially a poet of the fields. His father was a pauper and a cripple ; not even young Cobbett was so pressed to the glebe by the circumstances of his birth. But the thrushes taught Clare to sing. He wrote verses upon the lining of his hat-band. He hoarded halfpence to buy Thomson's "Seasons," and walked seven miles before sunrise to make the purchase. The hardest field-toil could not repress the poetic aspirations of such a boy. By dint of new hoardings he succeeded in printing verses of his own

but nobody read them. He wrote other verses, **which**
at length made him known. The world flattered the
peasant - bard of Northamptonshire. A few distinguished patrons subscribed the means for equipping a
farm of his own. The heroine of his love-tales became
its mistress; a shelf or two of books made him rich;
but in an evil hour he entered upon some farm-specu-
lation which broke down ; a new poem was sharply
criticised or neglected; the novelty of his peasant's
song was over. Disheartened and gloomy, he was over-
whelmed with despondency, and became the inmate of
a mad - house, where for forty years he has staggered
idiotically toward the rest which did not come. But
even as I write I see in the British papers that he is
free at last. Poor Clare is dead.

With this sad story in mind, we may read with a zest
which perhaps its merit alone would not provoke his
little sonnet of " The Thrush's Nest " : —

> " Within a thick and spreading hawthorn-bush,
> That overhung a mole-hill large and round,
> I heard from morn to morn a merry thrush
> Sing hymns of rapture, while I drank the sound
> With joy ; and oft, an unintruding guest,
> I watched her secret toils from day to day, —
> How true she warped the moss to form her nest,
> And modelled it within with wood and clay,
> And by-and-by, like heath-bells gilt with dew,
> There lay her shining eggs as bright as flowers,

> Ink-spotted over, shells of green and blue;
> And there I witnessed, in the summer hours,
> A brood of Nature's minstrels chirp and fly,
> Glad as the sunshine and the laughing sky."

There are pretty snatches of a Southern May in Hunt's poem of " Rimini," where

> " sky, earth, and sea
> Breathe like a bright-eyed face that laughs out openly.
> 'T is Nature full of spirits, waked and springing:
> The birds to the delicious tune are singing,
> Darting with freaks and snatches up and down,
> Where the light woods go seaward from the town;
> While happy faces striking through the green
> Of leafy roads at every turn are seen;
> And the far ships, lifting their sails of white
> Like joyful hands, come up with scattery light,
> Come gleaming up true to the wished-for day,
> And chase the whistling brine, and swirl into the bay."

This does not sound as if it came from the prince of cockneys; and I have always felt a certain regard for Leigh Hunt, too, by reason of the tender story which he gives of the little garden, "*mio picciol orto*," that he established during his two years of prisonhood.[*]

But, after all, there was no robustness in his rural spirit, — nothing that makes the cheek tingle, as if a smart wind had smitten it. He was born to handle roses without thorns; I think that with a pretty boudoir

* *Lord Byron and his Contemporaries*, Vol. II. p. 258.

21

on whose table every morning a pretty maid should arrange a pretty nosegay, and with a pretty canary to sing songs in a gilded cage, and pretty gold-fish to disport in a crystal vase, and basted partridges for dinner, his love for the country would have been satisfied. He loved Nature as a sentimental boy loves a fine woman of twice his years, — sighing himself away in pretty phrases that flatter, but do not touch her; there is nothing to remind, even, of the full, abounding, fiery, all-conquering love with which a full-grown man meets and marries a yielding maiden.

In poor John Keats, however, there *is* something of this; and under its heats he consumed away. For ripe, joyous outburst of all rural fancies, — for keen apprehension of what most takes hold of the susceptibilities of a man who loves the country, — for his coinage of all sweet sounds of birds, all murmur of leaves, all riot and blossoming of flowers, into fragrant verse, — he was without a peer in his day. It is not that he is so true to natural phases in his descriptive epithets, not that he sees all, not that he has heard all; but his heart has drunk the incense of it, and his imagination refined it, and his fancy set it aflow in those jocund lines which bound and writhe and exult with a passionate love for the things of field and air.

L'Envoi.

I CLOSE these papers, with my eye resting upon the
same stretch of fields, — the wooded border of a
river, — the twinkling roofs and spires flanked by hills
and sea, — where my eye rested when I began this story
of the old masters with Hesiod and the bean-patches
of Ithaca. And I take a pleasure in feeling that the
farm-practice over all the fields below me rests upon the
cumulated authorship of so long a line of teachers.
Yon open furrow, over which the herbage has closed,
carries trace of the ridging in the " Works and Days ";
the brown field of half-broken clods is the fallow (Νεός)
of Xenophon ; the drills belong to Worlidge ; their
culture with the horse-hoe is at the order of Master
Tull. Young and Cobbett are full of their suggestions ;
Lancelot Brown has ordered away a great straggling
hedge-row ; and Sir Uvedale Price has urged me to
spare a hoary maple which lords it over a half-acre of
flat land. Cato gives orders for the asparagus, and
Switzer for the hot-beds. Crescenzi directs the wall-
ing, and Smith of Deanston the ploughing. Burns em-
balms all my field-mice, and Cowper drapes an urn for
me in a tangled wilderness. Knight names my cherries, and Walton, the kind master, goes with me over
the hill to a wee brook that bounds down under hem-
locks and soft maples, for " a contemplative man's rec-

reation." Davy long ago caught all the fermentation of my manure-heap in his retort, and Thomson painted for me the scene which is under my window to-day. Mowbray cures the pip in my poultry, and all the songs of all the birds are caught and repeated to the echo in the pages of the poets which lie here under my hand; through the prism of their verse, Patrick the cattle-tender changes to a lithe milkmaid, against whose ankles the buttercups nod rejoicingly, and Rosamund (which is the nurse) wakes all Arden (which is Edgewood) with a rich burst of laughter.

THE END.

www.ingramcontent.com/pod-product-compliance
Lightning Source LLC
Chambersburg PA
CBHW021122270326
41929CB00009B/1003